# Gossip, Markets, and Gender

# WOMEN IN AFRICA AND
# THE DIASPORA

Series Editors

STANLIE JAMES
AILI MARI TRIPP

# Gossip, Markets, and Gender

## How Dialogue Constructs Moral Value in Post-Socialist Kilimanjaro

## Tuulikki Pietilä

The University of Wisconsin Press

This book was published with the support of
the Anonymous Fund for the Humanities of
the University of Wisconsin–Madison.

The University of Wisconsin Press
1930 Monroe Street
Madison, Wisconsin 53711

www.wisc.edu/wisconsinpress/

3 Henrietta Street
London WC2E 8LU, England

1      3      5      4      2

Library of Congress Cataloging-in-Publication Data
Pietilä, Tuulikki, 1963 –
Gossip, markets, and gender : the dialogical construction of
moral value in post-socialist Kilimanjaro / Tuulikki Pietilä.
    p.      cm. — (Women in Africa and the diaspora)
Includes bibliographical references and index.
ISBN 0-299-22090-7 (cloth: alk. paper)
ISBN 0-299-22094-X (pbk.: alk. paper)
1. Markets — Tanzania — Kilimanjaro Region.
2. Markets — Social aspects — Tanzania — Kilimanjaro Region.
3. Markets — Moral and ethical aspects — Tanzania — Kilimanjaro Region.
4. Gossip — Tanzania — Kilimanjaro Region.   I. Title.   II. Series.
        HF5475.T362K556        2006
    306.3′40967826 — dc22        2006008597

# Contents

*Illustrations*                                                                    vii
*Acknowledgments*                                                                   ix

Introduction                                                                         3

## Part 1. Women

1   Domesticating the Market, Marketing the Domestic                                29
2   Feeding, Drinking, and Eating: Market Women
    Restructuring Gender                                                            63
3   Constructing Moral Reputation: The Case of
    Mama Njau                                                                       89
4   From Captured Wives to Bound Men: Rethinking
    Female Respect                                                                 118

v

## Part 2.  Men

5    Urban Men in Their Home Lineages                              143
6    Making Sense of Failure: Stories of Businessmen and
     Wealth                                                        165

Conclusion                                                         191

     *Notes*                                                       203
     *Glossary*                                                    217
     *Bibliography*                                                221
     *Index*                                                       235

# Illustrations

## Photographs

1. Coffee and banana trees                                          18
2. Father's house and his youngest son's house                      19
3. Making dinner                                                     19
4. An urban Chagga man's rural house                                20
5. A local road scene on a market day                               21
6. Bananas to be transported                                        31
7. Tomato sellers                                                   35
8, 9. Selling and measuring of finger millet                        51
10. Sellers of cooking bananas and second-hand clothes              53
11. Bucketfuls of sweet bananas                                     53
12. *Klabu* next to a small marketplace                             67
13. A woman selling *mbege*                                         67
14. The bride in a send-off ceremony                               125
15. The lineage brother lowers the bride's *kanga*                 125

16. Chagga men who live in Dar es Salaam                    145
17. Women singing hymns at a funeral                        147
18. *Matanga* meeting                                       148
19. Women sharing *mbege*                                   148
20. A grandmother next to her house                         153

## Maps

1. Tanzania                                                 xii
2. Districts and former chiefdoms in Northern Kilimanjaro   15
3. Main road and railway connections in and from
        Kilimanjaro                                         16
4. Road and railway connections in Tanzania                17

# Acknowledgments

In the course of this study I have received support and assistance from a number of people and institutions. I owe my greatest thanks to the many Chagga market women, neighbors, and friends who allowed me to enter their lives and endured my endless questions. I am unable to mention all their names, but I would particularly like to thank Piliosi and Priscilla Temu and their family, who so readily made their home mine during my field work. What I had initially imagined would be the hardest part of my research—living with a foreign family—proved to be perhaps the easiest and most rewarding. Sharing their everyday life, the hilarious atmosphere in their family, and their courage to face the unanticipated gave me strength and helped to maintain my sense of reality during the field work. The personality and local knowledge of Haika Moshi, my first research assistant, undoubtedly affected the early stages of my research and the evolving research interests in a way I was unaware of at the time. Later, Elikaneni Makundi, Annense Moshi, Edlais Temu, and Flower Makundi provided important assistance with interviews in the Kichagga language and in transcribing those interviews.

Professor emerita Marja-Liisa Swantz paved the way for my research in Tanzania by including me in a seminar on women's economy that she organized with Professor Aili Mari Tripp in Northern Tanzania in 1994. Involving mostly entrepreneurial and other active Tanzanian women, that seminar gave me my very first contact with such women and their lives, and immersed me in the Kiswahili language. Thanks to the seminar, I found my way to Kilimanjaro when one of the participants, Mrs. Mfinanga, kindly invited me to stay in her home. Professor Swantz, a pioneer in African and Tanzanian studies in Finland, has also been a role model of stamina in thinking and acting.

Professor Karen Armstrong of the University of Helsinki has been a particularly invaluable source of advice and support throughout the course of my doctoral work—which she supervised—and thereafter. She has for years read and made valuable comments on several versions of the text that eventually evolved into this book. I am also grateful to Professor Richard Werbner of the University of Manchester, who has read and offered insightful comments at several stages of my work, each time challenging me to stretch my anthropological imagination to another level. Professor Jukka Siikala has been my mentor throughout the years I have studied social anthropology, and his enthusiasm and efforts to develop an ethnographically rich and theoretically ambitious line of anthropological research in Helsinki has had a profound influence on my thinking.

I have also benefited from discussions with Harri Englund, Jeremy Gould, Adeline Masquelier, Joel Robbins, and Brad Weiss. Furthermore, discussions in seminars and elsewhere with colleagues, teachers, and students in the Department of Social and Cultural Anthropology in Helsinki, the Department of Social Anthropology in Manchester, and the African Studies Center in Boston have been very valuable.

Much of the writing for this book was done while I was a visiting scholar at the Boston University African Studies Center. I am particularly grateful to Jean Hay for her good advice on editing and for her overall warm support and presence. James McCann eased my way mentally by making the writing of a book sound like a purely pragmatic matter, devoid of mysticism. I also thank him and Sandi McCann for their hospitality. The comments of the two reviewers of the manuscript for the University of Wisconsin Press were very helpful and constructive in the production of the final edition. I wish to extend my thanks to Simeon Mesaki for help with Kiswahili, Aili Mari Tripp and Stanlie James for taking my book in their series and all the people at the University of Wisconsin Press who have worked on finalizing the manuscript for publication. Any omissions or errors are on my own account.

The main funding for this research was provided by the Academy of Finland: first as part of a project on Changing Gender Relations in Africa led by Karen Armstrong in 1994–1996, and later for a visit to the University of Manchester. Additional funding was provided by the Sasakawa Foundation, the Graduate School of Anthropological and Ethnological Sciences at the University of Helsinki, the Alfred Kordelin Foundation, and the Scandinavian Institute of African Studies in Uppsala, Sweden. The Tanzanian Commission for Science and Technology enabled my field work by granting research clearance. An ASLA-Fulbright scholarship enabled my visit to the African Studies Center at Boston University. I thank all these institutions for making this project possible.

Finally, I want to thank all my friends and family for their support and shared joy. My sister Arja and brothers Arto and Jari have often helped me with practical aspects of my living in various places. Most of all, I want to thank my parents, Maija and Rauno Pietilä, for providing me with a home where I am always welcome. Probably the biggest help my friends and family members have provided has been in arranging diversions from my work and its immediate context. Without those diversions this book might have been completed earlier, but I would likely have "dried up" prematurely before that.

Tanzania (based on FAO 2001c; Shand 2004)

# Gossip, Markets, and Gender

# Introduction

Tanzania, like many other African countries, has moved into a neoliberal era. In Tanzania, the shift began in the mid-1980s, after two decades of socialist rule and heavy centralization of its economy and administration. The reforms led the International Monetary Fund to declare that "the [Tanzanian] authorities are transforming perhaps one of the most regularized economies in Africa into one of the most liberalized" (IMF 1995, 1).

The national liberalization policies changed the rules of the game in political and economic life by giving individual actors more room to maneuver.[1] With liberalization, the boundaries shifted between the official and unofficial, or the legitimate and illegitimate. This book looks at how these boundaries ultimately are negotiated at the local level in everyday life. It focuses on moral dialogue concerning the changing economy and social structure among the Chagga people in Kilimanjaro in the mid-1990s.

The Chagga are not newcomers to economic and political enterprise. Indeed, the Chagga are reputed to be especially ambitious, entrepreneurial,

and modern people in Tanzania and wider East Africa. Their ready acceptance of missionary education, coffee cultivation, and a cash economy in the
early twentieth century made the region stand out as more prosperous than
other areas in the nation when independence came in the early 1960s. The
newly independent regime took various measures to even out regional disparities and to combat the likely opposition to its socialist policies at the
same time. For the Chagga, educational possibilities were restricted, and
important local power bases such as chieftaincies, cooperative unions, and
the Chagga Council were abolished. Consequently, the Chagga were not
avid supporters of the post-independence regime's socialist policies. Yet
they were not simply antagonistic toward or excluded from state structure,
either. Thanks to early exposure to education, Chagga men held many jobs
in the public sector throughout the colonial and independence periods.
Nonetheless, the era of liberalization was largely accepted among the
Chagga with celebration as a time of freedom regained for material and political pursuits. This became evident in the first multiparty elections in 1995,
when Kilimanjaro stood out as the strongest area of opposition in the
country (Pietilä et al., 2002). Both the most important rival to the governing party's presidential candidate, as well as one of the most prominent opposition parties, originated in Kilimanjaro.[2]

Different forms of marketing and trading have been part of Chagga life
for a long time. Chagga chiefs already had connections with the export
trade of Mombasa by the early nineteenth century (S. F. Moore 1986, 30, 63;
Stahl 1974, 36–7). Later, in the second half of the nineteenth century, both
chiefs and ordinary Chagga people were involved in year-round exchanges
with caravans from Zanzibar that stopped at the southern slopes of Mount
Kilimanjaro (Koponen 1988, 83; Von der Decken 1869–71, 272; quoted in
S. F. Moore 1986, 31). In these situations Chagga women simply extended
their usual food exchanging activities in the local markets to barter with
the caravans.

Indeed, Kilimanjaro is one of the few places in Tanzania and greater
East Africa with a long history of regularly held markets, where women
have traditionally gathered to exchange and market produce. The old system in which neighboring marketplaces form a rotating market ring continues today on the mountain, and is comparable to the better-known and
old pattern of market cycles in different areas of West Africa (Hill 1963,
448). Some Chagga men had been dealing in regional markets earlier, exchanging, for instance, milk, hides, and other animal products with the
Maasai (Koponen 1988, 103–4). For several decades in the twentieth century, however, coffee cultivation and salaried employment were an important source of income for many Chagga men. As in many other parts of the
country, the importance of trade in the informal sector began to increase

among the Chagga at the end of the 1970s, when many men and women used it as a strategy to augment their earnings in an ever-tightening economic situation. Trade and business only continued to expand after economic liberalization. This was not merely due to new official legitimacy, but also to the increasing availability of consumer goods as well as rising school fees and health care expenditures, which increased households' need for ready cash.

In Kilimanjaro, the shrinking of the *vihamba,* inherited land plots, has contributed to an increased need for money and mobility. In order to provide for their households, people seek part of their livelihood away from the home *kihamba* and the mountain; women have most often intensified their market trading, while for several decades men have been seeking economic opportunities in the urban areas of Tanzania and abroad. The current situation is thus a combination of the effects of both national and local economic developments. Chagga people, whose access to economic resources (money especially) has improved, have gained enough power to challenge the prevailing sociocultural order. Successful women traders, urban businessmen, and middle-born brothers are categories of people who have been able to enhance their economic importance in their rural home communities. New resources do not, however, translate directly into acknowledged social position; they do so only through negotiation over their value. Indeed, regardless of the Chagga's long familiarity with trading and their initially eager acceptance of liberalization policies, there was rather vigorous moral discussion of markets, market women, and businessmen taking place in Kilimanjaro in the mid-1990s. I study this discussion as a dialogue in which the moral reputations of enterprising persons and the moral value of trading itself are constructed in the context of the new official legitimacy of individual profit-making.

The Chagga do not see traders and marketplaces as separate from their sociocultural surroundings as do the advocates of the neoliberal policies. On the contrary, the Chagga evaluate traders and businessmen as members of their communities, and they ponder the wider sociocultural repercussions of the increasing importance of markets, enterprise, and money. For many people, the topic of trading and business seemed to condense many other controversial developments in society, especially changing gender and kinship relations. Therefore, this book begins with the markets of Kilimanjaro but expands, through conversations, beyond the marketplaces, to the larger concerns that trading, traders, and businessmen were closely associated with among the Chagga.

The book studies the small stories, moral reflections in everyday conversations, and interpreted life histories that are typically shared in small informal settings in markets, bars, and homes. Frequently a small group of people is involved in discussing and evaluating the life and doings of a mutual acquaintance, so much of this talk can be described as gossip. The word "gossip" has a bad reputation as a form of idle and malicious talk, which in the end demeans those—typically thought to be women—who occupy themselves with it. In this book, however, I argue that gossip plays a central part in socioeconomic transformations and the construction of moral value.

## Gossip

In Kilimanjaro, gossip is often expressly used to talk about and reveal secrets (siri). "Secrets" refer to a situation that does not comply with "how things should be" (that is, cultural conventions), but where the people involved behave as if it did, and others around them use discretion to act accordingly in the presence of those concerned. Such secrets often relate to unconventional domestic or kinship relations as, for instance, when a wife is believed to be socially or economically stronger than her husband, or a sister in relation to her brother. The public appearance of an obedient and subservient wife or a minor sibling is maintained, but the "real" state of affairs is discussed and debated in small informal circles.

There is indeed a persistent idea that any "secrets of the home" (siri za nyumbani) should be kept strictly within the family. A good home is often described as "one from which one does not hear any quarrel" (husikii ugomvi wo wote). This means that whatever discord might be at home should be kept there, for as soon as it is let out, even at a small lineage meeting, it tends to become common knowledge. Consequently, one of the crucial characteristics of a good and loyal wife is considered to be her ability to keep the secrets of the home and not reveal anything degrading about her husband or his relatives to others. This concern with keeping "secrets" only seems to encourage gossip as a way to probe into them.

What enhances such curiosity nowadays is the fact that today people's economic situations often appear more obscure to neighbors and kin than was the case earlier. With the retreat of the state and the opening-up of new economic and political arenas, the dividing lines between official truths and unofficial "secrets" are shifting. Socioeconomic differences between men have been a reality on the mountain for a long time, but during the socialist period wealthy men had to hide their accumulated riches for fear of government confiscation or anticorruption campaigns. Concealment required cooperation not only between the rich, but frequently also the help and good will of poorer relatives and neighbors (Kerner 1988, 223–24, 333–57; S. F. Moore 1986, 308–9). Thus, where there was need for an official front for rich men to hide their secrets from the state earlier, this is now more often the case in relation to some of their rural kin and neighbors. Wealthy people, men and women alike, often remain deliberately vague about their money and property in order to avoid arousing jealousy or attracting requests for assistance from their rural kin and neighbors.

Obscurity and curiosity concerning the economic situation of enterprising people is enhanced also by current forms of resources and how they are located. Wealth accumulated in the form of money is less visible and more dispersed than many of the more customary assets such as land, livestock, coffee, and food. When a person achieves prosperity outside the home community, rural neighbors can take note of it, but such a person's overall economic situation often remains a topic of speculation in the rural neighborhood. And where rapid economic or other successes are apparent, suspicions of witchcraft tend to arise.[3]

Gossip is by definition related to the "back stage" of social life. It usually takes place in informal circles behind the backs of those being discussed, and it is often occupied with revealing the back stage of the ones under discussion. In the anthropological literature, gossip has often been seen to play rather important social and political functions in community life. Early explanations emphasized gossip as a means by which group norms and values are strengthened via criticism of those who do not comply with them (Gluckman 1963, Epstein 1969). Many of the more recent theories have tended to retain this core function in their explanations, while at the same time broadening their scope to considerations of intergroup relations. Scott (1985, 1990), for instance, portrays gossip as a safe way for a subordinate group to resist and criticize the formal power structures. Gossip's ingroup impact is stronger for Scott, however; like Gluckman, he sees gossip's main function in the confirmation of norms and the obstruction of social differentiation, which strengthens group unity in relation to the outside world. The view of gossip as a way to voice anti-hegemonic views within a subordinate group is also found in White's (2000) understanding of gossip. In her analysis, gossip and rumor were genres through which Africans articulated their understanding of colonial social reality, ways for them to talk about economic and political relations. For White, gossip is also a way to delineate group bonds and boundaries by asserting the common values and standards, even though this involves debate and not merely the affirmation of those values.

This literature emphasizes the functions of gossip in defining the group; it creates and recreates the gossiping group itself by establishing a feeling of intimacy and community between the gossipers and by strengthening their common values. My approach is different. Rather than focusing on what gossip does among the gossipers, I am interested in the interaction between the gossipers and their targets, who seldom share the same conversational situations yet are always aware of each other. This awareness is largely sustained by informal talk, especially gossip and circulating stories, which make even the most aspiring individuals responsive and answerable to the surrounding community—although not necessarily compliant, as the functionalist explanations would have it.

Much of the gossip described in this book occupies itself with revealing the economic situations, means of enrichment, and main motives of entrepreneurial people. I apply Bakhtin's (1984) ideas on the interplay of official and unofficial forces in the cultural world in considering the situation as a constant attempt by successful people to present a virtuous face or official appearance in any public situation, and the perpetual undoing and opening-up of such to alternative understandings by the gossipers. Bakhtin used his distinction to describe the relationship between state power and civil society, where the official forces represented the hegemonic aspirations of the state and the unofficial forces were the anti-hegemonic practices of the public at large. Some post-colonial studies have criticized and deconstructed Bakhtin's opposition. According to Mbembe (1992), for instance, instead of a contradiction between overt acts and gestures in public and covert responses behind the scenes, the post-colonial situation is best characterized as illicit cohabitation and "conviviality" between the dominant and the subordinate, especially as played out in the ceremonies and feasts organized by the former. This conviviality, an atmosphere of mutual fun and play, results in the disempowerment of both the ruled and their rulers, their mutual "zombification" (see also Stoller 1995).

For my purposes, the distinction between a front and a back stage remains a useful starting point, even though their relationship is eventually better described as dialogical rather than oppositional. In post-socialist Kilimanjaro, too, one can observe conviviality in public encounters between the newly rich and the less well-off. Such spirit is common at feasts arranged by the wealthy, as well as in marketplace encounters between traders of different means or between traders and customers. However, there is always a back stage in a corner of a feast or a marketplace, often coexistent with the front stage event, where people evaluate and discuss their understanding of the public scene. What is crucial, nevertheless, is the fact that gossip does not remain on the back stage, that is, restricted to the small gossiping group and offering the weak a temporary safety valve for voicing their frustrations (Scott 1985). Even though initially it is discussed in small informal circles, gossip usually reaches the ears of the subjects of the gossip sooner or later, in effect requiring them to respond in one way or another. What ensues is an indirect dialogue; a person who hears what is being said about him or her through the grapevine typically does not address the criticism openly. A response by a person criticized of greediness and self-ishness, for instance, can be a display of generosity or a verbal explanation of his or her state of affairs. In the latter case, that person typically expresses her perspective in a public situation (such as a conversation in a bar) in a seemingly spontaneous way, as part of a casual conversation. In this way, gossip in Kilimanjaro eventually expands to create a semipublic sphere between the official and the unofficial—or the front and the back stages— that enables a dialogue about moral reputations and value.

Indeed, many of the casual conversations of female and male traders in bars and marketplaces are part of a larger dialogue beyond the particular face-to-face situation. The traders are aware of the talk and opinions around them, and they address that surrounding talk in their conversations and actions. Bakhtin's polyphony, or multiple voices, thus exists within what appears as a single voice or a monologue (Bakhtin 1981, 263, 271–72). In this way, gossip is the prime medium through which truths and appearances presented as definite and unambiguous are persistently subjected to dialogue in Kilimanjaro. My position leads to a very different view of power from both the theories based on the opposition between the front and the back stages and those based on the abolition of such an opposition altogether. The unofficial anti-hegemonic forces described by Bakhtin (1984) provide only temporary relief for the subordinates without any real effect on official hierarchy and structure, just as gossip remains a back stage weapon for the subordinates in Scott's (1985) depiction. In Mbembe's (1992) view, both the superordinates and the subordinates end up being powerless, trapped into mutual conviviality as performed at public feasts and events. By focusing not only on the back stage gossip or the front stage feasts and appearances, but also on the dialogue in between them, it will be possible to see how both are involved in the construction of cultural ideas and moral values.

Terms like "dominance" and "resistance" or "dominant discourse" and "counter-discourse" are too polarized in their conceptualization of the distribution of social power to capture the inescapable intertwining of the competing representations of reality. The public talk and conduct of traders and businessmen can either represent dominant ideas or depart from them. Back stage talk, for its part, does not necessarily express anti-hegemonic views; it can express dominant or conventional ideas of "how things should be." Such talk can be critical of and oppositional to the wealthy and the powerful and possibly, but not necessarily, subversive and resistant. It can also be reflective, ironic, or astounded in tone. Moral reputations and value emerge from this dialogical encounter of divergent opinions in the semipublic social sphere.

## Moral Value, Personhood, and Economy

Individual persons, even the most ambitious, are thereby dialogically entwined with the surrounding community through talk and shared concepts. That these persons are not thought of as separate but rather as par-
taking in other people's persons is shown in life stories narrating how an
individual's success or downfall often reverberates with the fate of one or
more significant others.

Anthropological studies of personhood have long been characterized by
the dichotomy between the individual and society. This precedent was set
by Mauss (1985 [1938]), who distinguished between the social concept of
"the person" *(personne morale)* and a human being's awareness of his or her
unique individuality, "the self" *(moi)*. Like Mauss, many later researchers
considered the former—the social or the public side of the person, or the
person in the roles assigned by society—as the proper object of anthropological research (e.g., Beidelman 1993, 291; Fortes 1987, 265; Radcliffe-Brown
1952, 194). More recently, researchers have been interested in the private and
inner dimensions of personhood, for which Mauss used the word *moi.*
Instead of examining roles played in society, these scholars focus on how
individuals experience the self through their senses, emotions, bodies, in-
tuitions, and movements (e.g., Jackson 1989; Jackson and Karp 1990;
Jacobson-Widding 1990). They argue that conceptualizations and verbal
statements cannot capture the shadowy, unofficial, countervailing set of experiences that represent the domain of individual freedom and agency,
hence their emphasis on bodily and sensory modalities.

According to this persistent dichotomy, the individual and private
side of personhood is something elusive and inarticulate, while the public
side is something normative, ideological, and verbally conceptualized. In
contrast, my view is that language is a means to express, build, and debate
an understanding of often ineffable events and experiences, and thus to
construct a social reality. In many ways, gossip in particular brings personal
issues into social contemplation. Although occupied with other people's
private matters, gossip simultaneously reveals issues relevant to the interlocutors themselves (cf. White 2000, 69). The subjects of the gossip, for
their part, attempt to elaborate on their own motives and life situations.
Much of the talk described here, both gossip and responses to it, involves
revealing and evaluating a person's inner qualities, aspirations, achievements, and orientations. It addresses the moral quality of people and their
acts—their moral reputations. A person's reputation emerges from between the rules and roles of society and the individual self. It is a social evaluation of and a probing into a person's inner self. In this sense, gossip forms

a bridge between the private and public aspects of the person, both that of the gossipers and their subjects.

Recently, some researchers have applied findings from Melanesian studies to examine personhood in Africa, especially the idea of persons as "dividuals" rather than individuals (Strathern 1988). A dividual person is a composite of relationships that encompass other living humans as well as the world of spirits and ancestors. Exchange and gift-giving are central in the realization of such personhood. Material exchange and giving are either depicted as establishing social relations and extending the boundaries of persons (Piot 1999, 56, 66), or they are described as acts that make visible the person's constitutive relations (Englund 1999). Individuals in these societies are the ones regarded as abnormal because they deny their relatedness by not exchanging or sharing with others. Individuals appear to others as nonrelational persons, and thus as witches (Englund 1996, 260; Piot 1999, 68; see also Taylor 1992, 13).

My focus is on how people *use* conceptions of personhood to discuss their own and others' moral quality. Among the Chagga, the criteria for evaluating moral value is based on the perception of the generative faculties and orientations of a person and his or her acts. A morally adequate person enhances the personhood of others by giving or "feeding," which refers to actual acts of giving or feeding and also to a person's more comprehensive inclination to take care of others. People who appear to appropriate the endeavors of others and to limit their possibilities for realizing or enhancing their personhood are regarded as selfish and individualistic. But such people are not depicted as "nonrelational" (Piot 1999, 68). Their selfishness lies not only in their unwillingness to exchange but also in that—directly or indirectly—they deprive others of the possibility for self-realization. In this way, even such persons and their acts are depicted as related and relational, but the nature of these relations is socially negative and damaging. Consequently, instead of "individual," I will use the term "individualist" in this book to refer to this kind of disposition.

In the anthropological literature, exchange and gift-giving are also conventionally seen as community-level means for maintaining social relations and social order in a pre-capitalist or non-Western society (e.g., Mauss 1990 [1925], Sahlins 1972). Material exchange in such societies is described as being an integral part of social relations (Polanyi 1957). Some researchers have seen the prevalence of gift-giving, reciprocity, and sharing as the characteristic features of a non-capitalist society and its "moral economy," in contrast to the emphasis on monetary transactions and individual autonomy in capitalist societies (e.g., Bourdieu 1977, Gregory 1982, Mauss 1990, Scott 1976). What seems to be a resurfacing of witchcraft suspicions and

accusations in many parts of Africa has in recent scholarship been explained by the problematic aspects of accumulation and other new forms
of inequality. Some researchers view current concerns about witchcraft as
reflective of anxiety among Africans about the encroachment of capitalism, commoditization, and modernity, which threatens the moral economy
of a local community (e.g., Comaroff and Comaroff 1993, Geschiere 2000).
Others argue that modernity, money, and accumulation as such are not
considered by Africans to be morally problematic; accumulation is acceptable as long as the enterprising person shares part of his profit by gift-
giving, patronage, or feasting. Those who do not, find themselves accused
of witchcraft (Englund 1996).

In Kilimanjaro few acts are unambiguous, however, not even such seemingly simple acts as feeding, gift-giving, feasting, or patronage. An act of
giving has several potential meanings; it can indeed be motivated by the
giver's willingness to make his or her constitutive relationships visible—
that is, to acknowledge their importance in public—but it can also be
motivated by the giver's attempt to extend her social relations or to influence others' possibilities for realizing personhood, either by expanding or
restricting them. Or it can be an attempt to mend or avoid damage to the
giver's reputation that arises from accusations of stinginess. It is this ambiguity in acts and the motivations and intentions behind them—as well as
lack of knowledge about a person's overall economic situation and material
capacity for sharing—that creates speculative discussion in gossip.

The application of concepts developed in other regions is risky because
it entails a bundle of presumptions, such as the foregrounding of acts and
distrust in the ability of words and talk to reveal people's intentions and
motivations, which is a prevalent attitude in Melanesia. In Kilimanjaro, it
is not only acts of giving and exchanging that are meaningful, but also the
ceaseless discussion and evaluation of those acts and the persons involved.
Acts of giving or not-giving do not establish the moral value of a person
and her action in and of themselves; valuation only comes about by means
of the talk that accompanies and evaluates those acts and thereby constructs their meaning. In this book, I will follow how individuals attempt to
manage the image of their own and others' moral value by revealing the
motivations, reasons, and intentions behind actions.

Rather than reflecting the advance of individualism and the encroachment of capitalism and commoditization, accusations of witchcraft and
selfishness are better seen as arguments in a dialogue about moral reputations and value, the other side of that dialogue being the justifications and
explanations those who are criticized offer for their actions. This does not
mean that money and modernity are not issues for the Chagga. In fact, despite the Chagga's reputed modernity, money and commodities do generate

a special appeal and moral concern for them. These concerns are heightened by liberalization policies, but they cannot be interpreted merely as responses to those policies or to other global economic forces invading a moral community. The relevant context for the Chagga discussions and debates are the combined effects of local, national and global developments that have enhanced the importance of money and mobility in the reproduction of life.

## Moral Imagination

The swirling ebb and flow of gossip continuously reopens to discussion matters presented as unambiguous and completed. For this reason, in my apparently sleepy, rural field site, everyday life and reality is in fact highly speculative and under constant imaginative contemplation and re-creation. In gossip, witchcraft discussions and circulating stories, other perspectives and alternative visions are continually being constructed that present life in a light other than the apparent, visible or conventional.

Rather than being simply malicious, there is a good measure of contemplation, curiosity, and imagination in gossiping. This is not to deny that gossip is sometimes harmful and destructive. My understanding of gossip draws on certain distinctions that the Chagga make between different kinds of talk in Kiswahili. They usually use a specific word for purposefully malicious or ill-intentioned talk *(kumsengenya mtu)*, and consider such talk to be demeaning and worthless. What I describe in this book is better captured by three other Kiswahili words; *porojo, soga,* and *mawazo. Porojo* and *soga* refer to light, everyday conversation or banter—they are often translated as gossip, idle chatter, or conversation. *Mawazo* means basically "thoughts" or "ideas," but it is often used for reflective thinking and discussion (cf. Fabian 1996, 311). What makes bars and marketplaces both attractive and potentially dangerous places in Kilimanjaro is the fact that people there are believed to be occupied in "exchanging thoughts" *(kubadilishana mawazo)*, that is, opening their minds to different ideas and ways of seeing things. These reflections usually include value judgments on the topics and persons under discussion. This is indeed the prevalent disposition in gossiping in Kilimanjaro, and it is best described as moral imagination.

It is in and through talk that people reflect, interpret, evaluate, discuss, and give meaning to reality. In this book, speech and talk as acts of definition are understood as inherently political and polemical, which does not mean a reduction to politics and power struggles. When discussing a particular person's moral reputation, people are simultaneously explicating, debating, and reflecting on their cultural ideas and values. In this sense, gossip is, as Haviland (1977, 170) has suggested, "a primary metacultural tool" by means of which cultural rules are learned and redefined. Here, the cultural categories concerning gender and moral value are not merely applied, but also creatively expanded to encompass new situations. As much as they are political, the conversations followed in this book are about imagination, play, and deliberation whereby the cultural notions of what is possible, appropriate, right, and desirable in gender and kinship relations are reflected on and reconsidered.

## The Research Site

### Moshi Rural, or Vunjo

The material for this book was gathered in the rural Moshi district of Eastern Kilimanjaro. I did my fieldwork in two parts: from the beginning of April 1994 until the end of January 1995, and from the beginning of February until the end of March 1997. In this book, I mostly use the ethnographic present to describe the events I observed. This is for the sake of readability and does not imply a view that life is unchanging in Kilimanjaro—it is changing as much there as in any other place in the modern world.

I lived in a former chiefdom that I will call Mayanka. Although such chiefdoms no longer formally exist, they are still alive in the sense that two or more present-day administrative units (called wards) acknowledge the boundaries and name of a chiefdom that had existed previously. People also talk about the former chiefdoms as entities and of their inhabitants as sharing common characteristics. A similar preference for older distinctions applies when we see that people often more familiarly use the word "Vunjo" when referring to the larger area with which they associate themselves, instead of the district name of Moshi. Vunjo was the middle of three administrative divisions into which the chiefdoms of Chaggaland were grouped between 1946 and 1961; to the west was the Hai division and to the east was Rombo. Vunjo included five chiefdoms (Kirua Vunjo, Kilema, Marangu, Mamba, and Mwika); the present-day rural district Moshi is larger, and includes three former chiefdoms in addition to these five.

The main road runs through the former chiefdoms and connects them to each other, to Moshi town at the foot of the mountain, and to the Kenyan border. It also connects them to the road that leads southeast to the Tanzanian coast and Dar es Salaam. On the way from Moshi town to Mayanka, the scenery changes gradually as the road curves slowly but persistently upwards and the maize fields of the plains are left behind. After the vastness of the plains, the view becomes obstructed by the banana trees that line both sides of the road. Family houses lie hidden among the banana trees.

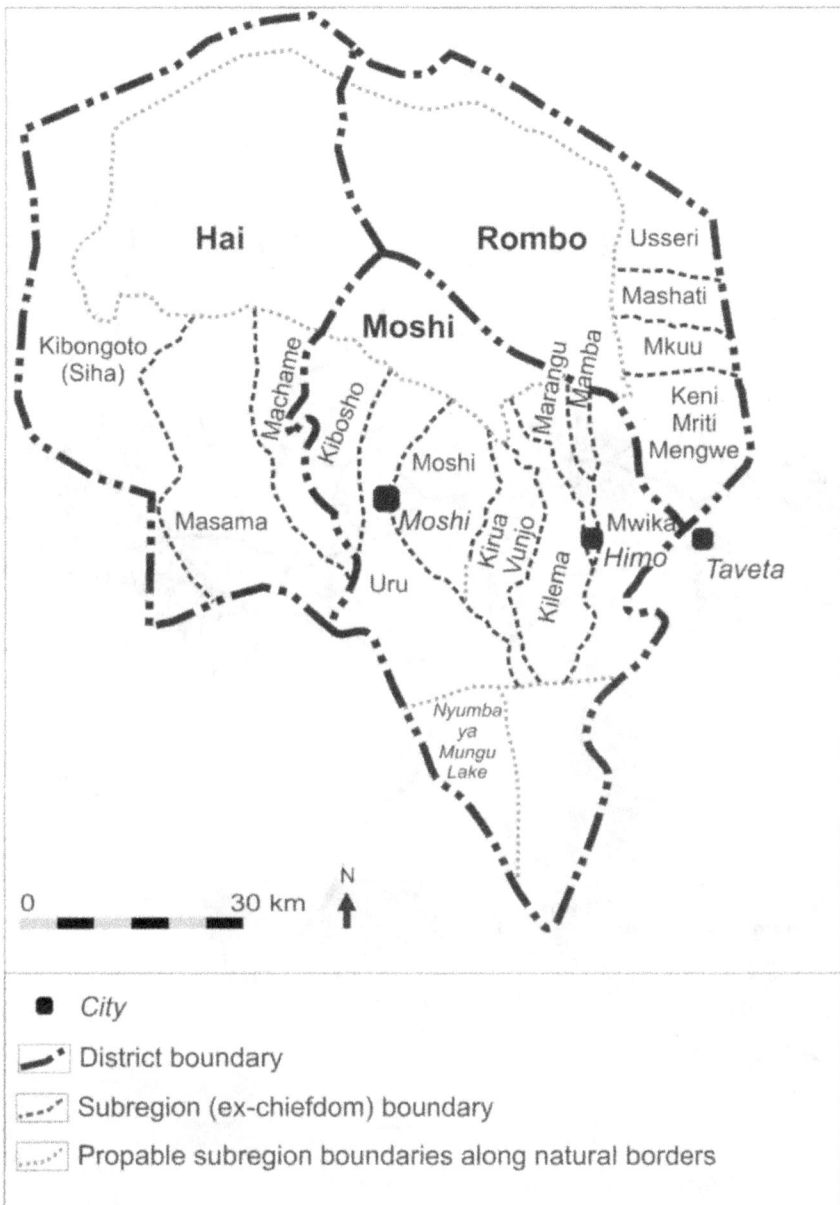

Districts and former chiefdoms in Northern Kilimanjaro (based on BP Tanzania Ltd 1990; FAO 2001a–c; Microsoft 2005; Shand 2004; Stahl 1964; Kilimanjaro Regional Statistical Abstract 1994)

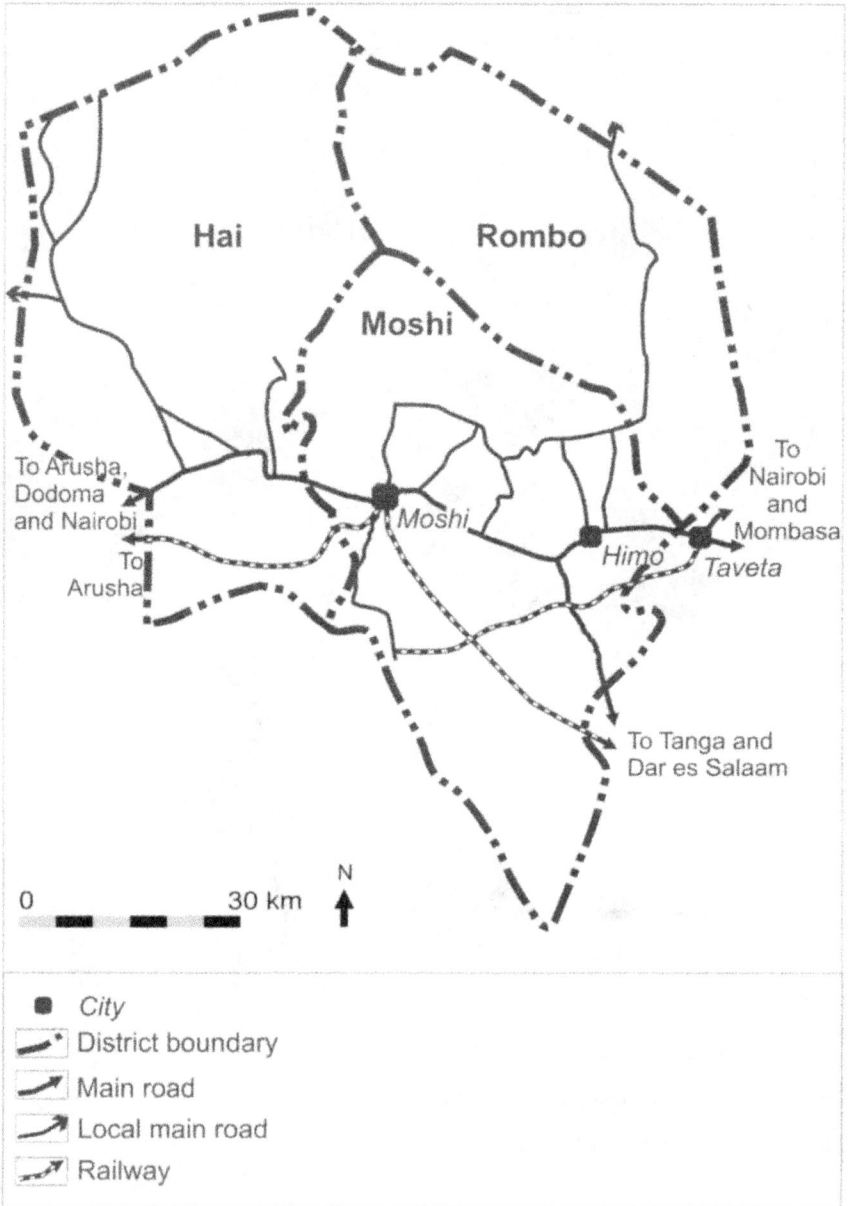

Hai

Rombo

Moshi

To Arusha,
Dodoma
and Nairobi

To
Arusha

*Moshi*

To
Nairobi
and
Mombasa

*Himo*

*Taveta*

To Tanga and
Dar es Salaam

0          30 km

N

■ *City*

*District boundary*

*Main road*

*Local main road*

*Railway*

Main road and railway connections in and from Kilimanjaro (based on BP Tanzania Ltd 1990; FAO 2001a–c; Microsoft 2005; Shand 2004)

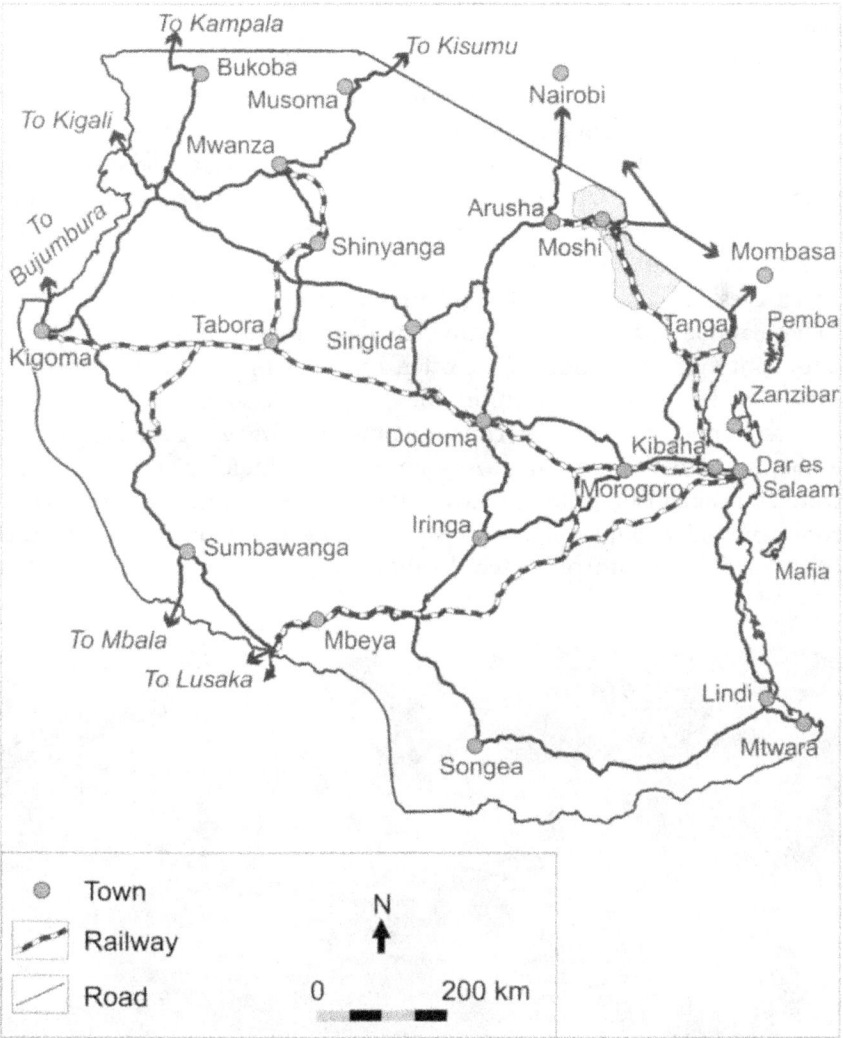

Road and railway connections in Tanzania (based on BP Tanzania Ltd 1990; FAO 2001a; Shand 2004)

## *Houses in* Vihamba

The cultivatable mountain area is densely occupied by *vihamba* (sing. *ki-hamba*), each separated from its neighbor by fences of live dracaena *(sale)*. A *kihamba* is a patrilineally inherited plot of land on which bananas, the staple food, and also coffee and vegetables are grown. Families of agnatically related kinsmen often live next to each other, each family having a house and other buildings in the middle of the banana trees on the *ki-hamba*. Families usually also have *shamba*[4] land about ten to twenty kilometers away in lower areas, where maize, beans, sunflowers, and eleusine (a type of finger millet) are grown. Due to the increasing squeeze on land and shrinking of the *vihamba* plots, maize has become a more important part of the diet than it used to be.

Houses with concrete walls and aluminum sheet roofing are common today. Families that still live in wood and daub houses are usually relatively poor. But even those houses are often roofed with sheet iron instead of grass thatch, and their condition does vary: while some wood and daub houses seem on the verge of collapse, others are in very good shape with a coating of white limestone. Among today's middle-aged and younger couples, husband and wife often live in the same house and sleep in the same room, but older couples tend to occupy separate houses or rooms. This was common practice until only a few decades ago. The wife used to live with the

Coffee and banana trees next to the main house in a *kihamba*.

Father's house *(right)* and his youngest son's house *(left)* in a *kihamba*, where both of them reside permanently.

Making dinner on a hearth of three stones.

An urban Chagga man's rural house in his home *kihamba* on the mountain.

small children and her older daughters in a traditional conical building that also housed the hearth and the animals. If a man had several wives, each woman had her own hut. The husband lived in a separate house with the older sons.

The most modern houses today are made of concrete, have glass windows, and are self-contained. These boast a fully equipped kitchen, flush toilet, bathroom, and bedrooms all inside the house. Even so, a traditional kitchen building with a hearth of three stones often stands beside such modern houses and is in active use. This reflects the continuing symbolic importance of the hearth and the food the mother cooks on it. It also reflects the unavailability and unreliability of electricity. Some people cannot afford electricity, while other houses might be situated too far from the main roads that power lines tend to follow. Infrastructural problems in the poor country often hamper the full utilization of the facilities in fully equipped houses in any case. The flush toilets tend to lack water, and the unreliable flow of electricity makes the effective use of a modern kitchen and other electric facilities difficult. People with money can solve these problems by acquiring a generator or a biogas system, both of which require a relatively large initial outlay of capital. Since the largest and fanciest houses usually belong to men who live outside the region, however, they are often empty most of the time.

A local road scene on a market day.

## *Connections*

The first European travelers to the area wrote that there were no compact villages or towns but only isolated enclosures, separated from one another by open space. Later researchers also noted the absence of compact villages or village centers. In a way this is true. Instead of forming a village center, it is more appropriate to say that commercial and other services such as post offices, gas stations, kiosks, small shops, bars, butcher shops, churches, dispensaries, schools, ward offices, courtrooms, and buildings belonging to the local coffee cooperative are situated along the road. And where there is any kind of service, there is usually also a gathering of people. The marketplaces that exist in each former chiefdom often form a kind of center, however, as there is usually a concentration of shops and services around them.

The markets and the market cycle create a pulse for the area and lend a rhythm to the scenery, the changing location of centers, and people's lives. In every marketplace, markets are held twice a week and the market days of adjacent marketplaces are arranged so that they do not overlap with each other, and so form a cycle. The women of a family usually go to the nearest market on the day it is held in order to acquire foodstuffs and to do other errands such as taking maize to be milled. Others are attracted to the market in order to meet people or perhaps send a message through a market woman to someone living farther away. Many people arrange to travel on market days, when transportation is much better, and privately owned buses and pickup trucks carry people and their loads to where they need to go.

The numerous bars *(vilabu,* sing. *klabu)* selling *mbege* (a traditional brew made of finger millet and bananas) have their own rhythm. They become lively in the afternoons, when elderly men begin to arrive. Many married women regularly go to *klabu* as well, usually between five and seven o'clock in the evening. By ten or eleven at night, the *vilabu* are usually closed because there is no *mbege* left. After that, bottled beer is available in many of the grocery stores and other kinds of bars that are often open as late as there are customers—rarely, however, after midnight.

Sunday is a day of rest. Most people go to church services, or at least feel the social pressure to go. Sunday church service is the event for which people enjoy the luxury of applying good-smelling oils and creams to their skin and hair and wearing their finest clothes (properly washed and ironed) and their best shoes. After services on Sunday, or later in the evening, many people head for a *klabu* to meet with others.

Very few houses had television sets in the mid-1990s, as there was no national television network. There were only three private television channels that served the coastal area. Those in Kilimanjaro with televisions watched Kenyan programs and videotapes of European and American drama and action films, Indian love stories, and a variety of music videos ranging from Michael Jackson to the very popular Zairean (Congolese) music and dance.

Almost every house had a radio. Men especially listened to the news, though they did not always take it at face value since the radio was still firmly controlled by the government. Rather than being considered fact and truth, radio news offered important raw material for political discussion; the end of the news was frequently the beginning of speculation as to "what really happened" or "what else happened." Radio also served the important function of providing daily announcements of deaths that had occurred; for the Chagga, who live scattered all over the country, the radio is sometimes the main way news of a deceased relative or acquaintance is received. The 1990s also saw the proliferation of new private newspapers, which were replacing the government-owned newspapers in popularity.[5]

Even those who live on the mountain and have traveled not much further than Moshi town have links to the greater world through relatives and family members. There is always someone who has studied in the United States, Europe, or China, and many more who bring news from, and their opinions of, various places like Nairobi, Mombasa, Dar es Salaam, or Mbeya. Tourists coming to climb the mountain, development project workers, visiting foreign teachers, researchers, and various "friendship society" members have all contributed to the image that the Chagga hold of Europe and Europeans. Few people bother with distinctions between Europe,

America, and Asia; all are usually referred to as "Europe" *(Ulaya)*. The change in the nature of the Chagga's global connections—if not in the orientation—is evident. The German missionary Rebmann was the first European to visit the Chagga, in 1848 (Krapf 1860, 239). Already accustomed to trading with outsiders, the Chagga confounded Rebmann by asking what he had come to trade. In the mid-1990s, I was clearly taken as a development worker and was frequently asked what I had come to do to develop the people and the area. The tone of these questions was certainly not submissive.

## The Art of Talk

This research project began as a study of Chagga market women's economic activities and household economics. The inadequacy of a survey-type approach soon became apparent. Rather than neat economic facts and data, I was confronted with different kinds of talk: gossip, stories, debates, casual conversations, and joking. All the talk seemed more elusive than clarifying, and I felt that I had been drawn into a game of whose rules I had no idea. I was simply not allowed to remain an outsider to these games, nor did people show any interest in bending to my rules: instead of replying politely to my questions, they presented counter-questions and made demands on me. They asked why I did not buy their produce instead of asking questions; they wanted to know what they would get in return if they told me about their trading; they persistently asked for gifts and drinks of soda and beer; and they wanted to know if I was able to trade or count in my head.

I found all this quite perplexing, but I gradually began to realize that the way people talked to me was not very different from how they talked and joked with each other. Instead of questioning people, I started to listen more to what they talked about, how they talked, and to ponder what their talk meant. Rather than mere callous mocking and snubs, what I had encountered was the market women's preoccupation with verbal exchanges and persuasion. I also encountered issues that they considered topical in their lives and trade.

What first seemed a game of evasive talk was the problem of overly straightforward, survey-type questioning. When answering a researcher's questions, people often have an idea of what the expected or "right" answers are, especially in a place where people have been studied, converted, and developed by Europeans for decades. But even more fundamentally, people's responses and their whole way of talking is culturally molded and constructed, which has several repercussions for conducting research. In Kilimanjaro, no one is expected to readily disclose personal matters, especially not in the marketplace, nor to a stranger—and economic "facts" are considered highly intimate matters. The father of my host family, who had had several European colleagues, more than once wondered about the European obsession with honesty and candor, and did not quite appreciate the value of it. What might be called an indirect or evasive manner of talking is appreciated in Kilimanjaro for its social flexibility and capability for avoiding conflicts. People behave smoothly and are not usually openly hostile or negative even when they do not agree—and if someone is adamant, they do often answer direct questions. Such answers can be, however, politically correct and at the same time clearly incorrect, in which case the implicit and more important message of the answer may be: "It is none of your business." Schmoll (1991, 17) calls this "the African no," an attitude of "acquiescing verbally while passively resisting." I think that responses of this kind and the evasive way of talking are also a call for the researcher to "come in" and learn the rules of the game—that is, how to talk and where to talk about what—rather than being simply a means for keeping outsiders away.

To grasp the content of the talk, one needs to learn not only the language and the words, but also to understand the concepts, the semantic meanings of the words that people use and modify as they use them. Why, for instance, do market women strenuously deny making any profit when it is obvious that they do? What exactly does "profit" or "food" mean to them? The answers to a researcher's questions on economy are often molded by different or broader concerns than the narrowly economic. Often people are speaking to wider issues and more locally momentous topics than what the researcher has in mind; in the case of Kilimanjaro, traders' answers were also comments on current local debates about gender, generational, and kinship relations. The economic is not detachable from the larger sociocultural and political environment. The most compelling and current socioeconomic concerns are often talked about through topics like witchcraft in more informal speech genres. Thus, to understand what people say, one has to learn the wider sociocultural context for their talk.

The bulk of my material comes from following fifteen trading women in the markets, bars, homes, and home communities. In the beginning, I paid most attention to how they bought and sold their goods. Because I spent several long days every week in the markets, usually sitting beside the women and occasionally helping them sell, I had abundant time to observe their selling techniques, tricks, and rhetoric, as well as their other conversations and practices. After several weeks of participation in the market, I started to spend more time in the village, bars, and homes of the market women and other people. I continued to visit the markets on a regular basis, however, in order to keep contact with the women and to gain an idea of seasonal variations in the markets.

Living in the village, I was constantly engaged in discussions with many different people, and taking part in such different occasions and celebrations as burials, inheritance meetings, church services, confirmation feasts, and bridal send-off ceremonies. My emphasis in this book is on market women, on their own talk and practices, as well as the larger public's evaluative talk about market women. Another category of people that attracted much public discussion was businessmen. Therefore, I have in this book included material on entrepreneurial Chagga men, which I will use to discuss gender-related differences in conceptions of personhood and moral value.

All in all, my material is mostly based on observation and on numerous informal discussions with market women and other people. The verbal material contains everyday conversations, circulating stories, gossip, jokes, and what I call "interpreted life histories," that is, stories people tell about themselves and about other people that often contain more or less hidden moral valuations and explanations for a person's fate. The only occasion when I made notes in the presence of people was in the market as I gathered price information; I avoided even that in the beginning until several of the market women, after having decided to cooperate with me, started to demand that I take notes, which they saw as the only way to accomplish my work properly. Otherwise, I did not make notes in public but used any brief moment of solitude to make quick notes on the conversations, which I then wrote up more properly in my own room as soon as possible. Toward the end of my stay, I recorded some twenty-five unstructured interviews, consisting of life-history interviews with middle-aged and elderly market women and some male traders. Whenever I use quotations from recorded conversations in the text, I mark them by an endnote giving the date of the conversation; other quotations come from my field notes. All the names of people that appear in this book are pseudonyms.

In fact, I realized the rather dialogical nature and bias of my field material only after I had returned home. Listening to a colleague's detailed presentation about the colors, orientations, and timing in funerary practices in Malawi, I realized that my presence in the numerous Chagga burials had been decisively different. As the formal ritual was going on, I would often be out of view of the gravesite, sitting under a banana tree, listening to an acquaintance reflect on the turns the deceased's life career had taken and the reasons for his or her death. These informal interpretations persistently surrounded and contested the formal life-histories read at each funeral, and were one example of how the informal conversations continuously challenge and call into a dialogue any attempt at formalization, closure, and official "truth."

Part 1 of this book focuses on women. Chapter 1 examines market women's sales techniques and rhetoric at Himo market. Chapter 2 shows how discussion about markets and market women spans the economics of trading to address the gendered behavior and personhood of the market women. Chapter 3 studies the construction of the moral reputation of a prominent market woman in her own conversations and those of the surrounding community. Chapter 4 considers how female respect is being reconsidered by examining several market women's recollections of their marriages by capture.

Part 2 shifts the focus to men. Chapter 5 discusses how urban-based men have become more important and visible actors in their rural home lineages. Chapter 6 considers how the moral reputations of ambitious men are discussed by examining stories about businessmen who failed to turn their resources into wealth and status. The conclusion summarizes the implications of a dialogical approach for the study of a changing economy, with a comparative discussion of the social importance of gossip in building moral reputations and value.

*Part 1*

# Women

# *1*

# Domesticating the Market, Marketing the Domestic

At present, open marketplaces are the most important marketing channel for food in both rural and urban Tanzania. Grain marketing was for a long time outside the control of private African traders. Under British colonial rule, grain marketing was organized through marketing boards and Asian traders. The post-colonial government tightened state control over economy and created a national, single-channel marketing system in the 1970s. Tanzania remained officially committed to this marketing system until 1986. In fact, however, from the late 1970s and through the 1980s, parallel markets for grain were expanding; in the mid-1980s, they were estimated to be handling as much as over two-thirds of nationally marketed production (Bryceson 1994, 17). After trade liberalization, private traders soon became dominant on the markets for food products; a study in Arusha region found that 88–93 percent of the marketed output of maize was being handled by private traders in 1990 and 1991 (Parsalaw 1996, 82).

This chapter deals with Himo, one of the largest marketplaces on Eastern Kilimanjaro and an important center for the food trade. The liveliness of Himo is much due to its strategic location at the junction of important roads, plains, and mountain areas, and its proximity to the Kenyan border. Sited next to the biggest river in the area, the Ghona, Himo has long provided a natural oasis for a variety of visitors. Himo was one of the first places to be visited by early European travelers and Swahili caravan leaders (Stahl 1964, 281, 294–95). In the second half of the nineteenth century, caravans of hundreds of men used to stop at Himo to purchase food and animals for the journey inland to Lake Victoria or to the south, as well as on the way back to the coast (S. F. Moore 1986, 31–32).

Today Himo is best regarded as a trading center and a developing town with a growing population of permanent residents and a diversity of shops and services. Although it is active on any given day, Himo becomes especially lively on market days, when buses full of people and truckloads of saleable goods are transported to and from the mountain and across the Kenyan border. All kinds of foodstuffs, both raw and processed, various factory products, petty commodities, and artisan goods can be found at this marketplace, and most articles are sold both wholesale and retail. What distinguishes Himo from Mwika, the other large market on Eastern Kilimanjaro some thirty kilometers away, however, is its importance as a center of the food trade. Himo functions as a center where different kinds of foods and grains are transported in bulk to be broken down into smaller quantities for sale. Thus, truckloads of maize, rice, beans, millet, vegetables, fruits, and tobacco are brought to Himo for redistribution at this and other rural markets in Tanzania and in Kenya. On the other hand, bananas are brought to Himo from the surrounding mountain areas to be bulked for transportation and sale elsewhere.

Markets are held twice a week at Himo as at the other nearby marketplaces; market days in different locations are so arranged that they do not overlap, but form a rotating market ring. This practice dates at least from the late nineteenth century (Gutmann 1926, 382–83). Apparently the trading scene was rather mixed at the times when the caravans stopped at Kilimanjaro; the chiefs held a monopoly over the most valuable goods, but ordinary people exchanged minor items with the caravans. Chagga women flocked to the grounds where the caravan porters camped in order to exchange foodstuffs (Meyer 1891; quoted in S. F. Moore 1986, 31–32). However, in the nineteenth century, regular rotating markets were strictly a woman's sphere where adult women gathered to exchange their foodstuffs, and it was not considered appropriate for men to enter (Gutmann 1926, 382–83). This association with women was strengthened by the fact that marketplaces used to be the first places where women ceremonially appeared in public at

Bananas to be transported from a marketplace in Kilimanjaro to Dar es Salaam.

the end of the seclusion periods marking life-cycle transitions such as initiation, marriage, childbirth, or the death of a husband.

Today the weekly market scene is more varied: while a majority of traders are still adult women, there are also men, boys, and girls involved in trading. Another significant change is the fact that while in the nineteenth century women most often exchanged goods they themselves had produced, traders today are usually involved in selling goods they have purchased; in other words, the markets have become commodified.

In this chapter, I will study the spatial and social organization of the Himo market. I will describe the layout of the marketplace and show how participation in trade is structured by gender, age, wealth, and nationality. The latter part of the chapter looks at the location of the marketplace and trading in terms of a more conceptual map, and I will focus on how the morality of trading is constructed in the greater public's critical discussion and in women traders' market discussions and practices. This emphasis on market women partly reflects my fieldwork methods, but also highlights the fact that critical discussions concentrate on market women rather than men. While this chapter focuses on the techniques of trade and the moral evaluation of them, the following chapter studies how moral dialogue extends to issues of gendered behavior and spheres of contemporary Chagga society beyond the marketplace.

Issues of morality in economy and markets have been discussed and debated in economic anthropology. One persistent practice has been to distinguish different spheres of exchange and societies on the basis of their differential logic and code of morality. Thus, a distinction is frequently made between noncapitalist societies where the economy is "embedded" in and subject to social relations (Polanyi 1957, 250) and where "gift logic" (Gregory 1982; Mauss 1990 [1925]) prevails, and capitalist societies where the economy functions as an autonomous sphere and "commodity logic" prevails. In this literature, marketplaces in otherwise noncapitalist societies are often singled out as morally distinct spheres, where profit-seeking, exploitative behavior is expected and accepted because exchanges take place among strangers (e.g., Bohannan 1955; Bourdieu 1977; Piot 1999).

The problem with these views is the rather rigid and predefined image of the different economic systems, exchange spheres, and the moral code that they prescribe. This chapter will show that both utility-seeking cunning and "gift logic" coexist in the markets of Kilimanjaro. It will describe how Chagga market women domesticate the marketplace by drawing on familiar domestic and kinship values. Most of the female traders define themselves as "mothers" *(mama)* and "farmers" *(wakulima)* rather than traders. This was also revealed in a census of a hundred households that I took; even the biggest and most dedicated female traders gave cultivation as their primary occupation. In the market, they talk about feeding children instead of profits. And many women call their trading capital a "hoe" *(jembe)*. Yet, the competitive market situation does require skill in cunning and negotiation.

I will argue that negotiability is the key characteristic of Kilimanjaro markets; women traders create both profits and social relations through negotiation. It is this negotiability, the manipulation of and experimentation with moral ideas and social relations, rather than the fixity of moral norms and spheres of exchange, that makes the traders seem shifty and the marketplace morally suspect in public opinion. For rather than trading and its morality being "embedded" in predefined social relations, as is often claimed in various theories, social relations are continually being defined and redefined in the marketplace.

## Himo Market

### Entering the Market

I used to enter the marketplace with my female friends from one side. Instead of the main gateway, most women use one of the narrow rutted paths near all the bus stands, which are more accessible and quicker than the main entrance. The main gateway is also usually blocked by large cars and trucks entering and leaving the marketplace with their loads of onions, tomatoes, cabbages, tobacco, bananas, and sometimes well-concealed Kenyan beer.

The vast and calm landscape, the infinite flat country with its maize fields and great vault of sky, vanishes rapidly when one dives onto one of those paths between the little shops. The narrow path is crowded with people entering and leaving the marketplace, dodging each other in order to get through, women carrying full baskets or bags of food on their heads or backs or in their hands. Every now and then a young boy rushes onto the path pushing a wooden cart bearing a sack of maize, rice, or millet and making a whistling sound or any loud noise to clear a way through the crowd.

At the main gate, and even in the marketplace itself, car drivers have little sympathy for the other passers-by or for the sellers sitting on the ground. Drivers do not hesitate to force their way through the crowds, even into the middle of the busy marketplace, considering it the responsibility of others to ensure they do not get hit by a car or splashed with water from the puddles in the bumpy way. Bicyclists, mostly young boys, zigzag between the cars, pushcarts, sellers, and pedestrians, carrying two to five cases of beer on their bike racks, and making their presence known by constantly ringing their bells.[1] As one tries to be quick and alert in order to avoid bumping into people or vehicles while trying to make one's way through, one cannot help but get a sense of the fast-paced and frenetic atmosphere of the marketplace.

## The Organization of Trade

Like other marketplaces on Eastern Kilimanjaro, Himo is surrounded by small shops, bars, and grocery stores that have sprung up over the past decades. Those with permanent premises are expected to possess an annual license for their trade. The marketplace itself is an open space without much infrastructure where, in principle, anyone can enter from any point and start selling his or her goods without paying a regular market fee or obtaining a license. Instead, taxes are collected daily from traders present in the market and the amount depends on the quantity of the trader's goods. While officially legitimate market attendance requires only the payment of the daily tax, in practice any newcomer or occasional vendor faces a rather fixed spatial organization where already established traders have staked out market spots that they will not let anybody else invade.

Market space is divided into sections according to the type of commodity sold and the level of selling. Sellers of beans or secondhand clothes, for example, sit next to each other. Wholesalers and retailers of one type of product are usually located in separate areas that are typically close to each other. Nevertheless, the goods do not simply pass from a wholesale to a retail level; most goods undergo a chain of redivision and redistribution via retailers of different levels.

For example, truckloads of sacks of millet brought in from other areas by wholesalers are sold to retailers who buy multiple sacks, perhaps twenty, and resell them individually to the next chain of retailers, who will sell them in the market by the bowlful. The beer brewers, depending on their capital, buy either a sack of millet from the first-level retailers or a few bowls from the second-level retailers. For rice, maize, and beans there are wholesalers from whom retailers typically buy one or two sacks at a time. The retailers resell them by measures at Himo or another marketplace both for home consumption and to yet another level of retailers who take the millet to sell in other marketplaces.

The situation changes with the market. An upper-level retailer always prefers to sell her goods to lower-level retailers, but if sales are slow on a given day, she might choose to sell both to retailers and to ordinary market customers. Such a situation is disadvantageous for the lowest-level retailers, and is one indication of their relative powerlessness in respect to the larger traders. Often, however, the smaller retailers decide to stay in the same section and sell at the same price as their suppliers, while trying to reduce the quantity measured for the customer. This is the most common strategy, since the upper-level retailer usually finishes her selling early. Other options for the lowest-level retailers are to move to another section in the market where small quantities are sold for home consumption or to move to a smaller market.

Most food product wholesaling takes place from trucks and storerooms, while most of the retail food trade and some of its wholesaling takes place on the open market. The marketplace is an open space that enjoys no natural shade. Traders spread a sack on the ground and their articles upon it, sitting on a sack or using a bucket, box, stone, or small stool as a chair. When the day begins to grow hot, sellers cover their heads with anything handy or move to sit in the shade of nearby shop roofs or terraces, provided they can keep an eye on their goods at the same time. During the rainy season, traders run a few times a day to these small terraces with their articles wrapped in plastic in an effort to seek shelter from the heavy torrents that turn the marketplace into a muddy arena of channels of running water. After each downpour, sellers return to their spots and lay out their goods again until another comes.

There is one section in the marketplace with permanent wooden stalls, built by people who rent them out to sellers. Those who rent them are people

Tomato sellers. Wooden market stalls with plastic roofs in the background.

who live close to the marketplace, perhaps in a rented flat, and use the stall
for selling foodstuffs, tea, or snacks on a daily basis. Sellers of goods brought
in from Kenya have a simple wooden table that is usually left standing even
though it is used only on market days. These traders spread plastic for cover
over their tables. Unlike many other products, Kenyan goods are usually sold
by the same traders in the same locations both wholesale and retail.

## The Traders

The spatial layout of the marketplace tends to be gendered, as most of the
retail food traders are women. Although some women are involved in
wholesaling, there are more men involved in wholesaling and transporting
truckloads of food products. Most of the shopkeepers and bar owners
around the marketplace are men.

Young boys can be found on different levels and in different sections of
the market, ranging from hawkers of trinkets, cheap cosmetics, drinks, and
biscuits and pushcart users, to importers of grain and exporters of bananas. They are especially well represented in the section where Kenyan goods
are sold. These Kenyan goods are minor factory products, usually illegally
imported from across the border, and include such items as toothbrushes;
toothpaste; shampoo; hair coloring; hair straighteners; skin lotions; skin-
whitening creams; soaps; toilet paper; cooking oil; tinned butter; packed
salt and tea; bottled juices; packed spices; kitchen utensils made of plastic,

aluminum, and enamel; flashlights; padlocks; and mirrors. There are also articles of ready-made clothing, such as plastic shoes from Kenya, dressing gowns from China, T-shirts, socks, and women's underwear, and some of the traditional women's cloth known as *kanga*. Most of the *kanga* and *kitenge*[2] cloths as well as scarves come through Dar es Salaam and Zanzibar. Young Tanzanian boys and men dominate the trade in these minor factory goods, but some younger female entrepreneurs are also involved in bringing them in from Kenya and Zanzibar.

In 1994, one of the most important Kenyan products was illegally imported beer, transported through the forests by bicycle and car and redistributed to rural and urban bars and grocery stores. Both women and men were involved in this illegal trade. Here again were operators at very different levels, ranging from those attempting to smuggle a few bottles to those who transported carloads, to as far as Dar es Salaam, Machame on Western Kilimanjaro, or other parts of the country. This was a risky business. The police were after these people all the way, and if a person was found with smuggled beer, he or she had to pay duties on it or, more likely, bribe the policemen. Every now and then a group of armed policemen went around the market area and smashed every bottle of Kenyan beer they could find, no matter if it was a smuggler or a bar selling the beer.

Whereas minor factory products flowed from Kenya to Tanzania, food was the most common product taken to the Kenyan side of the border. Both Tanzanians and Kenyans were involved in this trade. Kenyan men and women came regularly to Himo market to buy maize and beans in large quantities, fruits like oranges and avocados, and pottery from the neighboring Pare Mountains. Much secondhand clothing was also taken from Tanzania to the Kenyan market, because Kenya had restrictions on the import of cloth and clothing. Tanzanian women and young men dominated the cross-border secondhand clothing trade, and almost all the secondhand clothes sellers at the large market near the border on the Kenyan side were Chagga. The trade was still relatively profitable in 1994, but less so than during the heyday of the 1980s.

On the Tanzanian side of the border, both women and men sell secondhand clothes. Most of the sellers in Himo buy the clothes in Kiboriloni market, close to Moshi town, from traders who transport them from importers in Dar es Salaam. Some Himo traders occasionally travel themselves to Dar es Salaam to buy clothes. While men are more numerous than women in this large-scale and long-distance trade, women have become relatively prominent on the market for secondhand clothes. The presence of women in this trade is often remarked upon, because trade in clothes had been the business of men, and clothing was one of the first products that brought men to the market.

## Gendered Performances

The presence of men in Chagga markets is not a completely recent phenomenon. Some Mayanka men entered the local markets in the late 1920s
and 1930s to sell cloth and clothes imported from Kenya or purchased from
Indian merchants in Moshi town.[3] Some sold cloth and clothes at the marketplaces, while others established shops. Other men owned butcher shops
at that time, and by the 1940s still others had set up shops where they sold
millet purchased from women traders.

As parallel markets spread during the 1970s, some men became involved
in selling scarce items like salt and lamp oil, and they also sold millet in certain markets. Several market women remembered, however, how the number of men in the markets increased during the 1980s in particular. This was
because of the worsening economic situation on the one hand, and trade
liberalization on the other. One female rice trader described the men's behavior as a rather aggressive attempt to take over the women's trade: male
traders came and "molested us [female traders] a lot, because they came by
force, in order to win us. . . . He takes by force [saying] 'I'll take that load, I'll
just take it.' By force."[4]

Although there are fewer male than female traders at the market, at first
glance men are the loudest and most visible. They force their way through
with their cars, trucks, bicycles, and pushcarts. In the mid-1990s, two men
selling secondhand clothes in the large market area were the only ones using
microphones and loudspeakers to attract customers. Other traders had
to rely on their own voices. The loudest of these sellers were also men. For
instance, there was a group of young boys employed to sell secondhand
T-shirts, scarves, and underwear for women. They often tied a woman's scarf
around their heads and donned a brassiere over their shirts, filling them
with cloth to resemble breasts. The boys used to dance and sing a wedding
song with slightly modified words; "These T-shirts are shining and spark-
ling, we sell them with grace and mercy."[5] Like the traders with microphones
and loudspeakers, they managed to attract a steady crowd of people, with
potential female customers trying on the brassieres on top of their clothes.

The market performance of both men and women should be seen in the
context of cultural ideas and expectations of gender-specific behavior.
Their ways of moving about in the market reflect the gendered ways of the
greater society. Men's "forceful" and straightforward style in buying their
produce, in forcing their way through the crowded—and mostly female—
marketplace with their cars and other vehicles, and in their sales patter, res-
onates with the expectations of male visibility and publicly dominant roles
in other contexts.[6] Indeed, aside from young boys, men do not usually feel
comfortable using the small passageways between shops to enter the market,

even on foot, but prefer the larger passages. Women traders, on the other hand, make their way through the market day by slipping through the small passageways and attracting their customers by indirect means.

## Market Qualities

Many researchers have expressed frustration with trying to make sense of the chaotic marketplaces. For instance, Appleby (1985), who has studied Gambian markets, writes: "Marketplaces are also bewildering phenomena. Most last only a few hours. People are constantly coming and going. . . . Even the distinction between buyer and seller blurs. It just seems impossible to sort out all this activity in the few hours any market is functioning. Fortunately, both the theory and the methods necessary to make sense out of this seeming chaos are available." Appleby applies central place theory, which was developed by the German geographer Christaller in the 1930s, and later elaborated by Skinner (1964) and Smith (1985). In these studies, real-world chaos that did not seem to fit the model was usually treated as an aberration.

In what follows, I am more interested in how traders and the public conceptualize markets and how those conceptions are acted upon in the market proper. Instead of viewing the apparent chaos of the marketplace as a nuisance that clouds the underlying reality, I consider it an integral part of the making of the market, its transactions and its people, and attempt to plunge into the noise rather than slide beneath it.

### Ujanja—*Cunning*

In Kilimanjaro, markets are often categorized—along with bars, roads, and schools—as spaces outside the domestic sphere of *kihamba*. They are depicted as places where different people "mix" *(kuchanganya)*. Market women often say that trading requires speech *(mdomo*, literally "mouth"), experience *(uzoefu)*, intelligence *(akili)*, and cunning *(ujanja)*. This last aspect is perhaps the most common and controversial quality that both market women and others associate with traders, especially women. So frequent and strong is this association that *ujanja* can be said to be iconic or emblematic of trading.

*Ujanja* always relates to *akili* (intelligence), but it is more ambiguous in its moral value. When applied to a small child, *ujanja* usually means that she or he is not easily cheated, but knows to detect fraud and offers witty and clever responses instead of being unquestioningly obedient and kind. In a child *ujanja* is often considered a promising quality that can be channeled into a positive kind of *akili*. Similarly, *ujanja* is a positive quality in an adult, when he or she uses it to avoid being cheated. One can hear such proud comments as, "He tried to do some *ujanja*, but I was more *mjanja*."

The moral blame for being *mjanja* is then on the one who initially tried to cheat the other person.

As a personal trait, *ujanja* is considered a negative quality indicating a tendency to use a crooked form of intelligence and deceitfulness.[7] It can refer to actual and verifiable cheating but is more properly a suspected inclination to cheat. To call a person *"mjanja"* is to say that he or she tends to shuffle and swindle, and for that reason can never quite be trusted. In Kilimanjaro, *ujanja* is often considered the most descriptive attribute of the coastal Swahili people. For that reason, instead of *mjanja*, a person might also be called a Swahili when judged to be giving indirect answers or suspected of cheating.

While both the traders and others consider *ujanja* a central feature of markets, their opinions differ as to what using *ujanja* actually involves and what its moral quality is. As potential customers, nontraders see themselves on the defensive in the face of the traders' cunning, especially that of female traders. At the beginning of my fieldwork, when I told a local man that I had come to study market women, he replied, "All traders are thieves, especially the women traders." Many nontrading people do indeed claim that women traders are very experienced in cunning and far outdo the male traders in that respect. This is one reason men say that they would not go to the market to buy things, since they—like children and foreigners—do not know all the tricks that traders use and would surely be cheated.

The traders' definition of the term is more flexible. Market women often maintain that there are two kinds of *ujanja*, the good and the bad. While in their minds only the bad kind of *ujanja* is cheating, they consider the good kind of cunning a necessity both in the market and in other contexts. Basically, they describe it as the capacity to plan and count in order to avoid loss. *Ujanja* is also frequently described as a necessary asset in surviving, enduring and combating the ever-present possibility of fraud and betrayal in the market. In this usage, *ujanja* is again legitimized as something needed for defense and mere survival.

This is shown in the story of a woman who came home from the market one day in a rather agitated state of mind explaining how she had sold seven bundles of bananas on credit to a boy who would transport them to Dar es Salaam and who, having temporarily run out of money, had promised to pay for the bundles on the coming market day. It was now the second market day after the transaction and she was still waiting for her money. Feeling uneasy, she searched the market for the boy and found him just as he was about to leave for Dar es Salaam with a new load. She rushed at him, screaming angrily that she was still waiting for the money that she was supposed to have received a week ago. The boy agreed to pay her part of the amount and promised to pay the rest on the next market day. The woman was not happy to receive only part of the money she was owed, but declared that without *ujanja* she would not have gotten even that: "Had I been standing there like this [silently, her arms hanging down loosely] I would never have gotten my money! Really! Really! In the market one has to be *mjanja!* Otherwise you die of hunger!"

However, what morally acceptable *ujanja* exactly involves is often both flexible and ambiguous in market women's usage of the term. One market woman said quite matter-of-factly that "market trade is deceiving";[8] it is the "making of conjuring tricks" *(kumziba mtu macho)* so that the customer thinks she is getting something more and better than she actually gets. The other frequently mentioned quality, *akili* (intelligence), often carries the insinuation of cunning in market women's usage as well. A woman can, for instance, explain the difference between the purchase and sale prices for her produce of the day as what she has "got" (i.e., the profit), plus the extra that she got "by using intelligence" *(akili).*

By manipulating and extending the meanings of such words as *ujanja* and *akili,* traders often blur the difference between cheating and "healthy" cleverness. One tomato-seller assured me that there were no tricks to her trade. But even so, she explained that when arranging tomatoes into piles of three she might put two smaller tomatoes on the bottom and a large one "of dignity" on top so that it would seem like they were all big.

Market women would often distinguish between different kinds of trade and traders on the basis of the moral acceptability of their selling techniques. Many market women who are not involved in the trades that require measuring quantity (finger millet, maize, rice, and beans) share the greater public's complaint against those traders and the deceitfulness of their measuring techniques. These sellers are considered particularly experienced in using "conjuring tricks" that include skilful techniques in the process of measuring and the use of different-sized containers, as will be discussed below.

As always, there is more to the "conjuring" than pure technique, however. It also involves the creation of an air of attraction that enchants the customer, makes him or her feel satisfied with the transaction and eventually return to the same trader at another time. The creation of this magic involves both the seller's *ujanja* and *mdomo.*

The close association of *ujanja* with *mdomo* (mouth) was revealed in a discussion with a man who had been selling clothes in the market since the 1930s. Like other traders, he maintained that there are different kinds of *ujanja,* not all of which are bad. He explained:

There is *ujanja* of a good mouth and *ujanja* of a bad mouth, and there is *ujanja* of secretive stealing that one does not realize. You can talk with a person, and s/he has another friend here [behind his/her back] who s/he shares with; [good] *ujanja* is deceiving by mouth. Eeh, s/he laughs with you, and yet s/he has another one there [behind the back], and they are together. There is another [bad] kind of *ujanja;* a person makes you laugh, and while you are laughing s/he has other *wajanja* there [crafty people behind the back]. When s/he has gone, [you realize,] "ooh, that thing of mine has been stolen, I have been robbed!" And s/he asks you: "what has been taken from you, my friend?" You tell him/her that s/he has taken your thing, and s/he claims that s/he does not know about it, and yet s/he does.[9]

With this description, this man was saying that there are at least two kinds of *ujanja,* and the one necessary in trading is that of a "good mouth"; you talk nicely and behave in a friendly manner with a customer and keep your aim and purpose concealed, in the background. Entertaining talk makes a customer purchase from and return later to the same trader. By contrast, the bad *ujanja* is equivalent to cheating and involves making use of pleasant behavior and talk to conceal the aim of stealing. Interestingly, in both cases the man describes "the background" as other people with whom the trader actually shares even though he or she creates the atmosphere of sharing with the customer.

The attributes of "mouth" and "craftiness" are only associated with the larger markets. A small village market is instead called *soko mjinga* ("a fool's market"), since there is not much action or negotiation. One of the local markets that used to be pretty lively in 1994 had entered a quiet phase at the beginning of 1997 and some of the traders had stopped going there, saying the market had earned the nickname *soko bubu* ("a dumb market," also "unofficial market"). In contrast, a lively, populous market is said to be "mixed" [with people] *(kuchanganya).*

## Morality in Exchange

The smaller markets are thus conceptualized as being closer to "village" values and what Bourdieu (1977, 185) calls "good faith economy" than the large markets. In much of the economic anthropological literature, market and kinship relationships are seen as incompatible and antithetical, since market relationships are neither long-lasting nor personal. Between strangers, market exchange is characterized as profit-maximizing behavior (Bohannan 1955, 60), negative reciprocity (Sahlins 1972), or sacrilegious cunning (Bourdieu 1977, 185). According to these models, people follow different moral guidelines according to the context of an exchange and the goods involved (Bohannan 1955, Piot 1999), and to the predefined social distance between the actors (Bourdieu 1977, Sahlins 1972).

What is common for the theorists mentioned above (Bohannan, Sahlins, Bourdieu, Piot) is the "substantivist" baseline first formulated by Polanyi

(1957), according to which economy in a noncapitalist society does not function as an autonomous sphere nor is it integrated by a market principle in the way that economies in modern Western societies are. In a noncapitalist society, economy is embedded in social relations instead, and the prevailing exchange modes are redistribution, reciprocity, and gift-giving, which define and sustain the community. Mauss (1990 [1925]) postulated that gift exchange ties the exchanging parties and the objects exchanged together, and is thus the basis for integration of a primitive society. By contrast, monetary exchange in modern societies dissolves the relationship between people and objects exchanged, as well as between the transacting parties. This opposition was further sharpened by Gregory (1982) by naming these two exchange modes as "gift" and "commodity" logic. Gift logic refers to an exchange of inalienable objects between interdependent transactors, while "commodity logic" refers to an exchange of alienable objects between independent transactors.

The view of money's disruptive effects on sociality has a long intellectual history that stretches back to Aristotle, Thomas Aquinas, and Karl Marx (Parry and Bloch 1989). All of them condemned money, market exchange, and commodities on moral grounds, because they believed these caused the dissolution of communal bonds. Marx and Simmel saw money as enhancing anonymity in exchange, because money itself is anonymous (ibid., 2–6). Since then, many researchers have considered money and markets important agents in transforming once personal relationships into impersonal ones. Indeed, in addition to the social distance between transacting parties, another reason for the alienation from customary moral norms in exchange is often found in anthropological literature in commoditization and the entry of money economy. Even many of the substantivists have believed that the spreading monetary economy would destroy the distinctions both between the distinct spheres within a society and between the different kinds of economies (e.g., Bohannan 1955, 1959).

Comparable distinction between different economic logics is expressed in the literature on "moral economy." This concept, derived from Rudé (1959) and E. P. Thompson (1971), was applied by Scott (1976) to describe the ethos of sharing and securing subsistence to all members of peasant communities. Scott portrays the peasant "moral economy" in Southeast Asia in the twentieth century as threatened by the capitalist farming system and logic. In Scott's usage, "moral economy" comes to refer to a stable, traditional, homogenous, and norm-bound peasant culture attempting to defend itself against the state and the market system. A similar view of a local community defending its integrity and moral economy in the face of a more immoral and socially destructive but stronger economy and logic of capitalism is repeated in various recent studies. For instance, Yang (2000) describes the coming-together of two different economic logics on the southeast coast of China; that is, the archaic economic logic, which is subversive and opposed to the expanding capitalist logic. Comaroff and Comaroff (1993, xxv), for their part, portray post-colonial African societies as struggling against the "immoral economy" imposed by modernity and capitalism.

Parry and Bloch (1989) have criticized theories that attribute different kind of logic to different societies, and proposed that this distinction rather be seen within, not between societies. This is, however, not an entirely new view; similar ideas of the distinct logics within a society exist already in Bohannan (1955) and Sahlins (1972), for instance. Parry and Bloch (1989) suggest that there are two related but separate transactional orders within each society: long-term transactions concerned with the reproduction of the social and cosmic order, and short-term transactions that are the arena for individual competition. The latter is subordinated to the former; as long as this is the case, individual acquisitive aspirations are not morally condemned. This model is, however, rather structural-functionalist and presupposes shared culture and values. In the real world there is seldom such a consensus about which actions belong to short-term and which to long-term cycles, and therefore about their morality. Members of a society might also hold very different views of the highest values, the ideal social order, and the best ways to achieve and maintain them.

Many of the newer studies in the field of the exchange spheres emphasize the flexibility of the spheres. Guyer (1993, 1995) and Guyer and Belinga (1995) have sensitized anthropologists to the multiplicity of the categories of wealth, resources, and valued human qualities in pre-colonial Africa and their changing composition and character over time, which models of discrete spheres of exchange fail to capture. Others emphasize the continuous reformation of the spheres through political maneuvering. Appadurai (1986), for instance, stresses the calculative and interested dimension in all exchange, which always leads to diversions from the conventional regimes of value and to the creation of new paths and spheres of exchange. Ferguson (1985, 1992) has provided some concrete examples of the politics and conflicting interests involved in attempts to maintain or redefine spheres of exchange in Lesotho.

A comparable development has taken place in the conceptualization of "moral economy." After Scott, this term has been used in various ways and contexts. Spear (1997) and Tripp (1997), for instance, employ the concept in their studies of mountain farmers in northern Tanzania and the informal sector operators in Dar es Salaam, respectively. The way they use the concept resembles Scott's usage in that the "moral economy" tends to remain a normative and idealistic group-level denominator, describing a value system and logic in opposition to the ideology and economic rationality of the state. Tripp, however, develops the concept into a more dynamic view; rather than as a traditional culture on the defensive, she sees the moral economy among the informal sector operators as fertile ground for new institutions and a form of influential resistance that eventually pressured the Tanzanian state towards liberalization policies.

Some of the newer studies view "moral economy" as something that emerges in the encounter between dominant and subordinate groups. Munro (1998) describes "moral economy" as emerging in negotiations between state agencies and rural citizens in post-colonial Zimbabwe, and Rubert (1998) in the encounter between tobacco farmers and laborers in colonial Zimbabwe. Glassman (1995) views "moral economy" as an ideological or discursive language shared by both "patricians" and "plebeians" along the nineteenth-century Swahili coast. This language was one of paternalism and reciprocity, and the struggle between the two groups was about the meaning of the ideal of paternalism, as well as about the two differing perspectives to it. Glassman's view is evocative in its emphasis on "moral economy" not as a binding norm but as a shared language and ideology that people use and redefine as they act and argue with each other. The way Glassman uses the concept of moral economy comes close to my own, yet the difference is that in my Kilimanjaro case the question is often not only about the restructuring of existing relations but about extending the ideas of moral economy to new relations in the market.

I view moral economy a language and an ideology that provides familiar concepts, ideas, and practices for unfamiliar people to encounter and negotiate with each other in the market. Women traders use the moral economy language in order to combat the popular conceptualization of the marketplace as a morally suspicious sphere and to convert stranger and commodity relations into more personal relations.

## Women Creating the Ambience

### Attracting Customers

Male traders are quite straightforward in their sales rhetoric: they declare aloud that their products are good and state the prices, making a loud show of it. Female traders try to build an atmosphere of familiarity and trust instead. They try to master the potentially hostile market situation by drawing upon idioms for other kinds of situations, especially from the kinship and domestic domains. It is not just the words they speak, it is as importantly the ambience that they create by means of wheedling, cajoling, and amiable banter that is crucial in their construction of the social setting for trade.

In diverse ways, female sellers try to achieve more personal contact with the passers-by, for example, by constantly shouting, "Tomatoes, tomatoes, customer, come here, have a look at these tomatoes." If the seller sees a person she knows, she might call out, "Teacher, come, have some tomatoes, you certainly need tomatoes, come, teacher." Depending on age and gender, the customer is also frequently addressed as *mama* (mother), *bibi* (grandmother), *dada* (sister), *wifi* (sister-in-law), *kaka* (brother), or *baba* (father). For a customer who has bought a larger amount of product, the seller can show respect and gratitude by saying: *Asante mzungu* ("Thank you, European"). This is one of the ways by which a trader praises and inflates the value of the customer while belittling her own position.

While drawing upon the values of familiar sociability in their interpersonal etiquette, the traders may appeal to images of newness and modernity to enhance the value of what they are selling. A woman seller often takes a potential customer by the hand and pulls her closer, saying, "Customer, see, these beans are not from yesterday [= old]; no, look how they are shining, look, look!" or, "There's music and video in my beans, have a look!" while simultaneously digging a handful of beans from deep in her pile and showing them in her open palm, urging the potential buyer to do the same. Other sellers may look appealingly at each passer-by and plead in a humble voice, "Customer, look at my rice, look, and buy some," holding out a handful of rice at the same time. If the passer-by pauses and seems undecided, the seller may start opening the bag the customer is holding tightly folded in her hand. Many times traders try to attract a buyer who has already begun a transaction with another seller.[10] If a passer-by says that today she does not need any beans, the seller may urge her to buy some beans for a relative, her father's sister *(shangazi)*, for example.

A seller might also appeal to a potential or dissatisfied customer by praising her appearance. For instance, when one customer considered the price of a bundle of bananas too high, the trader started to wheedle: "How can you say that it is too expensive, a woman like you! . . . Wearing such expensive clothes; a scarf of 2000 shillings [Tanzanian Shillings, or TZS], shoes of 5000 shillings, a dress of 10,000 shillings, earrings of 1000 shillings, bag of 1500 shillings, and still she says she cannot afford 900 shillings for a bundle of bananas!" While she said this, the seller was smiling and touching the clothes of the customer, whom she finally got to smile and accept the seller's price.

The Kiswahili expressions *kuvuta wateja* ("to pull customers") and *kumbembeleza mteja* ("to coax the customer") aptly capture the market women's style.[11] Outside the market context, coaxing is also the usual way a woman tries to influence the decisions of others—of her husband or any other person whose help or consent she needs.[12] By beseeching and praising the other person, the woman presents herself as subordinate to and dependent on that person, his or her decisions and kindness. In so doing, the trader suggests the existence of a patron/client relationship between the customer and herself. Consenting to the trader's wish is like accepting the implied superiority of the one appealed to. In this way, female traders extend their domestic techniques of persuasion to the marketplace, and at the same time try to suggest that they are just humble, ordinary, and trustworthy mothers.

Arguments of motherhood are indeed frequently used in the market. In the course of sales negotiations, both traders and customers often appeal to their maternal responsibilities and need to feed their children. A customer may demand a lower price on the basis of her children's "need to eat." A trader can refuse an offered price on the same grounds. In addition to presenting these basic needs as grounds for fixing price at a certain level, the motherhood argument on the part of the trader is also a deeper moral argument for the honesty and respectability of her trade. If a customer criticizes the quality or price of the articles on offer, and the seller proudly finishes her defense with a sentence, "Me, I raise children" *(Mimi nalea watoto)*, it is meant as the ultimate guarantee of the quality of her goods and her honesty as a trader.

### Evoking a Moral Community

Indeed, market women always present themselves as mothers rather than traders. They usually deny making any profit *(faida)* and insist they are just seeking food *(chakula)* for their children and basic necessities *(riziki)* for their home by means of trading. For many market women this is quite true; after selling their products they often use the money acquired to buy household necessities. Interestingly, however, the larger sellers use the very same arguments even though it is obvious that they sometimes make sizable profits.

In their market rhetoric, women traders try to evoke the atmosphere of a moral economy where those who are better off should help the needy. A trader frequently tries to persuade others, both customers and other traders, of her own neediness and relatively low position. Thus, a larger-scale trader can be addressed by others as *mzungu* (a European). Such a trader might also be called *tajiri* ("rich" or a "wholesale trader/capitalist") or *kizito* (literally "heavy," meaning "wealthy"). All these words posses a flattering tone, but one that is double-edged in emphasizing the far superior position of the one addressed as compared to the speaker. The word *tajiri* is generally used for an employer, but its connotations are often extended to encompass more than the formal relationship between an employer and employee. When a person says *tajiri yangu,* the literal meaning is "my rich person," but more properly it means "the one that I am dependent on" or "the one who helps me." These expressions are used by lower-level traders to suggest a kind of patronage relationship to a larger-scale trader, with implications of mutual help and moral obligations.

A comparable evocation of a mutual relationship is traders' habit of calling each other "husband" or "wife." For example, a woman who regularly bought her products from a female wholesaler used to call her "my husband." She explained that as her husband is dead, she is dependent on this particular wholesaler. This also includes an appeal that the wholesaler not set the terms of trade too harshly. One female trader said she used to call another "my wife" as a joke, with the explanation that any time she called the other woman over, she came immediately.

Additionally, gifts and gift rhetoric frequently feature in various market relations. It is not unusual for a trader to ask a customer for a gift, whether they are familiar with each other or not, especially if the customer looks like she has benefited from a trip to a location farther away. The trader typically makes her request simply by saying "Give me a gift" *(nipe zawadi)*. Most commonly and importantly, however, gifts feature in relationships between traders of different levels as, for instance, between a wholesaler and a first-level retailer or between a first- and a second-level retailer. Even though either party can appeal for a gift, it is more often the one hierarchically higher, for instance, a wholesaler, who asks the gift from a retailer. Such requests are typically made in the phase of sales negotiation, where the wholesaler can, for instance, reply to the retailer's solicitation for a lower price by asking the retailer for a "gift" *(zawadi)* or a "soda" or a "beer," or simply say "I'm thirsty." Gift requests can also be made immediately after a transaction, in which case they are no longer part of the present negotiation, but rather attempts to influence future encounters between the parties.

In the market, the rhetoric of gifts is more common than the actual practice of gift-giving. However, gifts are made every now and then; most often they are drinks like soda, beer, or *mbege,* but also other gifts are sometimes given. One woman who regularly sold her banana bundles to another woman (a wholesaler who transported them to Dar es Salaam) sometimes agreed to a lower price than she would have asked from other customers and lower than the common price level of the day. She also earned extra small amounts by carrying all the wholesaler's banana bundles to her truck. In return for her flexibility and services, the wholesaler kept on promising her a gift. Throughout 1994, the wholesaler kept her promise only once to my knowledge, giving the woman one *kanga* and a pair of cheap sandals. For a wholesaler whose business was large and stable, these were meager gifts.

The symbolic importance of market gifts rests on the fact that, being clothes and drinks, they imitate the form of gifts exchanged in nonmarket relations. Clothes, food, and drinks are things that will be incorporated into the receiver's body and person; they are extensions of the giver's person and subsequently enable the extension of the receiver's person. For this reason, market gifts are more than compensation intended to balance accounts; their purpose is rather to instill a sense of indebtedness and thus of a continuing social relationship. Similarly, gift *rhetoric* in the market suggests a relationship between the traders; by requests and promises, another person is persuaded that there is a relationship of mutual dependence.

The tone of gift rhetoric in the market is significant, however. It is usually amiable and half-joking, and so intended to overcome a potentially hostile and competitive market situation. At the same time, it is a way to obscure or play with the seriousness of promises and make them more ambiguous and less binding. Just teasing someone else by a gift request has the effect of bringing an atmosphere of familiar sociability to the market. Often it remains just playful and teasing small talk replied to with laughter and a witty answer, and the setting for the forthcoming transaction is created. Beyond sociability, however, the gift rhetoric is always also somewhat wishful and experimental—the other person might agree, after all, and if she does not consent to give a gift, she might still become persuaded to offer favorable terms of trade.

By constantly using motherhood, kinship, and patronage terms, and through the talk and practices of feeding and exchanging gifts, market women bring cultural models of more stable sociality and reciprocity to the market. Combined with their mutually shared silence concerning matters of money and profits, this rhetoric helps the traders evoke a sense of moral community. Neither the playfulness nor the strategic dimensions of these conversational pragmatics should be disregarded, however. Nor should it be ignored that the traders' shared ways of appealing to others in the market frequently conceal very real differences in their respective economic possibilities. In the case of the two banana traders mentioned above, the security that the regular relationship gave the retailer was apparently important. The value that such continuity brought to the retail seller was shaped by her poverty. Market rhetoric works to conceal socioeconomic asymmetries both between traders and between traders and customers. As pleas for sharing by subordinates, they are also attempts to negotiate and narrow the differences between the parties.

In their way of talking and presenting themselves as humble mothers, the women try to enhance symbolic value for themselves. The appeal is to the trustworthiness and transparency of both their persons and their trade. Amidst this rhetoric of transparency, however, a trade transaction often contains a sequence of skillful impression-management tactics aimed at concealing certain technical tricks a seller employs to her own benefit. The whole trade transaction is best seen as a sequence of negotiations by means of which parties evaluate each other, and the customer tries to assess the trader's performance. It is through this negotiation that the terms of the trade and the morality of exchange is established in each case.

## Negotiating a Profit

At first glance, it would seem that there is little bargaining in Chagga markets. At the retail level there are barely negotiable margins in price, no matter how vigorous the customers' attempts. Price can be somewhat negotiated at the wholesale level or sometimes at the retail level for a regular customer who buys in large quantity. There is indeed some bargaining going on in each transaction, but it concerns quantity rather than price. I intend to show how this bargaining, which I describe as negotiation, extends through the whole sequence of the transaction at the retail level—beginning with "coaxing talk" to the throwing in of *nyongeza* (an addition or supplement) for the customer.

The conceptualization of the transaction as negotiation is also evident in some of the words used in the process. A customer urges a seller who seems unwilling to lower the price, "Come on, talk!" The Kiswahili word for the supplement, *nyongeza,* derives from the root verb *ongea,* which means both to talk and to increase. The negotiations that ultimately determine a trader's profit are extended beyond the transaction itself through a one-day credit system and also through the traders' habit of negotiating the amount of tax they have to pay.

### The Transaction Process

The process of negotiation includes establishing the quality and price of the goods involved, the legitimacy of the sales container and the way it is filled, and the "extra" given on top of the bargain. All these steps are negotiable and are usually negotiated, except in cases involving uninformed and uninitiated customers such as men, children, and foreigners. There are, however, clear differences in even regular female customers' knowledge, daring, and aggressiveness in making their demands on traders.

Discussion of the quality of a sales item often includes assessment of its age, color, and where it was produced. A customer and trader can debate these issues at length, with neither conceding the other's evaluation, because it would mean acknowledging the other person's claim for a better price. For a small quantity of product especially, the customer usually has to accept the trader's price. Assessing the quality of a product is, however, the initial opportunity for both customer and trader to judge how informed, yielding, or "stern" *(mkali)* the other is.

Quantity is the point more properly negotiated at the retail level, not price. Clark (1994, 130, 132) has reported a comparable prevalence of quantity bargaining in the retail sales of foodstuffs at the Kumasi market in Ghana. She has perceptively noted that it is more concealed than price bargaining, and is advantageous to the seller by enabling her to better control information about the transactions and manipulate the quantities bought by customers.[13] This applies to Kilimanjaro markets as well, and is the very reason why quantity bargaining requires cleverness and alertness on the part of both customer and trader.

A constant topic of negotiation is the sales container, particularly for products that are measured by containers. This is the case especially in retail trade involving rice, maize, millet, beans, and ripe bananas. Many traders have two or three measuring vessels that they claim are all of one size—one kilo, for example. These can be used tins or plastic containers that might originally have contained butter or cooking oil. On top of the differences in their original sizes, these containers are often treated further in different ways to make them even smaller. Plastic containers can be shrunk in hot water, or by cutting out a section from the side or bottom and reattaching the remaining sections with the skillful use of heat or fire. Metal cans can likewise have a slice cut out of the bottom. Often these cans are so worn out—presumably on purpose—that their sides are full of deep grooves and indentations. It is difficult to know what a tin originally contained, as all markings on it have been worn off.[14] Reducing the size of such vessels is often so skillfully done that it is hard for the customer to prove if there is no unaltered vessel around for comparison. Retail traders often use unaltered vessels to buy grain from wholesalers, after which the trader carefully hides it in her basket. It is common for a customer to demand a better measuring container if she is suspicious of the one being used. Often the trader acquiesces and borrows her neighbor's vessel—which has been similarly modified. Some traders have two or three different containers and choose a suitable one after sizing up the customer.

The measuring of the amount to be purchased is an equally delicate process. Both trader and buyer have an interest in how the vessel is filled. A container should usually be filled to at least slightly above the top, but by how much varies from one transaction to the next. A skillful trader does her measuring very rapidly, each time filling the vessel and pouring it into the customer's sack in a twinkling of an eye. This speed may conceal the fact that the vessel stands unevenly on top of the grain pile each time it is being filled, thus shorting the customer a bit more every time. The informed customer is aware of these tricks and keeps her eyes on the traders' hands during the measuring. Such a customer often keeps demanding "Fill it! Fill it!" (*Jaza! Jaza!*) A dissatisfied customer might repeatedly correct the position

Selling and measuring of finger millet *(ulezi/mbege)*.

of the vessel or add another handful of grain to the top of the vessel just before the trader pours it into the buyer's sack or basket. Sometimes a customer might snatch the container from the seller's hands and start measuring herself. No trader will let a customer do the measuring, however; she will grab the container back immediately and continue with the measuring herself. If the customer remains dissatisfied when the measuring is done, she might turn her sack upside down to pour out the grain and thus cancel the transaction.

After measuring, it is customary for the buyer to ask for a little more on top of the purchased amount by using the noun *nyongeza* (addition, supplement) or the verb *ongeza* (to add). The trader is then expected to throw another pinch of grain into the buyer's bag or basket, the understanding of the correct amount again being flexible and negotiable, and varying from a real handful to a few grains or beans. Some customers ask for yet a second addition, but whereas a trader can seldom refuse giving the first, she can refuse giving a second or give so little that it amounts to a mere token gesture.

There are some changes in the terms used for requesting *nyongeza*. According to the older women, it was always asked for twice early in the twentieth century; the first *nyongeza* was requested for "the husband" (*ngao*, Kichagga), and the second for "the grandchild" (see also Gutmann 1907, 50). A customer might even continue asking for more than these two additions in the name of other relatives. The first two supplements used to be customary, however, and could hardly be refused by the trader. Today the supplement is most often asked for simply with the word *nyongeza*. More rarely, a second supplement can be asked "for the child" (*nyongeza ya mtoto*). I myself never heard *nyongeza* requested "for the husband." Some traders refuse to give even the first supplement to those who buy only a small amount, such as one kilo of rice; a second supplement is more easily given to a buyer of a larger amount when it is called "for money" (*mapesa*), since the buyer is going to resell the grain at another market.

## Display Tactics and Types of Articles

Selling goods and making profit is different with bananas, tomatoes, onions, other vegetables and fruits, as well as other goods not sold in bulk. Cooking bananas are sold in readily examinable bundles, and there is not much to speculate about other than price and quality. Vegetables and fruits are usually arranged in piles that the customer can examine, evaluate, and compare with other piles.

Perishability also enters into speculation and planning. Tomatoes are ideally sold within two days, while onions can be kept for about a week. While this can give traders some flexibility in when they sell, they often prefer to reduce prices somewhat and sell out in one day, rather than having to

Sellers of cooking bananas. Second-hand clothes sold in the background.

Bucketfuls of sweet bananas sold for making *mbege*.

deal with storing and transporting their product to another marketplace. There are storage and transport charges that cut significantly into profit. Banana bundles can be stored, but that is rarely done. Retail traders prefer to stay even until dark sometimes, rather than have to store the rest of their bundles. In order to speed up their sales, they might cut the last bundles into bunches of a few bananas each and sell them for home consumption. Or they might sell their last bundles on credit, although that is risky.

The preference for selling-off instead of storing goods reflects the fact that these traders are operating on low capital and relatively low profits. Indeed, the kind of products sold and the scale of trading often reflect a trader's capital as well as her potential for "skillful arranging" and making profit. Even though piece goods offer fewer opportunities to use arranging tactics in small quantities than do grains, on a larger scale piece goods do enable such strategies, since they are then sold mostly in opaque containers. Thus, for instance, the buyer of a wooden box of tomatoes cannot check to see whether the tomatoes in the middle are good. And the seller of a bucket of onions or ripe bananas (sold for making *mbege*) can put the worst ones at the bottom or in the middle. A more discreet way of using such tactics is to array the items in such a way that as much space as possible is left in the bucket by filling the bottom and the middle of the bucket with the largest items, covered by the smaller ones on the top. For this reason, when buying ripe bananas that are sold peeled in buckets, an informed customer goes around and hefts various buckets one by one, searching for the heaviest and thus most tightly filled bucket.

One can see how small amounts count and how profits are made on these tiny amounts in the situation of a retailer buying a bucket of onions from a wholesaler. Allowed to arrange the onions in her bucket herself, she sits a long time among the onions concentrating on how to make maximum use of her bucket. When she has filled the bucket to the top, she still painstakingly fits in the last onions by attaching them in a neat circle around the rim of the bucket and piling as many more as she can on top so that finally they are about to fall at any moment.

In addition to measuring tactics, grains also make possible the use of other strategies. For instance, finger millet and rice can be stored for a long time without any problems. A trader with enough capital and a storeroom can invest in grain by buying large amounts when prices are low and selling when prices are high. Large amounts also make other tactics possible. A trader might buy millet of varying quality and at different prices and mix it all together so as to even out the quality. And when the mixed millet is re-bagged it can also be short-weighted. A further "conjuring trick" is using new sacks for the millet to make it seem fresher than it is. But buying and storing up large amounts requires significant capital that is economically beyond the reach of most market women.

## A Chain of Credit

Traders do not readily extend credit to ordinary customers, especially at the lowest retail level. Between traders of different levels, however, one-day credit is common. A wholesaler or an upper-level retailer will write down the names of traders to whom she has given articles on credit; when those traders have finished their selling in the afternoon, they will return to pay for their goods.

Such one-day credit is extended for different kinds of articles, from produce to secondhand clothing (mostly in Kiboriloni market). The system in which the chain of credit can extend from wholesaler all the way down to the lowest-level retailer is very common at Himo. It sometimes extends to food stall keepers who acquire cooking bananas from a retailer, for example. The retailer collects the money from the stall-keeper in the afternoon when she is preparing to leave the market, the stall-keeper having by that time prepared and sold at least some of the bananas as snacks and meals. These one-day credit arrangements require that both parties operate in the same marketplace and that the creditor trusts the borrower. In practice, this usually requires that they know each other outside the market context or as regular and established traders in the market.

The pervasiveness of the one-day credit arrangement and its use throughout the trading chain reveals prevalent liquidity problems; in practice, traders operate on borrowed capital through these arrangements. While often a simple economic necessity for a lower-level trader, this credit system simultaneously lends a degree of negotiability to the entire trading chain. At the end of the day, a retailer can appeal to her supplier to reduce the original price, arguing that either the quantity or quality of the articles had been less than expected or that low trade volume had forced the trader to lower her selling price or store part of her goods. Suppliers are resistant to such appeals, although they sometimes yield.

These kinds of short term credit systems have been reported from other marketplaces, as in Java (Alexander 1987) and Ghana (Clark 1994, 174–76). In Kumasi Central Market in Ghana, such credits do not seem to be as prevalent as they are in Himo, but Clark (ibid., 175) reports similar attempts at renegotiation of the amount by the buyer at the time of payment and thus at making the seller share her misfortune. In Kilimanjaro, the one-day credit is used both by traders with little capital as well as those upper-level traders who often would be able to pay for their goods immediately. This credit practice thus offers a way to try to push the risks and losses of trade up the chain.

## *Taxes*

The amount of money a trader has in her pocket at the end of the market day is also affected by the tax every seller must pay according to the sales amount. For a seller with a sack of 200 kilos of rice, the tax was 100 TZS in 1994, where one kilo of rice sold for about 230 TZS. For people selling smaller amounts, such as retailers of tomatoes or beans, the tax was usually 50 TZS. Even though the tax is not large, a seller might use that money to buy herself tea and a doughnut, perhaps the only thing she eats during the market day. The taxes paid over a few days or a week might equal one market day's profit. On other days a seller might incur a loss or make only a tiny profit, but the tax is levied every day.

Traders do their best to evade or reduce the tax. There are frequent quarrels and at times brawls between the female traders and the tax collectors, who are all men. The women try to postpone paying the tax, for instance, by arguing that they have not sold anything that day and thus have no money to pay the tax. Or they might simply slip away from their market spot every time the tax collector approaches. When doing so, they leave their articles on the ground but take along any measuring implement, because otherwise the collector will take it as security. The collectors know the women who come to the market regularly, but they cannot always keep an eye on each of them, so every now and then some women succeed in escaping the tax. One can frequently see the collector pointing at some sack or bundle and shouting, "Whose is this?" The surrounding sellers usually remain silent. The collectors may sometimes ask one trader to pay another one's tax, but that is always futile even if the two are good friends. As one woman said, "There is no grave for two persons."

If a collector sees that somebody is attempting to escape the tax by running away or refusing to pay it, the collector takes some of the trader's goods as compensation. Often the woman runs after the collector, trying to get her articles back. On one day, it seemed particularly difficult to get the banana sellers to pay the tax. The collector confiscated a bundle from each and carried them away. But the women kept fetching them back over and over. Surrounded by the angry women, the collector ended up getting only a small part of the required tax. In addition to physical confrontations, the women often insult the collectors, as on this occasion when one of them shouted, "I will rip off your pants if you don't return my things!"

Misrepresenting the amount of a product for sale is another common strategy among the traders. A seller of beans may seem to sell only a few bowlfuls per day, but can actually sell an entire sack's worth as she goes to buy more beans from a wholesaler several times a day. Likewise, a rice-seller might buy and sell a second and even a third sack in the course of a day but, if she's lucky, pay tax only for the first one.

Coaxing *(kubembeleza)*, sometimes accompanied by suggestive teasing, is a less antagonistic way of negotiating tax. For instance, one day a tax collector realized that two women had separated their bundles of bananas into a few piles, each claiming that only one of the piles was theirs. As he was angrily demanding the tax for the other piles, the younger of the traders took him by the hand and walked a small circle with him, speaking quietly. What she said made the man snicker and excuse them from paying the total tax amount. When I asked what she had said to the man to make him so cheerful, the woman told me she had asked him, "What shall we eat today?" *(Leo tutakula nini?)* The other trader was quick to reveal that "eating" connoted having sex by grabbing the first trader's crotch and repeating her words in a very sweet voice, only to receive an angry but giggly blow from the other.

Some of the larger traders come to an understanding with the collector so that the seller pays a smaller amount of tax without a receipt, or buys the collector a beer or two every now and then. I once observed a young boy who had just recently started collecting taxes and was having a hard time trying to tax a larger female trader. The woman was already irritated by the boy's officious and insistent way of demanding the tax when he happened to point his finger at her, which the woman took as an insult. She exclaimed: "I am your mother, and you point at me with your finger! I am your mother!" After that she refused to talk with the boy at all. The boy could do nothing but call an older tax collector over. With this older man, the trader could get on with her usual practice of negotiating the tax amount and eventually paid less than the official tax the boy had demanded. This is also another example of the strategic use of the motherhood argument in the market.

Towards the end of the market day it is often easy to see that the tax collectors have enjoyed some of the perks of their work and are clearly intoxicated. It is also obvious that the tax collectors have not succeeded in getting rich. Most of them are elderly men with shabby clothes and ragged appearances. Their work seems rather like a series of confrontations; they are received mostly as illegitimate intruders, and mocking is seen as a more normal response to their tax demands than quiet payment.

These attitudes and behavior have their roots in history. According to Gutmann (1926, 383–84), there used to be a "market taster" *(mosuhura)*, and the women could not start bartering before he collected the toll. The taster reached into every basket and collected a handful of its contents. In return, each woman was entitled to pummel the man and, according to

Gutmann, they all made use of that privilege. Gutmann calls this "ritual beating." He reports that the "tasting" ritual assured that food sold in the market was not harmful or dangerous; produce that had not been tasted beforehand could not be offered to children.

Today, the collection of the tax and the conflict it creates do not have the same ritually cleansing purposes. I never heard of cases of poisonous market produce, and to avoid paying the tax was not considered a dangerous or illegitimate practice among the traders. It was rather an expression of their dissatisfaction with the district administration. The association of the "market taster's" or "toll collector's" office with the political powers-that-be is customary. According to Gutmann (1926, 383), the office of *mosuhura* was granted by the clan that controlled the market place. According to the old market women in Mayanka, the job used to be given to a poor man who asked the chief *(mangi)* for it. It was his way to make a living; he took home all the food gathered as tolls as compensation for sweeping the marketplace after each market day. Today, the District Council pays tax collectors a small salary. The collected tax is to be used for the maintenance of the market place, for cleaning the market area and the toilets, and for developing the market. In practice, however, sweeping the grounds was usually the only visible administrative effort in the market. Evading taxes was the traders' comment on the administration; negotiating the tax with the collectors was their way of making power relations informal and personal.

## Markets and Morality

A trade transaction thus involves a process of negotiation and mutual evaluation that begins with the trader's coaxing talk and ends in the customer's assessment of what she has gained. A transaction is characterized by a constant back-and-forth between concealing and revealing, as the trader tries to convince the customer of the transparency of her trade and at the same time conceal her little tricks, while the customer tries to figure out and uncover those tricks.

The trader's negotiation skills, comprising her behavior, techniques, and verbal and social skills, can be summarized as *ujanja*. It involves skill in persuading a customer and acquiring and concealing market information. I heard several people make the distinction between market and shop trading on the basis of negotiability and the related lack of transparency. For instance, one woman maintained that market trading is deceitful *(udanganyifu)* but not shop trading, as the latter is based on fixed pricing (cf. Kapchan 1996, 34–35). When I remarked that prices for the same items do vary between the shops, she started to talk about deceptive measuring in the market trade. Strictly speaking, it is the marketplace where the prices are fixed—between the traders of the same item, and also over time—but actual amounts vary, while the opposite is true for the shops.

In West African markets, too, prices tend to remain stable over long periods of time, and changes in scarcity and demand are reflected instead in the shifts in the quantity and quality of a given item (Guyer 1995, 25). Thus, for example, the price of an enamel bowl of cassava flour may remain constant for a long period of time, while the amount of flour in the bowl varies. Berry (1995, 308) suggests that this practice manifests the underlying ambiguity of commercial transactions. Coping with shifts in scarcity and demand by adjusting the volume and retaining the familiar container seems less risky than allowing prices to fluctuate in response to external forces.

Trading practices in Kilimanjaro can also be seen as ways to stabilize and domesticate market fluctuations caused by such factors as seasonal changes, inflation, the commodity form of exchange, and the presence of strangers in the market. However, I consider such practices more strategic than simply communal ways of combating the fluctuations of the market economy. Berry (1995) does not use the term "moral economy," but her interpretation does evoke it. It resembles Scott's usage of the term, whereby a pre-capitalist community tries to defend itself and its continuity in the face of the disruptive market system.

It would be misleading to apply such fixed concepts as "market economy," "moral economy," or "gift logic" to the reality and perceived morality of market transactions in Kilimanjaro, however. The Himo market is part of a market economy in the sense that money is used as a generalized medium of exchange and the articles exchanged are commodities. At the same time, however, traders persistently invoke "moral economy" in the market by drawing on the ideas and values from the kinship, domestic, and patronage spheres. Comparable usage of gentle and persuasive language and the female market traders' practice of addressing the customers with terms of kinship and patronage is found in other parts of Africa—for example, among the Congolese traders (Ngolé 1986, 291), the Baganda in Kampala (Musisi 1995, 132–33), and the Moroccan traders (Kapchan 1996, 40, 67–69).

By drawing on the values of more stable sociality, the traders in Kilimanjaro attempt to turn stranger and commodity relations into more personal relations, and thus domesticate the marketplace. Traders also attempt with their rhetoric to create such symbolic value as honesty, trustworthiness, and neediness, and turn it into material value (cf. Bourdieu 1977). But the traders' familiarizing rhetoric also disguises their manipulation of sales quantities at the same time.

The different sizes of selling vessels and the varying quantities behind the homogenous prices quite effectively conceal differences in the terms of trade between the customers (cf. Babb 1989; Clark 1994). Final quantities do vary between customers. Proving such differences is not very easy, because quantities also change according to the daily market situation, and because verifying the differences would require an open comparison between different buyers' amounts. A trader might try to influence her customer into a positive evaluation even at the very end of the transaction by saying: "You'll give me a gift." This is her implication that the deal was favorable to the customer, who is thus indebted and obligated to show appreciation at least by returning to the same trader the next time. But in the end, it is up to the customer to evaluate the trade and decide whether she is convinced or skeptical of the seller's assurances.

Is the traders' rhetoric then just an attempt to conceal underlying calculated self-interest in trading? What is interesting in the rhetoric of moral economy is the fact that most of the people involved are conscious of it being a marketplace tactic. Customers are usually aware of traders' *ujanja* and therefore keep their eyes wide open during trading. Because of this awareness, this is not the kind of "good faith economy" that Bourdieu (1977) describes, where traders' calculated interests would remain naturalized and mystified, and symbolic and material capital could easily be converted into one another.

The rhetoric of moral economy in the market and people's alertness to it makes the ideology of gifts and reciprocity transparent to the extent that traders and customers joke and play with it among themselves. Indeed, the traders' way of talking is taken not merely as an inevitable nuisance and harassment by customers; they also see it as entertaining. There is thus a hint of a Bakhtinian carnivalesque anti-structure in the marketplace—a temporary revelation of the underlying constraints and expectations of the everyday life outside the market. The rhetoric of moral economy should not, however, be reduced to just a shared joke, because it does have some real social impact in the market.

This rhetoric is important and effective in creating an amiable atmosphere and consequently a social setting for trading. Under the persuasive influence of this atmosphere, a customer might indeed become receptive to favorable terms or she might want to return to the same trader later on. And as mentioned above, the ideas of reciprocity borrowed from the extra-market relations do not always remain mere rhetoric; they are also sometimes actually realized in the market through the practices of gift-giving and the more hidden, giftlike, measurings of a trader. As they vary the terms of trade between buyers, traders define and redefine intimacy and strangeness between themselves and their customers.

Behind the quite homogenous rhetoric, both "sacrilegious cunning" (Bourdieu 1977, 185) and gift logic are thus realized in the market. All of Sahlins's (1972) continuum of reciprocity can be found in the marketplace.

Negative reciprocity is always a possibility—hence the alertness of the transacting parties. A certain balance between appearances and what is considered fair has to be achieved if any regularization of the trade relationship is sought, however. The orientation of regular market exchanges is indeed rather close to a balanced reciprocity, in which some time lag is often tolerated, especially between traders of different levels. This balance—the measure and understanding of a good trade—is achieved in the negotiations and mutual evaluation of the transacting parties.

Gifts and the constant rhetoric of gifts in the Kilimanjaro markets are not pure gifts in Sahlins' sense, however. The spirit is closer to the way some other writers understand gift-exchange to include compulsion, calculation, and strategy.[15] Strathern (1992, 188) remarks that, instead of providing some secure integrative framework, uncertainty is always present and "reinforced at every stage" in gift-exchange. This feeling of uncertainty as to the other's intentions and the continuity of the relationship is even stronger in market relations and market gifts as compared to the domestic and kinship sphere. The traders' joking tone constantly hints at this vagueness in the market relations; it is their way of playing with the seriousness of the promises and appeals.

Does all this have anything to do with a "moral economy" then? It depends on how "moral economy" is defined. The problem in Scott's and his followers' way of using the concept is that it amounts to a kind of "gift logic" on the community level. This is problematic in that it provides a very homogenous view of any community, as if reciprocity were an overall and shared norm applied among the members of the community quite without distinction or qualification, and remaining beyond reflection. Rather than a shared norm or culture, moral economy is better viewed as a shared language and ideology, as Glassman (1995) does. It provides common ground, familiar concepts, for people to negotiate with each other. I would even expand the concept: more than a language, moral economy is a set of ideas, values, and practices that members of a given culture use and recognize as ways of forming and maintaining social relationships. Traders in Kilimanjaro bring their cultural ideas from the domestic and kinship sphere to the marketplace and use them as a cultural resource and a strategy in their market negotiations. The traders' familiarizing rhetoric not only conceals deceit, but keeps the door open to experimentation, change, and development in market relations.

It is thus not simply that the pre-existing social distance between parties transacting in the market determines the terms of trade. Relatives and kin expect to be treated as a special category of customer exempt from being cheated, but sometimes even they remain somewhat unsure as to whether they received special deals. Trading is thus not merely "embedded" in predefined social relations. By means of the little extras—be they outright gifts or the more hidden, somewhat generous, giftlike, measurings of a trader or simply promises of gifts—social relations are constantly defined and redefined, and new relationships formed and experimented with in the markets.

All this also means that "gift" and "commodity" do not exist as pure and distinct categories in the market. All the rhetoric, persuasion, play, entertaining atmosphere and style, as well as the mutual evaluation of the transacting parties, play a crucial role in constituting the categories of gift and commodity, and also the traders' relationship. The unending talk in the market is thus not "only talk"—to play with the Kiswahili word *ongea* (to talk, to increase), from which the term for trade supplement *nyongeza* derives— market rhetoric is "increasing talk," that is, it is essential to the creation of value and social relationships in the market.

Moral economy in this context involves the way traders extend extra-market values and the ideas of more binding social relationships to the market as strategy, play, and practice. Moral economy is thus not a shared and stable value system used to combat an encroaching market economy; it is something created in market relations by using cultural ideas about sociability as a model. This extension of extramarket values is often carried out in a tone and style the public finds slippery and shifty. This is also the central concern in the moral criticism of traders' *ujanja;* behaving as if strangers were friends often makes it difficult to discern who the people "behind the trader's back" are. In other words, who are the ones that she in fact shares with. This concern extends beyond the pure economics of trading to the social associations and gendered qualities developed in the marketplace, a theme that will be dealt with in the next chapter.

# 2

# Feeding, Drinking, and Eating

## Market Women Restructuring Gender

I once observed a situation in the market place where a prominent female trader was having a loud dispute with a male customer. Another important female trader, with whom I was sitting nearby, snorted disapprovingly: "That woman!" A man, next to her, echoed her contempt, and added, "And, at that, a wife of someone!" *(Na tena ni mke wa mtu!)*

The conversations in markets and about market women span both the economics of trading and the sociospatial boundaries of the marketplace to address the current concerns of gender relations and gendered behavior in the Chagga society. Women are often suspected of being prone to develop inappropriate gender qualities and sexual behavior in the market. In this chapter, I will study how conversations among and about market women address current concerns of larger society, especially in the domestic domain. It is only by studying the wider connotations and context that, for instance, the market women's rather fierce emphasis on their motherly responsibilities becomes fully intelligible.

The market and the domestic sphere are confluent in many ways; a fact that shows how artificial a strict separation between public and private would be. The intensity of a woman's trading depends on her domestic situation, which both determines needs and provides possibilities for trading. The husband's contributions, the household's land situation, the number of children and their ages, and the available help all affect the scope of a woman's marketing. Her success in trade and in combining the diverse tasks eventually affects the domestic situation. Thus, trading both reflects and influences the gender relations and their transformation within the domestic sphere.

Women's earnings have become ever more crucial for the maintenance of families, and they most commonly make money through market trading. Thus, more and more women are trading on a regular basis, and many spend several days a week in the market. Most are there for two to four market days a week, but there are women who are involved in trading six, some practically seven days a week. These are either the quite large-scale traders who hire people to do domestic and cultivation work, or women who mostly depend on small-scale trading for their livelihood because they have either very little or no land at all.

Earlier studies of African female traders have shown that a woman's increased economic contribution often leads to her having more say in household issues and possibly in more public matters as well.[1] Many studies done in different parts of Africa and at various times have found that female traders are frequently suspected of immoral behavior, especially sexual promiscuity. I consider such allegations and other forms of the public criticism as well as market women's conversations as a dialogue that addresses and constructs transformations in gender relations, and even in the gendered constitution of society. The intense dialogue shows how such transformations are not simply economically driven—in other words, money and economic success do not automatically lead to changes in acknowledged social position, but only through cultural conceptualization and social negotiation.

Research on African marketplaces and market women has most often concentrated on the economic and material aspects of marketing. The most important of these studies, such as by Sudarkasa (1973), Clark (1994), and Robertson (1997), provide detailed information on the economic and pragmatic sides of trading and marketplaces as well as their wider social context and impact. There are relatively few studies on the more symbolic and social construction of marketing and marketplaces. An exception is Bastian's (1992) study of the cosmological construction of the Onitsha market system. Van Donge (1992) studies the social construction of markets in Dar es Salaam. Somewhat paradoxically, however, by "social construction" he ends up meaning the traders' goal of "maximum independence from other people" (ibid., 197). In what follows, I will study the social and conceptual construction of marketplaces, marketing, and gender in Kilimanjaro by focusing on the giving of meaning to market women's practices and qualities, by both the women themselves and the nontrading public. Kapchan's (1996) approach comes close to mine in her focus on women's discourses in a Moroccan marketplace as a way to construct and transform identities. I will go beyond the marketplace context, however, and study discussions in and about markets and market women as a mutually and socially constitutive dialogue. I pay particular attention to the symbolism and politics of the current dialogue in Kilimanjaro and its preoccupation with the notions of knowledge, feeding, drinking, eating, and binding.

## Moral Discussion about the Market Women

### Market-wise: Knowledge and Worldliness

There is a persistent gender dimension in the moral evaluation of markets and traders. *Ujanja* (craftiness), even while seen as a defining feature of market trading, is believed to characterize trading women much more than trading men. Shops, thought of as a more respectable and honest mode of trading, are mostly owned by men. The moral evaluation of markets and market women assess the impact of market presence on the traders' gendered behavior and personhood, in addition to business acumen. So, too, do the qualities of *ujanja, akili* (intelligence, resourcefulness), and *uzoefu* (experience) have meanings beyond the economics of trading; they connote the accumulation of knowledge and a certain worldly attitude in the market.

As places where different people(s) "mix" *(kuchanganya)*, markets in Kilimanjaro are comparable to bars, roads, and schools as prime places to learn of the latest news, diverse ways of life, and changing fashions. An employed woman once said of market women that because they are frequently "amidst crowds of different kinds of people" *(jumuiya ya watu mbalimbali)*, "they know the news and information before the radio" *(wanajua habari na taarifa kabla ya redio)*.[2] A nontrading woman said that a market woman is like a person who "goes to school" *(anayekwenda shuleni)* and becomes thus "animated" *(mchangamfu)* in contrast to a woman who only stays at home and is in comparison like a "stupid person" *(mjinga)*.[3] Several market women also compared markets to schools, yet they emphasized their need to go to the market by saying that nowadays they head for the market each morning as diligently as children going to school.

One example of the fashions that the market women are thought to learn is the "new words" *(maneno mapya)* that are often disparagingly described as *maneno ya kihuni* (vagabond or street language[4]) and which their fellow villagers do not understand.[5] Market women themselves express the conceptual association between learning new things and the "outside spheres" and their familiarity with those spheres and "street language" in their habit of jokingly comparing not only the markets but also the bars with schools. Depending on the size of the bar, they might call it a "university" *(chuo kikuu)*, "secondary" *(sekondari)*, or "primary school" *(shule ya msingi)*. The sellers in the bars would be called "teachers" *(walimu)*, whereas the women themselves as customers are "pupils" and the money to purchase *mbege* is called "exercise book" *(daftari)*; without an "exercise book" a pupil naturally cannot go to school.

Cunning, intelligence, and experience are not only considered prerequisites for market trading, but are also believed to increase through mere presence as well as trading in the market. In addition, both trading and non-trading people often mention *maarifa* (knowledge) among the qualities that one "gains" *(unapata)* in the market. The most apt English phrase for someone characterized by this bundle of concepts is "a knowledgeable person."

Being informed and having knowledge are crucial for trading success in many ways. For instance, a trader can reap large profits by being informed earlier than others about changes in trade opportunities, policies, and prices across different regions and markets. And she could also incur major losses by not having heard, for instance, about policy changes and stricter control on the Kenyan border. As discussed in the previous chapter, learning how to acquire, share, and hold back information is essential in even normal and small-scale market trading. As they exchange different kinds of news, traders also create and maintain the social networks that are crucial in their trade. Different kinds of knowledge are usually passed on informally and by word of mouth in the market. Aside from the marketplaces, bars are the main places where all kinds of information is exchanged.[6]

Market knowledge is, however, more than an accumulation of facts and networks useful in trading. The expression used for market and bar conversations where women are believed to enhance their knowledge and *ujanja* is *kubadilishana mawazo*. At its simplest, this means the "exchanging of thoughts/ideas," but it more inclusively refers to a meditative, imaginative and reflective kind of thinking.[7] Fabian has described the semantics of *mawazo* in Zaire (Democratic Republic of Congo) as "popular thought" that is connected to processes of dreaming and remembering, and of conception and elaboration. Such thinking is challenging and includes the idea that (African) people have to think or imagine themselves out of problems and suffering through popular knowledge.[8] Fabian (1996, 311) describes *mawazo* and the verb *kuwaza* as "a purposeful intellectual activity, not a

*Klabu* next to a small marketplace.

A woman selling *mbege* that she has brewed in a *klabu*.

handing down of something that had been passively received" from authorities such as traditional elders or colonial schoolbooks.

Among the Chagga, innovative and revolutionary possibilities are related to knowledge.[9] *Ujanja* and *maarifa* that Chagga women are believed to accumulate in the market connote certain learned worldliness and the expansion of women's personal qualities and the broadening of their horizons. The distinction in Kilimanjaro between informed and animated market women and the "stupid or ignorant" women *(wajinga)* who stay at home is similar to the fundamental distinction that the Bwiti draw between "knowledgeable people" and "simple and ignorant people" (Fernandez 1982, 68). The value attached to knowledge applies probably more widely in Africa; Guyer and Belinga (1995, 93, 117) have argued that the social organization of knowledge in African societies should be considered as significant a "resource" and "means of production" as "wealth in people" or material resources.

It is because of their acquired worldliness that market women are considered somewhat frightening and obstinate *(mbishi)*, and therefore imperfect marriage partners, as both men and women in Kilimanjaro often told me. Trading women's reflective faculties are thought to pose a potential threat to their ability to show domestic loyalty and respect. In addition to the cognitive and mental propensities, there are certain more embodied forms of worldliness that women are thought to become accustomed to in the markets and bars. Popular discussion of the dangers inherent in the market frequently concern the market women's increased exposure to the habits of drinking and eating in bars, to licentiousness, and the art of "binding" *(kufunga)* men.

### Eating, Drinking, and "Binding"

There are certain spatial and alimentary practices and expectations by which the open market space is imbued with meaning. They are yet another way in which the domestic design is extended to the market, and the violation of that spatial design is often considered to indicate a woman's more general disregard for domestic values.

Each trader has a fixed, regular spot that has become hers by consensus over time. It is extremely improper to invade another trader's spot. If that does happen, there is no doubt that the one who usually occupies that location is justified in driving the invader away—with the support of adjacent traders, if need be. A female trader's seemingly aimless wandering in the market, as well as eating and drinking in the bars and guest houses around the marketplace, is considered inappropriate. Many of the women spend long days in the market without eating anything at all, or having just a couple of doughnuts or some fruit, drinking a cup of tea or a bottle of lemonade, or sharing a calabash of *mbege* with the other women at their market spots. After finishing their trading, they usually go for *mbege* in a bar, but it is not considered appropriate to go to one of the bars around the marketplace. Trading women should first take their food and baskets home, and only afterwards head for a bar near to their home. This "settledness" in relation to a certain market space is comparable to a woman's "settling down" in her husband's patrilineage and *kihamba* in marriage, and is also an expression of the domestic orientation of market trading.

In popular discussion, certain disparaging expressions are, however, frequently used regarding market trading that build on the idea of the negation of the female settledness. A woman's presence in the market can be characterized, for instance, with such expressions as "to keep on passing" *(kupita pita)* or "to keep on jumping" *(kuruka ruka[10])*, both referring to restless and constant motion. For selling sexual services instead of food, such expressions as "to pass to the small paths" *(vichochoroni)*, "to go ten ways" *(kwenda njia kumi)*, or "to seek the corners" *(kutafuta makona makona)* are used. In addition to ceaseless motion, these expressions refer to concealment and hiding, and are thus reminiscent of the allegations of craftiness pertaining to women's trading techniques.

Market women's spatial mobility attracts attention because it is believed to include social, sexual, and mental dimensions as well. Because of their constant moving away from home, the dedicated market women are often said to be "hot" *(moto)*, which is the antithesis of "cool" and being "settled" (see more in Chapter 4). *Akili* and *ujanja* are understood as forms of mobility in and of themselves; they are already spatially and conceptually associated with roads, movement, and advancement. A distinction in mental qualities is commonly made between people who live close to roads and those who live farther away. Proximity to a road or roads—just like being in the markets—is believed to enhance people's *ujanja* and *akili*, because it increases their ability to observe and participate in anything new and unusual. Those who live on the upper areas on the mountain are thought to be more simple-minded, trustworthy, and bound to traditions, because they live away from the road and close to the "silent" *(kimya)* forest.

It is common to hear not only the market women but also many other people say that one is able to survive and prosper only by using *akili*. Intellect as mobility is also conveyed in the idiomatic expression *"akili inatembea,"* or "intellect is walking." For instance, one market woman who was recalling and reflecting on the constant economic and social problems of her life, concluded optimistically by knocking on her head with her knuckles and saying: "but this intellect is still walking" *(lakini akili hii bado inatembea)*,[11] implying that she believes she will find solutions to her problems by using her intelligence and mind. *Ujanja*, moreover, is considered a shuffling and shifting kind of mental mobility, as discussed in the previous chapter. Through their *ujanja*, market women familiarize themselves with strangers. Alluring talk and negotiation skills are integral to a trader's economic success and the creation of more regular trade relations, but the persuading and coaxing way of talking *(kubembeleza)* is also the language of seduction and "draw" *(kuvuta)*. Indeed, a regular trading relationship between a female trader and a male trader tends to arouse suspicions in the woman's husband and sometimes in other traders as well. One young man gave cross-gender trading relationships as the main reason for not wanting his wife to start marketing, saying that these could easily make him jealous. Another young man persuaded his girlfriend not to start trading, reasoning that in markets one tends to "meet with a lot of people."

The alimentary practices especially are considered to signify a trader's loyalty or disregard for domestic values. Therefore, women's eating and drinking habits in the marketplace are subjects of intense observation and discussion both among fellow traders and nontrading relatives, as well as the larger public. It is considered especially suspicious if a female trader eats meat and drinks beer in any of the bars around the marketplace. Such behavior is condemned as seeking individual and selfish "enjoyment and relaxation" *(kustarehe)* instead of "food for children." Beer consumption in the bars that surround the market can easily lead to suspicions of illicit sex. This derives from the cultural opposition of bars to home and *kihamba*, and the association of "eating" and "drinking" with sexual relations. As in many other parts of Africa,[12] "eating" is a common metaphor for sex among the Chagga, but so is also "drinking."[13] A woman desiring sex is said to be "thirsty" (see also Emanatian 1996). Men frequently remind others that going to the market may be only a pretext for a woman's "real business," which takes place in bars and guest houses where she enjoys food and drink offered by rich men in return for sex. Conversely, this charge can also be leveled at affluent market women who are often believed to go so far as to entertain men in bars by offering them beer and expecting sexual services in return.

In addition to possibly seducing a woman to indecent behavior, an intense market presence is often condemned on the grounds that it has harmful effects on the well-being of her children and husband. It is thought to endanger social and even biological reproduction. Trading is sometimes suspected to make a woman so blinded by money that she simply has no time to take proper care of her children, with the result that they go undernourished. Another common suspicion is that trading women use birth control and/or abortions to avoid the obstacle that children would pose to their own advancement and wealth accumulation. Additionally, successful and/or very mobile female traders are often suspected of having used "medicines" *(madawa)* to "bind" *(kufunga)* their husbands and make them stupid *(mjinga)*, which consequently allows such women autonomous decision-making and accumulation. More than one of these various suspicions are often associated with prominent market women: drinking in bars, meeting with boyfriends, "binding" the husband, and neglecting their children. The following account by a young male trader pictures the alarming side of a successful female trader.

This young man told me that he would not want to marry a trading woman because she could be difficult to control and "obstinate" *(mbishi)*. He said some trading women use "medicines" so that "the husband sits at home like a stupid person" while his wife goes out trading. The husband might even humbly escort his wife to the bus that takes her to Dar es Salaam to do her business. "The husband has become like a woman," the young man said.[14] The wife might spend a week in Dar es Salaam and upon her return does not go straight home, but spends the first night back in a local guest house with her boyfriend instead. All the while, the husband is sleeping at home with the children without knowing the whereabouts of his wife. After having thus made her husband stupid, the wife can freely meet with her boyfriend. When meeting with him in a bar, she offers him two beers and the man offers her four beers. As the boyfriend buys her beers and other small things, the woman can meanwhile accumulate the money with which she can finally build a house of her own. In this way, the woman becomes independent and can leave both her husband and boyfriend: she becomes totally free *(ana uhuru kabisa)* to choose any man she happens to fancy; she no longer needs a man for money. This characterization of a trading woman sounds very much like the stereotype of a prosperous Chagga man. The account paints a strong picture of gender-reversal.

## Changing Market Perils

The conception of the marketplace as a special sociocultural space where more flexible morals prevail than in the domestic sphere is not new. This is evident when we compare people's present concerns with Gutmann's 1907 description of Chagga markets and market women:

> The opportunity for wide conversations with the other women seems to be more important for the women than the exchanging of food items. Here, where they have all come together, the wise Chagga expression, "Of all your matters share only half, and keep the other half in your head," is quite ignored. No one is too shy to tell others about her most intimate matters. Here, a naïve wife has all her husband's weaknesses explained, here the faithful and modest are provoked to free enjoyment and initiated in all the cunning against the man. Here one laughingly explains how she has

betrayed her husband, and mercilessly puts her husband in the most embarrassing light through cynical mockery and laughter, which is regarded as the
price of the market. Should one make a mistake with men, s/he does not
need to worry over gossip because they know to keep silent. But should one
commit a mistake in front of the women, it spreads all over the country till
the person is being mocked even in the farthest huts. Such a market is also the
worst place for procuration. For instance, it can happen that a man asks his
own wife to mediate between himself and a beautiful woman via their market relations. Of this speaks the phrase, "The fall of the women is the marketplace" [Gutmann 1907, 50; translated by the author from the German].

This account reveals a conceptualization of the marketplace as a sphere of
female power, "cunning," and "mouth." However, experienced content and
meaning in market perils are historically specific and derive their significance in relation to the concerns in the surrounding world at the time.
Today the market is considered an even better place to seek illicit sex than it
was at the beginning of the twentieth century. This is because it is not only
women, but also men and other people from different places and of different ages, that gather and "mix" in today's marketplaces. The abundance of
various services, bars, and guest houses surrounding the marketplace attracts all kinds of people on market days, including those who seek sexual
companionship. When I asked the old market women about their views of
the biggest transformations in the markets, almost all of them mentioned
first the appearance of food-stalls, bars, and guest houses. This was also
usually a moral comment on today's marketplaces. Furthermore, nowadays
it is the women who are believed to be active and enterprising in seeking
male company in the market and bars rather than mediating their husbands' messages, which was the expressed concern in Gutmann's account
above.

Money and exchange in commodities have also had an impact on
the threats and possibilities that people relate to market trade today. Gutmann (1926, 386–87) described the Chagga markets as sacred places where
any spilling of blood required ritual cleansing. Older Chagga women in
Mayanka told me how fighting in the market among women used to be
"very bad" (mbaya sana) and "dangerous" (hatari); it was "a taboo" (mwiko),
the breaking of which brought "a curse" (laana) or "a calamity" (balaa).
The "calamity" would come from the food that a woman involved in a fight
cooked at home later on, and would only fall upon her husband and her
male children, who could even die from eating that food. To avoid this, a
woman would have to indicate her polluted state when coming from the
market by not entering the home in the usual way. Rather, she would stop
and squat on the path before the front yard. When asked what was wrong,
she would say, "I was hit by a baboon" (nimepigwa na nyani),[15] and everyone

would know what that meant and what was required. The husbands of the women involved in the fight had to take a goat to the market for slaughter, and with the slaughter and sprinkling of goat's blood a petition and apology was made.[16] Every old woman who told of this said that if these measures were not taken somebody would die, and many concluded by saying "and it has taken place" or "and I have seen it happen."

It is noteworthy that this deviant behavior brought misfortune only to a woman's husband and sons, not her daughters. This can be compared to present-day concerns of the potential dangers of women's trading. Trading is a central part of the wife's contribution to the growth of her home and her husband's lineage, but it can also cause their demise through different forms of behavioral deviation.[17] Today, however, it is seldom food brought from the market that transmits the danger. I never heard of any contemporary suspicions that market food contains harmful essences. Nor did I hear concerns about the polluting effects of market conflicts, even though quarrels and brawls are relatively frequent. More generally, purchased food and drink were not believed to contain poisonous essences[18] unless someone had treated them by sorcery after purchase in order to harm a specific person. For instance, I was frequently told that the *mbege* sold in the bars cannot be poisoned unless the person next to you treats it after you have bought it. In this regard, a distinction was drawn between the *mbege* and food sold in bars and that offered at a feast; the latter could be poisoned even before it was served. Thus, food and beverages in the form of commodities were not believed to be sources of harmful effects (cf. Rekdal 1996, 373–74). However, after they were purchased, they could rather quickly become a medium for personalized effects.

Money and the commodity form of exchange have modified the market threats in another way, too. Nowadays, the profit that remains after food and other necessities are purchased in the market can be brought home and accumulated in the form of cash money. Earlier, if a woman had any wealth, it was in the form of food or livestock.[19] Money is more easily concealed and transformable, less gender-specific, and a potentially more individual resource than food or livestock. Money is most often used for the benefit of the trader's family. Even so, it can be—and today increasingly is—turned into resources that are customarily considered to belong to the sphere, responsibilities, and priorities of men.

## The Symbolism and Politics of Drinking, Eating, and Knowledge

At first glance, today's accusations of trading women's selfish enjoyment and accumulation to the detriment of their children, family and overall domestic values appear to reflect concerns over their individualist, profit-maximizing behavior—that is, attributes classically related to markets and market economies. However, the criticism is not about individualism in the neoclassical economic sense. The concern is rather about the creation and maintenance of social relations, loyalties, and values both alternative to and subversive of those of the domestic and the patrilineal group.

Eating and drinking in bars is meaningful precisely because they are understood as highly social acts. Eating and drinking are the main ways to socialize and share and they frequently involve reciprocal hospitality of a drink or snack, referred to as "feeding." It is significant that beer and meat are always targets of the public condemnation and suspicion concerning market women: the provision of meat and beer is a quintessential male duty and a masculine way to form and maintain relationships in the domestic and wider social circles—with women, other men, and the ancestors. *Mbege,* and nowadays beer, are crucial in the initiation of different male-female relations; they form an essential part of bridewealth negotiations and payments, and offering *mbege* or beer in a bar is the standard means—and, indeed, the key metaphor—for initiating a commercial or casual sexual relationship. The sight of a market woman having beer and/ or meat in a bar at the market is readily interpreted as either her being treated by a strange man, or as her buying drinks and meat she might possibly offer to men. In both situations she is understood to be forming a reciprocal relationship with a man other than her husband.

With all these allegations—eating, drinking, and socializing in bars, and the valuation of money and mobility instead of children and home—the market women are blamed for adopting male spaces, roles, and aspirations. In their familiarity with the "outside spheres" and their knowledge and worldliness, the market women have acquired qualities that are customarily more properly associated with men. The complaint about trading women's attraction to bars echoes the standard and customary complaints about men and their habit of wasting their money in bars and with "outside" women instead of bringing it home. A trading woman's craving for masculine authority and control finds its extreme expression in the images of her "binding" her husband and "feeding" other men in bars. Both express a gender reversal and the feminization of a man by the woman—both her husband and the man whom she offers drinks to. In both cases, it is the men who become "bound" and "settled" in sexual, social, and spatial terms to the woman and not vice versa, as it is expected to be. In addition to being humiliating for a man on an everyday basis, such subordination is in its extreme seen as leading to a situation where the woman accumulates money and turns it into such wealth as house and land. The climax would then be the woman becoming materially self-sufficient, when she in effect becomes a male in her social behavior and person and is able to fulfill her ambitions without restrictions.

In addition to the above complaints that build on the idioms of drinking, eating, and "binding," similar understandings and concerns regarding
market women's aspirations to male-like authority were often expressed in
more mundane comments. For instance, when I once mentioned to an employed woman that most of the market women had introduced themselves
to me by their natal lineage names, the woman snorted, saying that those
women want to accumulate even their money in their own name. Several
times I heard complaints about market women's tendency to occupy large
spaces without any concern for others. A few men and women complained
that market women tended to take up space on the bus and not make room
for other passengers. A couple of women who were not regular traders, but
only occasionally went to the markets to sell their homegrown produce,
complained about how the established female traders were not willing to
give them any place to sell their wares. This clearly speaks to the competi-
tiveness of the market trade and the economic importance and informal
power that securing the best spots in the marketplace brings. However, the
identity and power of Chagga men and patrilineages are expressed in and
build on spatial control as well, in the form of land control. The market
women's alleged assertiveness in occupying space is taken as another indication of their aspiration to male forms of control.

## Market Women's Self-Exposure: Practice and Reasoning

### Feeding

The market women were well aware of the moral evaluation swirling
around them. Beer consumption in the bars around the marketplace was as
meaningful to them as it was to their critics. Many of the market women
avoided the bars, or if they did enter, they would have a quick soup, tea, or
soda. The more affluent and daring ones, however, were not shy about
going to a bar for a couple of beers during the market day.

It was also common for the more affluent female traders to boast of their
ability to buy their own beers as an indication of their relative freedom in
comparison to women staying at home. Additionally, market women of
widely differing means would often proudly emphasize their ability to offer
food and drink to their guests at home thanks to their trade earnings,
contrasting their situation to that of a woman with no income of her own.
Like some of the nontrading people, market women would often apply the
word *mjinga* (stupid)—which is the opposite of *mjanja*—to women who
stay at home and earn no income. They explained that such women lack
money and that it is likely that there is "hunger" *(njaa)* and "trouble" *(shida)*
in their homes, since what their husbands provided was likely not enough.

These comments reveal the constant monetary needs of households today. They are also expressions of gender politics where the "stupidity" of the stay-at-home woman means her total dependence on an allegedly unreliable male provider. The women who go to the marketplace bars and emphasize their ability to buy their own drinks by the same token express an autonomy that is usually considered the most revealing sign of deviant market behavior. But they also strive to shift the complex of connotations commonly related to such behavior, especially the strong conceptual connections between beer, bars, and illicit sex. Instead, they emphasize their "self-reliance" *(kujitegemea)*[20] and thereby their independence of and from being served or provided for by either their husbands or other men. The politics of beer-drinking was brought home to me one time when I was sitting with a woman in a marketplace bar. There were several men who we knew and who each wanted to offer us a beer. After being bought a few beers, the woman refused to accept any more and instead bought beer for herself and me, saying that we had better do so in order not to give the impression of being *wajinga* (stupid). Another prominent market woman explained to me how proud she was of being able to go to a bar in the evening if she felt like it, to buy a couple of beers, meet "peacefully" with other people there, and "then peacefully go to sleep at home."

The trading women's constant emphasis on "feeding" in the marketplace also has to be seen in the context of the surrounding moral evaluation and in dialogue with it. By saying that they do their trading only to acquire "food" for their children and the "basic necessities" for their family, the women emphasize the most serious and moral nature of their trading and fend off any allegations of "relaxing and entertainment." In addition to being a defensive counter-argument, the women are emphasizing their contributions to the reproduction of the household and the society.

In the case of the market women the stated aim and motive of "feeding" includes often not only the food but also fulfilling such male responsibilities as buying clothes, meat, and medicines, and paying school fees. There are families in which the wife has also built the house because her husband could not afford to. These are, however, "secrets" *(siri)*—transmitted through gossip—since the situation is shameful for the husband. Both the people involved and those around them act publicly as if the man had built the house. The wife does not make any display of being financially stronger than her husband, but acts as if she was both economically and socially subordinate to him. She gives her husband the money for the house-building so that he can buy the materials and take a public role in the construction.

Thus, when even the more prominent women traders claim they do their trading in order to "feed their children," it is not necessarily a bald-faced lie, as I first thought. Rather they extend the categories of "food" *(chakula)*, "feeding" *(kulisha)*, and "basic necessities" *(riziki)* to include the very diverse facets of the essentials of life. Simultaneously, they use the category of "feeding" as a rhetorical gloss that, when including the above mentioned diverse facets, in effect blurs the boundaries of both the category of "feeding" and "mother," and also "father."

As the daily work of feeding is what a wife and mother is expected to do, the women's appeal to the aim and importance of "feeding" is not openly subversive. By concealing shameful "secrets," it can present outer compliance to the dominant ideas and expectations of gender relations. In the market context, furthermore, it conceals the differences in the traders' economic possibilities. Frequently, however, a more or less open insinuation of a man's inadequate contributions is included in a woman's emphasis on her feeding responsibilities. This is the case when, for instance, a woman who should be in postpartum confinement comes to the market. When she responds to admonitions by saying that she has had to come in order to "feed her children," she is also saying that both her husband and his near lineage members are failing to take care of her and her children as expected during confinement. An indirect and commonplace reference to a husband's inadequate provision is also made when a woman emphatically tells how she has struggled to pay for her children's school fees and expensive medical treatments.

## Social Constitution through Feeding

Market women thus stretch the category of "feeding" to fit with their realities and expanded responsibilities. But there is yet another, more symbolic, dimension to the concept. As in other parts of Africa and South Asia (Carsten 1995), "feeding" is also a metaphor for taking care of another person in a broader sense and for enabling the establishment and development of another person's social personhood. Subsequently, "feeding" creates an emotionally and morally charged expectation of reciprocity from the one fed to his or her feeders later on. Such a relationship is asymmetrical until the time of reciprocation.

Through feeding and provision, social relations, persons, and ultimately the sociocultural order are created. In marriage, the wife's and children's lineage identities are established through their feeding and provision by the husband and his parents. The wife's task of providing her family with the daily food is culturally circumscribed by her husband's and his extended family's provision of the basics of life, such as house and land, as well as meat, clothes, school fees, and medicines. The subversive tone in women's emphasis on their "feeding" efforts derives from the unmet expectations regarding these items men are supposed to provide.[21] When the wife takes

care of some of the crucial male responsibilities, she in effect becomes—
even when it remains a "secret,"—the provider in relation to her husband as
well, which simultaneously casts the husband as dependent on her.

When they speak emphatically about "feeding" and their maternal responsibilities, these women stress the socially generative aspect of what they
provide and the practical kinship created by and through women. Bourdieu's term "practical kinship" is apt for describing these connections, which
are "continuously practiced, kept up, and cultivated" in everyday life and
"in the most intimate sphere of family life," in opposition to the "official
kinship" that is publicly manifested in ceremonies (Bourdieu 1977, 37, 43).
Bourdieu's emphasis on materialist and strategic dimensions as the driving
force for people's behavior does not, however, suit how the Chagga often
experience their "practical relationships." Such relationships—especially
mother-child bonds and women's natal home connections—are more often
in Mayanka experienced as emotionally close than simply functional and
utilitarian.

It is perhaps not too farfetched to claim that motherhood is the emotional core of the otherwise strongly patrilineal Chagga society. That is
probably not a new phenomenon. I frequently heard men talking about and
recalling their mothers and grandmothers with warmth. For instance, one
man had two large paintings on the walls of his house, one of himself and
the other of his grandmother. The man said that each time his father entered the house he became very emotional to the extent of almost crying
upon seeing his mother. One man, who opened a shop during my first visit,
had by 1997 named it after his grandmother. Another man, in his mid-
fifties, explained to me how natural it was that he likes his mother more
than his father. "Well, isn't it the mother who has cooked food and fed me?"
he said. Due to the increasing importance of women's economic contributions and their comments about it, the significance of "mothers" and their
"feeding" efforts seem ever more enhanced and visible today. Changes in
ways to ask for add-ons in the market perhaps reflect an increasing mother-
centeredness in Chagga society as well, since the add-on is not requested for
the "husband" as it was before, but is now asked only for the "child."

In addition to their children and family, women cultivate other relationships with their earnings. In their use "feeding" often includes some help
for natal lineage relatives, especially parents and siblings. For instance, one
prominent female trader had provided her brother with a rather large
amount of starting capital for his business—which was a "secret"—and another woman provided money for her sister for market trading. Small aid
and loans to friends were also sometimes included in the category of "feeding." Many women maintained that one could not expect much help from
relatives (*ndugu*) except at such special times as weddings, litigation, or

childbirth. Many traders said that friends—both female and male—are the persons to turn to in times of need.

As discussed in the previous chapter, kinship categories and expectations can be extended to friends and acquaintances with varying accents of seriousness. Several trading women adopted me, too, as their "daughter" *(binti)*. In addition to being a demonstration of warm-heartedness and acceptance, it often included the expectation of, or a claim on, mutual help. A scene in a bar serves as an example of such an expectation made explicit, and at the same time the spirit of such requests—often an insinuation or a half-joke—which leaves the person of whom the request has been made some room for formulating her stance and timing. As I passed a group of female acquaintances they asked me in deeply humble and coaxing voices: "I am your mother, so please bring me some beer." I responded, "Isn't it the mother who takes care of the child?" and the women burst into laughter and, as they pounded their thighs in amusement, one of them said: "She has learned!" *(Ameshajua)*. The women were applauding both my learned wittiness in evasive talk and my understanding of the present state of domestic relations and the woman's burden to provide.

By using kinship and conjugal terms outside the domestic sphere, even when it is done in a bantering tone of voice, market women attempt to extend the sphere of kinship, and the realized exchange and mutual help establishes a realm of kinship, which is simultaneously fictitious and practical. The everyday importance of friendship, motherhood, and women's natal home relations challenges the ideological emphasis on patrilineal connections.

## Restructuring Gender

Market women are often spoken about as a category when their propensity to violate expectations of womanly and wifely behavior is criticized. Distinctions are typically made between individual women only with further qualification; for instance, those women who really are burdened in trying to acquire the basic food for their families do receive pity. Instead of reflecting reality, the moral discussions should be understood as attempts to make sense of and control certain tendencies in society.

What is at stake is not a sudden rebellion by women or the enrichment of women in general, but rather the relative positions of men and women in the household and the greater society. Although sexual exchanges are initiated and take place in the bars and guest houses around the market, the "real business" of the majority of the market women takes place in the products market. There are also differences in women's ability to extend "feeding" beyond the bare essentials of life, as well as in the strength of their subversive tone. While the successful market women tend to be bolder, some of the poorer women can express quite open criticism towards male authority as well. Again, some of the successful traders make little of their contributions and economic strength. Yet, the situation of their home affairs is often revealed through gossip.

The inclination to talk about the market women as a category serves to address and symbolize the more general tendencies of the outward orientation from the *kihamba* and male authority. Markets are apt symbols for these developments because of the older cultural opposition between them and the domestic sphere of *kihamba*. Today, as locations where women produce and create value through their "increasing talk," negotiating skills and the extension of social relations, markets offer a contrast to the cultivation work in the *kihamba* that women gain access to only through a husband and marriage. As places where the genders mix and some people come for the purpose of seeking sex, the markets appear to be prime sites of subversive sociality and morality.

In those cases where the husband lacks any regular work and income and those where he lives and works outside the region, much of the daily providing falls to the wife. Often, when I asked a woman if she receives support from her urban-based husband, I was met with a counter-question, "Now, where would I see him?" Naturally there are men who do their best to provide adequately for their family. Some men can even be proud of their wives "not having to leave the house" *(mke hatoki nyumbani)*, because they can provide all that is necessary and needed. Today it is more usual, however, that even when a husband provides for the family as best he can, his wife still has to earn money outside to "feed the children."

Another development strengthening mother-centeredness is the increase in the number of single mothers who reside at their natal homes. Usually, the children of unwed mothers are affiliated with their father's patrilineage even though no marriage was forthcoming for the child's mother and father. However, acknowledging fatherhood is sometimes a cause for dispute and litigation. Even when it is agreed upon, the child usually remains several years at his or her mother's home. The affiliation and the concomitant compensations for the child's upbringing to the mother and her family take place only after many years, and can even then be disputed. The responsibility for providing thus falls on the child's mother and her parents for a long time. Many single mothers seek a livelihood for themselves and their children in the markets, some of them in the bars.

Economically strong women, publicly bold women, and pre- and extra-marital sex are presumably not new phenomena in Chagga society. What is experienced as threatening is the sense that such phenomena are increasing along with women openly violating or disdaining cultural ideals. The violation can be either verbal or enacted, and either intended or unintended. Children born to unmarried girls are open evidence of premarital sex. Going to the bar during the market day as well as any boasting about "self-reliance" is not how an "ideal" woman, wife, or mother is expected to behave. An example of unquestionably open deviance was provided by one rather prominent market woman who was living at her natal home with three children whose fathers she refused to reveal. To her parents' ceaseless questions she would boldly answer, "The children don't have any father. They are mine." This was indeed an open denial of the customary ideas of children's lineage affiliation. The continuing strength of the practice of affiliating children (even those born out of wedlock) with their father's patrilineage in Kilimanjaro was frequently expressed by such phrases as "The children do not belong to the mother. They belong to the father," and, "In Chagga land children do not get lost" *(Uchaggani watoto hawapotei)*.[22] The open boldness of this particular market woman, who denied her children's patrilineal affiliation, tried even the limits of what many women considered appropriate. Approved or not, women like her caused people to ponder the limits of the appropriate in gendered behavior and the ideas of relatedness and kinship.

The sense of women's increasing boldness finds an expression in the common complaint that contemporary women do not show "respect" *(heshima)*, which refers both to non-obedience to husband and other authorities and to perceived sexual looseness. It is not uncommon to hear men complain that women have taken over male businesses like the profitable selling of clothes and the long distance trade in millet or bananas, although there are still considerably fewer women than men in the latter businesses. A local priest, echoing many other voices, told me that present domestic problems arise from the general "lowering" or pushing down of men by women *(wanaume wameshushwa)*, and the respective "ascent by the women" *(wanawake wamepanda)*, a situation which he believed would only worsen.

Many of the trading women describe the present state of gender relations and gendered tasks with such expressions as "there is no woman and man any more; everyone has to run around" *(Hakuna mwanaume wala mwanamke siku hizi; kila mtu lazima akimbie huko na huku)*.[23] Nevertheless, women often use national political language to describe contemporary gender relations. In addition to "self-reliance" *(kujitegemea)*, they use the words *mapinduzi* (revolution) and *mageuzi* (reform) to describe their increased activity and assertiveness.[24]

By emphasizing women's eating and drinking in bars, the critics thus warn of market women developing behavior and personhood that is destructive to domestic order and values, and even for social and biological reproduction as women start adopting male qualities and aspirations. By their persistent appeal to their "feeding" responsibilities, the women themselves emphasize the socially constitutive importance of their trading. By extending the category of feeding, women extend their morally acceptable spheres of activity, emphasize their contribution to social generation, and make the claim that it should be acknowledged and supported. What is being debated in this highly moral dialogue are the emergent gender relations, gendered spheres, and the gendered constitution and bases of relatedness in Chagga society.

## Different views of Women's Trading Activities

Surprisingly similar images of economically strong women can be found in different times and places in Africa, and dialogues apparently comparable to the one on Kilimanjaro have been going on in many other societies. Researchers often adopted the view of one party to the dialogue in the early studies especially, initially often the image of women's trading as entertainment, socializing, and sexual rebellion, and later a view of their trading as respectable and demanding work.

In early studies, the significance of African women's trade was often belittled. This is especially the case with the exchange and marketing of food in the local markets, which has typically been women's domain in many parts of Africa. The view of such exchanges as of minor material and social value was expressed, for instance, by Bohannan and Dalton (1968 [1962]), who wrote about the moral and symbolic importance of the various exchange spheres. They proposed that transactions involving prestige items such as copper, bracelets, or cattle are the most important activities in precapitalist societies. They write (ibid., 5), "Transactions of goods necessary for biological survival need not be regarded *socially* as important as are prestige item transactions" [emphasis in the original].

On the other hand, women's marketing was described as primarily social in the early studies—yet, social in a certain trivializing sense. It was portrayed more as entertainment and fun than serious work. According to Bohannan and Dalton (ibid., 8), market women were not eager to sell all their wares quickly because "the market place is a source of entertainment and social intercourse." This kind of diminishing tone as regards the economic aspects of women's trade and the emphasis on the socializing and sexual aspects was present also in Gutmann's (1907, 50) account of the Chagga markets cited earlier in this chapter. In several studies, moral laxity, sexual rebellion, and prostitution were seen to accompany women's involvement in trading (see e.g., Little 1948; McCall 1961; Nadel (1965 [1942], 1952).[25] In the case of urbanized women, city life was often believed to further enhance their moral looseness. For instance, Nadel (1965, 152–55) wrote about developments among the Nupe in Northern Nigeria: "Sexual license has been greatly increasing in the last generation or two. . . . Women's trade involves a loosening of matrimonial and family ties and tends to become identified with licentious living. . . . The result is the close association between professional female trade and semiprofessional licensed prostitution. . . . We have heard that the kola-nut vendors on Bida night-market, all married women, are prostitutes at the same time." Here Nadel relied on the reflections of his "informants, all married men," (ibid., 152) on these worrisome developments in Nupe society. Comparably, women's trading in Nairobi in the 1920s and 1930s, and even the 1940s, was frequently related to prostitution in the minds of male researchers and authorities, who found in it a reason to control women's movements and trading (Robertson 1997, 93–96, 134).

In the 1960s and early 1970s, several writers described issues of gender and power in trading, arguing that women's increased mobility and economic possibilities enhance their economic independence.[26] Mintz (1971, 266–67) emphasized the importance of trading as the source for women's autonomy, for instance, and contrasted trading to salary-paying jobs, which, according to Mintz, were increasingly valued but conferred less autonomy upon women. For the African materials, Mintz relied on Marshall's (1964) then unpublished study on Yoruba traders, which appeared in 1973 (by the name Sudarkasa), titled "Where women work." Sudarkasa and subsequent (and mostly female) researchers have emphasized African women's trading as serious and laborious, but often undervalued work, thus giving an image quite opposite to that of women's trading as entertainment and socializing.[27]

The long history and economic, social and often political significance of women's trading in many parts of West Africa has since been established. For instance, Yoruba, Ga, Igbo, Hausa, Asanti, and Esan women have been trading since long before colonial times.[28] Women have historically been predominant in local markets, and some were involved early in long distance trade. For instance, the Ga women in Accra are known for having sold all kinds of products as early as the sixteenth century and for their long standing contacts with European firms on the coast (Robertson 1974; 1995, 110). In the Igbo, Ashanti, and Yoruba societies, successful female traders could even gain political titles and followings.[29]

A view that East African women's trading is of meager economic importance has tended to persist, however. It is often portrayed as nonexistent or of minor importance, in contrast to that of West African women. Indeed, the general historical absence of markets in East and Central Africa and their long history in West Africa has been described as one of the major geographical dichotomies of African history (Oliver and Fage 1962; quoted in Hill 1963, 447). East African women have indeed often been involved in quite small-scale food marketing, but there are areas where marketing done by women stretches at least as far back as the middle of the nineteenth century, for instance, among the Pare, Kikuyu, Kamba, and Luo people, in addition to the Chagga.[30] With the exception of Robertson's (1997) notable study on the history of the food trade conducted by Kikuyu and Kamba women and men in the Nairobi area, there has been relatively little research on the history of women's marketing in East Africa. The rise and growth of the informal sector increased the research interest on East African women's trading.[31] These have often been survey type studies made within a relatively short time span, mostly in the urban areas. A certain distinction has tended to remain in the research findings on East and West African trading women, however.

In the case of the West African women traders, economic independence and toughness, long distance traveling, and social and political strength are recurring and celebrated themes in the research and more popular understanding. But the materials on East African market women are full of such expressions as "necessity," "physical survival," and "mere subsistence," "marginal subsistence," and the "aim to earn the living rather than profit."[32] And the difference is often real enough: whereas West African women trade in a rather wide array of goods, trading by women in East Africa is often an extension of their customary domestic activities, such as selling food, brewing beer, or offering sexual services. Robertson (1995, 113), who has studied both the Ga traders in Accra and the Kikuyu and Kamba traders in Nairobi,[33] writes about the difference as follows: "When I went to Accra to study wives, I found traders; when I went to Nairobi to study traders, I discovered farmers." By this she means that while trading was the hereditary and primary occupation for the Ga women, farming was still the main occupation and trading only an extension of it for the Kikuyu and Kamba women.

Yet the differences between women's trade in the two regions are perhaps not as great as often thought. While large-scale women's trade has long been common in West Africa, there have also been large numbers of women involved in rather modest local trade. Most of the West African studies are conducted in well-established town marketplaces where trading by women is likely to be both of longer standing and of greater scale than in the more rural areas. As mentioned above, there are also areas in East Africa where women have been involved in long-distance trading for a fairly long time. Over the past decades, the number of women engaged in rather large-scale enterprise has increased in many areas. For instance, some Chagga women have created noteworthy businesses in Kilimanjaro and other areas in Tanzania, even though they still often prefer to call themselves "mothers" and "cultivators" rather than businesswomen. Tripp's (1997, 110–14) study found women with profitable, booming businesses in Dar es Salaam at the end of the 1980s and beginning of the 1990s. Perhaps the most important difference in the two regions is that increased economic activity by women in East Africa more often seems a response to economic necessity that forces women to seek a living outside their homes, whereas women's freedom to move and economic autonomy are more often set as the initial cultural expectations in West Africa.

Regardless of the historical differences in the initial acceptability of economic activity by women, trading women in different parts of Africa share remarkably similar aims and responsibilities. The aim of feeding, supporting, and educating children is often given as the first priority of women involved in trading. This is true especially in East Africa, but also comes up frequently in the West African studies.[34] Such findings are often seen as a confirmation of a persistent gender asymmetry in which women have to carry the responsibility of their children's and family's well-being, while men use their incomes in more individualistic ways. The inability of women to accumulate and invest money is often lamented in the research (see e.g., Kongstad and Mönsted 1980; Mintz 1971). Robertson (1995, 115) draws a distinction between the Ga women who invested in their trade and the Kikuyu and Kamba women who used their profits to educate their children, buy land, or to roof rural homes. She sees trading by Kikuyu and Kamba women as "increasingly a solution of desperation" (ibid., 116).

But what are educating children, buying land, and home improvement if not forms of investments and increased well-being? I do not intend to underestimate the wide diversity within and between these two regions, or to ignore the fact that men in these societies often have more options and resources for supporting their own economic and political enterprises and autonomy than do women. But what is of interest is the recurrence of certain common patterns of women's usage and investment of money in different parts of Africa. In addition to—and usually after accomplishing the aims of—feeding, education, and other support for children, the economically successful women often invest in real estate, regardless of the means used for generating money.[35]

Van Donge (1992, 197) explained this drive to invest in real estate among the Waluguru traders in Dar es Salaam on the basis that it ensured "maximum independence" for them. In both East and West Africa, women's increased economic activity or "economic independence" is often found to lead to increased "social and political emancipation" for women (House-Midamba and Ekechi 1995, xvi; Hodgson and McCurdy 2001). Concepts like "economic independence" and "accumulation" are problematic, however, because they entail an idea that a person is separate from the values of and relations to his or her sociocultural context. Economic strength rarely comes from individual effort alone, but requires the extension of social relations, even in order to get essential trade information. Economic proceeds are seldom used independently, either. Accumulation of money is not meaningful as such; the material becomes meaningful through processes of social and symbolic valuation. Food, education, and housing, as well as knowledge, are significant because they construct and transform social and gender relations, personhood, and identities.

What is "emancipatory" then is not an achieved "independence" but rather the changes in the relations of autonomy and dependence that women's increased economic activities and use of their earnings often lead to. Tripp (1997), for instance, has shown how in Dar es Salaam in the 1980s the increasing reliance on informal sector incomes reversed the dependencies in the households there, giving women and children more freedom and autonomy in regard to their husbands and fathers, respectively. Hodgson and McCurdy (2001) and the articles in their recent compilation provide ample evidence from different parts and periods in Africa of how such changes in the wider, gendered economic sectors and the household economy often both empower enterprising women in their domestic relations and create moral discussion and hostility towards them. With their increased economic activities women gain "better bargaining positions within marriages" and sometimes find that they can "survive and thrive outside marriage" (Cornwall 2001, 75). The moral vocabulary used against women who are economically strong or not dependent on a husband, as well as physically and socially mobile women, is wide but quite consistent. They are often called "prostitutes" (McCurdy 2001, 226) "wayward" (Cornwall 2001), "wicked" (Parpart 2001), "women who wander aimlessly" (Coplan 2001), or women who think they are "like a man" (Lovett 2001, 47).

On the other hand, women can become scapegoats in conditions of wider macroeconomic transformation that changes power relations without women's specific initiative. Clark (2001) has shown how even among the Asante, for whom trading by women is a well-established tradition, market women became targets of verbal and physical attacks in a time of wider economic changes, which worsened earning prospects in the male-dominated economic sectors while the female-dominated trading sector was initially less affected. As with the Chagga market women, these other African women who transgress the conventional gender boundaries, either because of economic necessity or of their own choosing, tend to become targets of moral criticism, but also the sites for rethinking cultural ideas about gender and gender relations.

The association between enterprising women and sexual services is not, of course, always imaginary; sexuality has been and remains a resource for some enterprising women. Women's use of their sexuality for creating and manipulating relationships to important men is described for some large scale "elite" businesswomen in Accra (Robertson 1984, 16, 133, 242) as well as for the successful female traders in post-independence Zaire (LaFontaine 1974; MacGaffey 1987, 177–80). The emerging colonial towns in the Northern Rhodesian (Zambian) Copperbelt and Nairobi attracted enterprising women as early as in the beginning of the twentieth century, where they lived by combining proceeds from sexual and domestic services, beer brewing, cultivation, and gathering, or petty trade (Bujra 1975, 213; Parpart 2001; White 1990, 40). The women in Nairobi managed to accumulate money, becoming an important category of house owners in the African settlements (Bujra 1975; White 1990, 118).[36] Selling of sexual services has been a realistic strategy for women in different places and throughout the times, but to accuse enterprising women as a group of prostitutition has been a recurring way to try and control women's enterprising and movements, because they are conceived as threatening the sociocultural order and its continuity.[37]

A comparable dialogue to the one in contemporary Kilimanjaro was perhaps going on in the societies where Nadel (1965 [1942]), Little (1948), and McCall (1961) once made their studies. And apparently the earlier decades' debate on the Zambian urban "bad girls/women" versus "respectable ladies," described by Parpart (2001), was going on in Lusaka in the 1970s, where Schuster (1982) studied women's increased involvement in trading. According to Schuster, the colonial time suspicion of traders as "no better than prostitutes" prevailed in the 1970s, and the traders took pains to emphasize their respectability both verbally and in clothing, and in developing an image of themselves as "poor-but-respectable." "We are not prostitutes," was a theme Schuster (ibid., 108, 117) heard over and over again when interviewing the market women. Acknowledging that the trading women were also admired because they managed to provide for their families, Schuster nevertheless concludes that women trade more out of a sense of necessity than privilege, that their trade provides marginal subsistence, and that altogether the marginal status of the traders is apparent in all aspects of their lives (ibid., 105, 123).[38]

In this chapter, I have shown how the charges of sexual looseness and selfishness form one side of a dialogue about proper gendered behavior and gender relations in a changing socioeconomic environment. The targets of moral criticism—the trading women—seldom remain passive victims of the moral criticism; their reasoning for their action forms the other side of the dialogue. We have to acknowledge both sides of the moral dialogue and examine the debated issues and meanings because it is through this dialogue that gender relations are ultimately reformed.

In this dialogue the meanings of the cultural categories are often extended and shifted to include talk about something more than "food" or "sexual laxity" per se. Although for many market women in Kilimanjaro the struggle to "feed" their families and to acquire the "basic necessities" are the very real and realistic aims for their trading, even the prominent traders state these very same aims as their motives for enterprise. Most market women extend these concepts to include the normative male responsibilities of provision as well as some help for friends and relatives. In using terms that emphasize the most moral, acceptable, and traditional purposes of their marketing, the market women both respond to the public criticism of their selfish enjoyment and accumulative motives and emphasize their generative contributions for their dependents' personhood and identity. By talking emphatically about their responsibilities for "feeding," women stress the increased importance and contribution of mothers to society.

It is through cultural conceptualization in the social conversation that meaning and value are given to people's actions and achievements, and gender relations and gendered spheres are constituted. An emphasis on the economic necessity and importance of women's trading should therefore not lead to the neglect of the social aspect of the markets and economy. By "social" I mean all that was in the early research disparagingly labeled as meaningless "entertainment," "fun," and "socializing" in the marketplace. It is in this social realm of gossip, conversation, feeding and other forms of interaction in the market that meanings and conventions are played out and experimented with and where material exchanges and reality are endowed with meaning.

*3*

# Constructing Moral Reputation

## The Case of Mama Njau

Mama Njau is one of the most prosperous and visible women traders in Mayanka, a "big woman" in every respect. Her affluence is indicated by her body weight, which has increased to a level many local people consider excessive. Her behavior in the market is unlike that of most other women; she usually sits on her millet sacks, prominent in both her physical and her social presence, joking loudly with men and with other women, and openly going to a bar to drink beer and eat meat and perhaps roasted bananas. At the beginning of my stay, when I asked people if they thought she would be willing to tell me about her trading, they frequently suggested that Mama Njau would not have any time for me—during the day she would be busy with her businesses and in the evenings out late in bars.

While most other female traders have to juggle domestic chores, child-care, cultivating *kihamba* and *shamba* land, and trading, Mama Njau concentrates her energies mostly on trading and on managing her children and hired hands in the performance of domestic and cultivation tasks. She began her trading career selling a few bowls of millet at a time, and later tried her luck in several other ventures. Today her main business is whole-saling millet, in which she is involved virtually seven days a week.

Mama Njau's trading profits, entrepreneurial skills, and her overall ac-tivity have enriched her family remarkably. However, like other women in Mayanka, she works within the structures of formal male authority and title to landed property. Her husband lives in Nairobi and runs several busi-nesses of his own there, and visits his Mayanka home only occasionally. He found another woman to live with in Nairobi, which Mama Njau experi-enced as a threat to her position.

This domestic situation, Mama Njau's entrepreneurial determination and success, and her simultaneous subordination to her husband's formal authority form an important background for the conversations of this chapter. In what follows, I will consider the conversations of Mama Njau—and those of others in the community about her—a dialogue in which Mama Njau's moral reputation is discussed and constructed. What is at stake is the acknowledgement of her social and moral value and the legiti-macy of her position, both as a wife and as a member of the community.

Mama Njau is the target of different kinds of gossip and suspicions of witchcraft. Her accumulation of property and wealth is rumored to involve the use of occult powers and the sacrifice of the health of her child, as well as other manifestations of selfishness. Comparable accusations of accumu-lation as a detraction from other people's well-being are reported from other parts of Africa in discussions of witchcraft.[1] I attempt to bridge the persistent division in the literature about gossip and witchcraft between ap-proaches that explain them as political instruments in struggles over mate-rial resources and power on the one hand, or as attempts to maintain group values and social order on the other.

In the understanding of British structural functionalists, gossip and ac-cusations of witchcraft were caused by social conflict, but they were often also interpreted as ways to solve those conflicts and thus to maintain and strengthen the social order (on gossip, see Gluckman 1963, and Epstein 1969; on witchcraft, see e.g., Marwick 1965, and Middleton and Winter 1963). The explanation of gossip as an index of and a means for solving social contra-dictions within a group is reproduced in some of the newer literature (e.g., Abrahams 1970; Bergmann 1993; Scott 1990). Where these explanations em-phasize the positive social functions of gossip and witchcraft in the mainte-nance of group norms, values, and unity, in other views gossip and accusa-tions of witchcraft are regarded as an instrumental use of such norms in political struggles. Paine (1967) emphasized these political functions of gos-sip, as later did Scott (1985), who viewed gossip as an instrument of resist-ance of a subordinate group in regard to those in power. Similarly, several recent studies on witchcraft have interpreted it as an idiom and weapon in local struggles over power and resources.[2]

The emphasis on politics and social order leads to an undermining of the dimensions of belief, knowledge, and explanation—issues that Evans-Pritchard (1937) found crucial in witchcraft. Recently, there has been an attempt to revive these aspects of explanation in analyses that interpret witchcraft accusations or gossip as ways to comprehend and control the inequalities that modernity, commoditization, or new regimes have created in African communities.[3] Nevertheless, these studies share the earlier research's understanding of witchcraft or gossip as a reflection of a social crisis. All in all, the emphasis on either the political or sociocultural functions of witchcraft and gossip has tended to persist in the newer literature.

However, when people were discussing Mama Njau's alleged use of witchcraft, these conversations have to be understood in terms of beliefs and values as well as politics. So extraordinary were her entrepreneurial success and her behavior that many people believed that occult forces were involved. I examine conversations about Mama Njau as both attempts to grasp the basis for her success and to be included in that success. These conversations were also ways to discuss the changing limits of the possible and appropriate in gendered behavior, resources, and spaces in general. Therefore, rather than as means to fortify social order and communal values, I examine witchcraft discussions as ways to rethink them.

The politics of these conversations is in the attempts to unveil Mama Njau's economic state by gossip. Gossip calls her to explain and make her intentions and resources visible, public, and transparent. We will see how Mama Njau's comments about herself, whether in public or private, were often responses to the critical and evaluative talk that surrounded her. These responses include politics as well, since Mama Njau tries thereby to assure others about her moral quality.

Mama Njau's discussions about herself and other people's conversations about her thus form a dialogue. My use of the word "dialogue" is very different from the way the term has been most commonly used in recent anthropology, mainly due to the reinterpretation of ethnography as dialogical enterprise. The reference has most commonly been to cross-cultural dialogue between the anthropologist and the people studied, resulting in reflexive personal knowledge in which the anthropologist comes to rethink and report his or her own struggles towards fresh consciousness and self-awareness through an exotic other (see e.g., Dwyer 1982; Okely and Callaway 1997).

I use the word "dialogue" in Bakhtin's sense (1994 [1986]), considering the interlocutors' words as polyphonous, so that there is a plurality of voices present even in the most private conversations. My reading of Mama

Njau's personal narratives resembles other researchers' creative use of life histories and their shift from the focus on a single individual to whole families. Oscar Lewis (e.g., 1959, 1961), for instance, looked at the differing perspectives on life of the members of Mexican and Puerto Rican families. More recently, Richard Werbner (1996 [1991]) studied the memories of several generations of a Zimbabwean family as a micro-dialogue in which the family members are in ongoing argument with each other and with the anthropologist. Instead of being on a single family, my focus is on the involvement of the surrounding community in constructing the life story and moral reputation of Mama Njau and her family. In addition, I examine the recurring idioms and categories with which personal difference and moral value are discussed and constituted. Rather than simple labels, these categories are signifiers of complex cultural values and expectations. Therefore, the mere use of those idioms in personal conversation makes the "voice" of an individual embedded, dialogic, and polemical.

In the following conversations with and about Mama Njau, the moral reputation of her husband and his second wife are also under consideration. For simplicity's sake, I will call the husband Wilfred; Mama Njau usually calls him *Mzee,* an honorary and respectful title for a male, literally meaning "an elder."[4] For this account I will call Mama Njau "Mary," even though people always call her Mama Njau or just shortly Njau, which is her natal lineage name. Her husband's second wife I will simply call "the Mpare," meaning a person of the Pare ethnic group, because this is how I always heard her called. I never came to know her real name, nor did I ever see her, even though she was strongly present in conversations and in gossip.

I will first present Mama Njau's life history, in her words but in my composition. This life history comes from two recorded interviews and numerous informal discussions we had in her home and in the markets and bars. In our discussions, I was able to cross-check and expand upon information concerning the different phases and events of her life. Furthermore, our conversations revealed certain recurring themes in her talk and their use in situationally changing arguments, all of which the life history interviews alone would not have revealed. My chronological presentation of her courtship, marriage, life in Nairobi, and return to Mayanka is mostly compiled from my discussions with her on occasions when there were only the two of us present. I examine her self-representation as an unfolding personal narrative where she reveals her transformation from a naïve young girl to a clever and artful woman and trader. After that, the chapter moves gradually to her conversations in more public contexts and to the other people's evaluating talk about Mama Njau. These conversations took place in 1994 and early 1995, and during a shorter visit in 1997.

## Mama Njau's Story

### Engagement and Marriage

Mary was only fifteen years old when she met a neighbor woman on her way to the market one day and the woman persuaded her to pass by a certain house. Mary did not know that the short visit was all planned and that she was being directed to the home as a potential wife for a certain local young man living and working in Nairobi. Mary was considered a possibility since the man's father had taken a liking to her when he had seen her on the road to confirmation classes. A few days after that short visit, Mary got a letter and an enclosed photograph from a man called Wilfred. She did not particularly remember him; he had moved to Kenya when he was about sixteen, and was now twenty-one. He earned money by sewing first in Mombasa, and later in Nairobi. In his letter, Wilfred told her that he would like to court her *(kumchumbia)* and asked for a picture of her. A few days later, Mary was again invited to Wilfred's home, where she met a man who resembled the one in the photograph. Wilfred asked if she had gotten his letter and why she had not answered. Mary said that she had been too busy *(shughuli nyingi)*. Wilfred wanted to know what she thought of his proposal; she answered that "it [courting] is possible, but I'm still young" *(bado mimi ni mdogo)*.[5] Wilfred impatiently asked why she had not already made up her mind before coming to visit his home, but he eventually had to leave for Nairobi without receiving any clear answer.

Mary later accepted Wilfred as her suitor, but there were three other boys who were also interested in wooing her. They sometimes came to visit and occasionally presented her with gifts. As Mary's confirmation day approached, Wilfred sent her cloth from Nairobi for a confirmation dress. Not knowing about this present, Mary's father gave her money to buy cloth for the dress, too. Mary did not hesitate to accept her father's money, and used it to buy certain small but crucial accessories for her confirmation dress, such as sunglasses and a small handbag. Mary was stylish and elegant on her confirmation day. She wore a dress made from the cloth sent by Wilfred, with accessories she had bought with the money given by her father. She was also wearing on her wrist a brand new watch given to her by a rival suitor. To this boy's courting proposals Mary had given the same answer as she had to Wilfred: that courting was possible, but that she was still very young.

After Mary's confirmation, Wilfred's father grew impatient as he noticed that many boys were visiting Mary at home. He urged Wilfred to hurry before someone else won her. Wilfred came to invite Mary for a visit to his home one day, just as Mary was seeing off another suitor at the road.

Hearing Wilfred's invitation, Mary lied to him, saying that she was not able to come since her father wanted to send her on an errand. Mary felt indecisive even though by that time her father had already been at Wilfred's home to receive the first bridewealth *mbege*. Mary explained to me, "Here with us, when your parents have received *mbege*, it means that the one who offered it is your fiancé."[6] Finally she had to agree to visit Wilfred's home on the proposed day, however.

Mary arranged with a friend of hers to escort her for the visit. As the day came, Mary was nervous, to the extent that her "feet refused to walk." She was afraid of being "carried"[7] on that visit. Finally she set off with her friend. While at Wilfred's home, Mary still felt so nervous that "beer *(pombe)*[8] would not go in."[9] Wilfred told her he had brought two pieces of cloth from Nairobi to have dresses made for her. He proposed taking her to Moshi town someday to have them cut and sewn. Mary agreed to the trip, suggesting that they go the following week. On that day Mary returned home with her friend, relieved that her fear of being "carried" had been groundless.

Wilfred came to Mary's home the next day in order to plan the trip to Moshi. It was already about eight o'clock in the evening when Mary saw him to the road, as is customary with visitors. She led him the usual shortcut way along a shady river slope. As she was about to return, Wilfred grabbed her hand, saying that he wanted to talk with her, and told her to come to his home. Mary resisted and told him that she could not "marry yet because she [was] still so young."[10] Wilfred was determined, however, and said that he would stay there on the path until she agreed to go with him. They began to argue. Mary kept repeating that she wanted to go home. Wilfred tried to convince her that it was already too late—she had stayed on the path so long that her mother would certainly assume she had "become married." As Mary continued to resist, Wilfred started to tear at her clothes. The harder she tried to wrench herself free from his grip, the more her clothes were torn as he pulled her in the opposite direction. Finally she was naked. Then Wilfred said he felt pity for her, and pulled out a new *kanga* that he had hidden in his coat, asking Mary to cover herself with it "so that this chill will not kill you."[11] It was then about eleven o'clock at night. Wilfred believed that Mary was ready to follow him, but, wrapped in the *kanga*, she stood there on the riverbank and refused to move.

Around midnight Mary admitted that it was too late to return home; to do so without proper clothes would bring her shame *(aibu)*, and the door would probably not be opened for her at that hour. After all, Mary recalled thinking, by that time Wilfred had been her "boyfriend" *(rafiki)* for more than two years and her father had drunk *mbege*; crying and returning home would be considered shameful. She finally decided to go with him. At his home, Wilfred told his male relatives, "I have a guest." A glance inside the house revealed that the guest had been expected; there was food, two plates, and *pombe* at the table. While Wilfred was talking with his relatives, Mary ran to hide herself behind a tree in the front yard. Wilfred came looking for her, but could not find her until he had fetched a flashlight. He pulled her from behind the tree, hit her lightly, and admonished her by saying, "You've troubled me all evening." "So, I decided to go in and I was married" *(Basi, nikaamua kuingia ndani nikaolewa)*,[12] she said. In the morning Wilfred went to tell his mother that "he had a guest inside," and a messenger was sent to Mary's home to inform her parents that she was married.

The other suitor had come later to Mary's home, only to hear that she was married. He sent Mary a letter through his sister and advised her to run away from Wilfred. Mary replied that they would see each other at a certain wedding the next Saturday. When she was talking with the boy at the wedding, Mary noticed Wilfred watching her from a distance. Gradually Mary began to feel more and more perplexed, and she remembers thinking: "I am married now. It is not appropriate to run away with another man." Mary told her friends that she was suffering from a bad headache and left. Noting Mary's absence, Wilfred asked her friend where Mary had disappeared. Suspicious, Wilfred himself hurried home, where he found Mary lying on the bed, crying. She told him that she was just suffering from a bad headache. Mary told me that it was not true, however: "I just cried. I was thinking that I have been confirmed. And I was thinking of these two suitors of mine."[13]

Although Mary often described herself as indecisive regarding her suitors, in other contexts she implied that she had taken a special liking to Wilfred from the beginning. Once Mary explained: "Even the other suitors I liked. But in my soul *(kwenye roho yangu)*, only to see that one [Wilfred], my soul would go 'tap.' I felt like I was afraid of him, but of the other ones I was not afraid." Mary explained that she liked Wilfred also because he was "calm" *(mtaratibu)* and always "spoke to the point" *(anaongea pointi)*.[14] Mary thus implied that in his firmness and wisdom Wilfred had earned her deference and had the authority over her a husband is expected to have.

A few days after Mary's arrival at Wilfred's home, the marriage was confirmed in church. The two pieces of cloth brought by Wilfred from Nairobi were sewn into dresses for Mary; one to replace her clothes that had been torn, and the other for the church confirmation of the marriage. Mary remained at Wilfred's home only one week before they set off for Nairobi. This was in 1967.

## Between Nairobi and Mayanka

Their first child, a boy, was born eight months after the marriage. Mary returned to Wilfred's home in Mayanka to give birth and "stay inside" for four months. The mother-in-law cooked food for her during that time, "after which," Mary said, "I went to church, I had the child baptized and returned to Nairobi." Soon she was pregnant again, returned to Mayanka a month before giving birth to a baby girl, and stayed three months inside, after which "I baptized the child and returned to Nairobi." The third child was born in Nairobi. But as this girl was sickly, Mary brought her to Mayanka when she was three months old, and some offerings were made to appease the spirits. After the child recovered, Mary returned to Nairobi. She soon found herself pregnant again and gave birth to her fourth child, another girl while visiting her ill father in Mayanka. After the usual three months' seclusion, "I baptized the child and returned to Nairobi," Mary reported.[15] That baby was only four months old when Mary found herself pregnant again, with yet another baby girl. Mary had begun to think about moving to Mayanka and having a house built there. Wilfred and Mary did not have a house of their own in Mayanka, and Mary lived at her in-laws' house when she was there.

Wilfred did not want her to move back to Mayanka; Mary said that she had to leave "by force," because she wanted to "learn to cultivate," and because in Nairobi she could do nothing but "stay at home."[16] The other reason she gave me was that Wilfred had started drinking beer and running around with young girls, which became obvious after they had bought a second car. The first car, a taxi, was bought after accumulating some savings from Wilfred's salary. Mary explained: "When the savings had reached 5000 TZS, I bought a car, a taxi."[17] The taxi had paid for itself in only two weeks, she said, and she and her husband were later able to buy a second and then a third car. When I asked Mary if it was really she who had bought the taxi, she said she was the one who received and kept the money at home, but that actually it was her husband's money. She implied, however, that she had made the decision to buy the car. She also managed the income that the other cars brought in, but said she was too "stupid" (mjinga) at that time to set aside some of that money for herself.

Mary likely exaggerated somewhat the profitability of the taxi business, by which she underscored her entrepreneurial abilities. According to Mary, the taxi business mostly benefited Wilfred, since he was able to leave his job as a seamster for an Indian man and open a dressmaking shop where he hired some tailors. And he began to spend more and more time away from home. He would return only at four o'clock in the morning, and when asked where he had been, would simply reply that he was "doing business."[18]

### Return to Mayanka

Mary returned to Mayanka while she was pregnant with her fifth child and started to build a house, the big cement "block house" where the family lives today. While the building was in progress, however, she realized that she would run out of money and give birth before the house was finished. She asked her father-in-law to give her a place for a small wood-and-earth house that she then had built in one week and in which her father-in-law placed the three cooking stones for her to have a hearth of her own. A few days later she gave birth and stayed inside for three months, after which "I came out, and we finished building this house, and I did not go to Nairobi again."[19] That was in 1975.

Mary explained that after having the house built, "I started to build the cattle shed. Until that time I had not been cultivating, so I started to cultivate and I bound[20] some cows."[21] Money for building the house was found from a cancelled land purchase; after first having sold the land for Wilfred, the seller sold it a second time when he got a better offer and Wilfred's money was eventually returned. When I asked Mary who had done the plans and drawings for the house, she said: "*Mzee* brought the drawings, but I searched for the stones, I went to carry them, and I searched for the car to bring them here, I carried the water, and everything. Then I called him and asked him to bring me a drawing, and so he did."[22] The wood for the cattle shed was given by her neighbor, an older man related to Wilfred's mother. Mary said that she bought the cows but was not forthcoming about where she got the money for them.

After moving to Mayanka, Mary started trading. First she would buy small amounts of millet and sell it by the bowlful. She would buy less than one sack at a time. When she had sold the contents of that one, she would go buy more and might sell as much as two sacks per market day. For start-up capital, she said, she used money that her father-in-law had given her at the beginning of her marriage, which was for the stated purpose of "eating in Nairobi" *(kwa kula Nairobi)*. This money was his compensation for the seclusion period after marriage, the costs of which the father-in-law would normally cover, but which was not realized because they had departed so soon for Nairobi. Mary did not use that money in Nairobi because they were able to live on Wilfred's income. Having started her trading in Mayanka, Mary was able to accumulate some savings from the profits and from the money that Wilfred gave her "for food."

During the 1970s, millet started to be brought to Kilimanjaro from greater distances away; before that time only locally cultivated finger millet (*ulezi wa Kichagga*, "Chagga millet") had been sold in the markets. Local millet is of better quality and more expensive than the transported product (sometimes called *ulezi wa Kizungu*, "European millet"). Mary explained that with her saved money she was able to buy thirty sacks of the new millet, which she stored at her home and waited until prices had increased. Around that time, her neighbor also gave her money to buy another forty sacks of millet. These are remarkable amounts of millet for a female trader to buy at one time, even by today's standards. Mary explained that she bought and sold the forty sacks on her neighbor's account, as he had asked. Later she returned the money to him with some of the profit, but not quite half of it as she "hid" part of the total profit for herself. She tried trading maize for a while, and at another time secondhand clothes, but soon returned to selling millet. Mary has been involved in the wholesale trading of finger millet as her main business since the end of the 1970s.

## The Mpare

Wilfred stayed in Nairobi and found another woman to live with, who was from the neighboring Pare ethnic group. According to Mary, their relationship started within a year after she left Nairobi. Hearing the rumors of his mistress only strengthened Mary's decision not to return to Nairobi. "If he has another woman there and I go there too, it's quarrels. One cannot know, you know, those [Pare people] are people of *pori*,[23] I decided that I don't want to go." A couple of years later Mary had her sixth and last child, the second boy, just a few months before the Mpare gave birth to her first child with Wilfred. "I was told that 'the woman who was with your husband has given birth to his child.' 'All right,' I said, and I just continued with my chores *(shughuli zangu)*, until today."[24]

I asked Mary if she had used some means of birth control after the last child, and she said, "Well, *Mzee* went and started to live with that woman, and I was thinking that if I continue bearing more children here, I'll get troubles. I started to use pills, but *Mzee* does not know."[25] Another time Mary explained to a few women and me in a bar how there was a point when she was tired of being constantly pregnant and giving birth. At that time she was living in Nairobi and went to a doctor in order to get contraceptive pills; she then happily showed them to Wilfred at home. He objected strongly and immediately ordered Mary to throw them into the toilet. At that point Mary realized her own naiveté; she should have used the pills in secret. Mary said that Wilfred expected her to bear him more sons. Their first child had been a boy, but the next four were girls. The last child was also a boy.

## Growing Clever

In these reflections Mary portrays herself as gradually coming to awareness while gaining wisdom about the nature of her own agency. A crucial theme in her recollections on her past is her growing cleverness, combined with a certain increased disillusionment and determination. In her description, as a young girl she was an object of boys' attention and desire. Although not merely a passive object or victim, she often portrays herself as confused and indecisive, and her "agency" lay mostly in her evasive behavior. After her marriage, it was in Mayanka that Mary found increasingly more space for creating and realizing her own agency. This is revealed by the recurring "I"-forms of her account, which are culturally incorrect[26] but which emphasize Mary as an actor and decision-maker. In Mayanka, she gives birth and baptizes her children and arranges to give offerings for the health of her ill child. Overall, the impression she gives is that Wilfred is hardly involved in these events. Mary's "agency" in Nairobi, most notably saving Wilfred's money and buying the cars, is successful in financial terms but a failure when it comes to the stability of their marriage; it contributes to Wilfred's self-realization and status but not to hers or to their mutual benefit.

A clear statement of Mary's desire for more autonomy is her oft-repeated description of Nairobi as the place and time of "just staying at home" (nilikaa nyumbani tu)[27] and Mayanka as the place to "cultivate" (kulima) or "learn to cultivate." "Cultivation" in this context is a culturally acceptable and respectable reason for her to return, but should also be understood as a metaphor for her overall activity in Mayanka as contrasted with her stay-at-home status in Nairobi. This passivity is linked to her alleged naiveté in Nairobi: Mary does not realize that she should tuck away any of Wilfred's money for herself, nor that she should just use her contraceptive pills without saying anything. Upon her return to Mayanka, she has grown clever enough to keep part of the profit made with the neighbor's money and to start using the pills without informing Wilfred.

Mary thus presents her increased cleverness as a justified response to her experiences as a young girl and wife whose trust and trustworthiness gradually become revealed to be naiveté. Little by little, she learns to start building, strengthening, and defending her own sphere and position. And this becomes a search and an argument for "her place" as both Wilfred's legitimate wife and in what is ultimately "his place"—that is, Wilfred's home and kihamba.

### The Two Wives Dispute Their "Place"

Because she had given birth to Wilfred's child and was living with him, the Mpare could be considered Wilfred's second wife. Wilfred never directly told Mary about the other woman; she found out from other people. When Mary told him that she heard these rumors, Wilfred denied having married the woman. "I just had a child with her, that's all," Mary said he told her.

The Mpare had visited Mayanka once. Mary recalled how Wilfred's brother asked her one day if he could borrow her pickup truck the next Sunday, supposedly to transport a "load" (mzigo) from Himo to his home. Rumors that the Mpare was looking for Wilfred's home had already reached Mary, however, and she guessed what kind of "load" he needed the truck for.

When Sunday arrived, Mary pretended to go to church but hid herself in the cattle shed instead. She waited until she heard her brother-in-law stop at Wilfred's house. Mary listened to him tell her father-in-law, "This is the co-wife of Mama Njau." He added, "And she is a better wife than Mama Njau is." According to Mary, her father-in-law answered his son angrily, "Mama Njau is the only one I know." The father-in-law added that if Mary were present she would cut the Mpare with a machete *(panga)*. Mary said he totally refused to accept the Mpare woman, telling his son to "Take her away."[28]

There was a party that evening at the brother-in-law's house, at which Wilfred's brother introduced the Mpare to Mary and said she was her "co-wife." Mary told me that she said nothing, but said she was thinking that even if she did hit the woman with a *panga* it would not result in any legal ramifications because that woman had "broken her marriage/house," and was thus herself the guilty party. Mary emphasized that the Mpare never entered her house in Mayanka while she was there, even though she had come in order to do so.

Mary said that whenever she goes to Nairobi she usually visits Wilfred's house, and might meet the Mpare there. I started to ask her, "When you go to her place . . ." *(unapokwenda kwake),* and she quickly interrupted to say that it was not "her," the Mpare's, place, but that it was where she, Mary, lived when she was in Nairobi and that she still had belongings there.[29] She said she does not stay at the house overnight or drink or eat anything while there. This was both a way to avoid any social association with the Mpare and to protect herself from contact with any substance of witchcraft.

Mary's neighbor also told me about the Mpare's visit to Mayanka. The Mpare, she related, had wanted Wilfred to show her his home. As he persistently refused to do so, the woman decided to find it by herself. The Mpare did not dare to enter Wilfred's house, and slept overnight at his brother's house a few kilometers away instead. She departed very early the next morning for Nairobi, passing but not entering Wilfred's house. According to the neighbor, Mary was deeply shocked by this strange visit and became very sick afterwards, but she did not want people to know how strongly she had reacted. "Mary was very sick, to the extent of almost dying. To the point of almost becoming mentally confused," the neighbor said. She also said that Mary was convinced her sickness had been caused by some witchcraft substance that the Mpare had secreted somewhere near her house as she passed by. Mary also accused the Mpare of having "bound" Wilfred so that he would not send any money home for her, the neighbor said.

Mary herself would air such suspicions somewhat indirectly, typically in bar conversations where her other, more general discussions would turn into reflections on "the Mpare women." Once, for example, a few women were sitting and chatting in the bar Mary owned and Mary commented on a story told by one of them by saying thoughtfully, "A Mpare is not a human being; they are like the Machame." When I asked Mary what she had meant, she explained that both Pare and Machame women steal one's husband by using "medicine," after which it is impossible to make the man return. "He leaves you. He runs away from you," she explained.

Mary once asked a local doctor in a bar if there were any pills available that she could use to reduce her weight. The doctor said they were not purchasable in Tanzania, and that the closest place to get them was Nairobi. Mary said she could ask her husband to bring the pills for her from that city. The doctor pretended sudden enlightenment, saying that now he understood that the reason for her weight gain was because her husband was not there to tease her at night. The doctor eventually left. After quite a long time Mary suddenly repeated what the doctor had said, thoughtfully and with a sad face, and the talk turned again to the nature of Pare women.

Wilfred had had three children with the Mpare by the time I arrived in Mayanka. The youngest lived in Nairobi, and the other two with Mary in Mayanka. The Mpare's first child, a girl, had lived with Mary since she was small, and was now attending a nearby secondary school. A woman in the neighborhood told me that Wilfred had brought this child from Nairobi to Mayanka when she was only a few years old, telling Mary that he was bringing her because he was just about to separate from the Mpare. He did not, however, and brought another child to live with Mary a few years later.

Once Mary was complaining to a few people in a bar about how Wilfred had "forgotten" her, and I suggested that it had actually been Mary herself who had first left her husband in Nairobi and returned to Mayanka. Mary said again that she wanted to come home "to cultivate" and not just "stay at home." Soon after she had moved out, "he came to find that Mpare," she added. I tried to provoke Mary a bit by noting that she had taken in the Mpare's children. Both Mary and another woman present were quick to assert that Mary had had no alternative. Should she have refused to take them, the husband would have immediately informed her that "This is my place" (hapa ni kwangu), thereby suggesting her only other option was to leave. The other woman suggested that Mary should invite the Mpare to her own daughter's confirmation feast. She thought the Mpare would probably be too frightened to come, however, as she knows that Nairobi is "her place." If she were to come to Mayanka and should "a panga be used," she understood that it would not result in any sort of court case.

"Using a machete" was a threat of physical violence and not of occult power. The differentiation between means of aggression was in fact an important aspect in the construction of and claim for moral distinction between Mary and the Mpare. Blaming the Mpare for using occult, hidden powers strengthened the image of her position having been illegitimately acquired and maintained, and of the overall immorality of her means and person. By claiming the right to use a "machete" Mary was maintaining the legitimacy of her own position and place and saying that using even the crudest physical means was justifiable.

## Jousting through Gossip

The Mpare's first child and Mary's own youngest child, who were born at around the same time, went through confirmation while I was staying in Mayanka. The approach of the confirmation feast brought the rather explosive nature of the two wives' relations to the surface, even though "that Mpare" had been a recurring theme in Mary's talk. The feast ultimately became an occasion for the reconfiguration and reshaping of the two women's moral qualities, relations, and positions.

Mary had talked about the confirmation in different places and situations long before it actually took place. The two main topics of discussion were the cost of the feast and the question of whether the Mpare would be present. The initial plan was to have a double feast for the two children in Mayanka, but sometimes when Mary became upset and angry enough she would demand that the girl's feast take place in Nairobi, where her mother lived. Mary was not shy about telling people how much money she had already spent on the Mpare's daughter's feast. She would say she had bought the girl four fine dresses and all the necessary accessories. The girl had been part of two of Mary's own daughters' confirmation feasts a few years earlier, and might have felt bad if she had to wear something less fine just because she was not Mary's child.

Mary had heard how the Mpare had by chance met and recognized her daughter at the Moshi bus station. She had allegedly approached the girl and asked her whose daughter she was. When the girl named her father, the woman asked who her mother was. When the girl answered that she did not know her mother, the woman exclaimed, "It's me!" She then cried out, "I have found my child! I had lost her!" According to Mary, the Mpare started shouting so joyfully that everyone around was staring at them. This was utterly inappropriate behavior, in Mary's icy opinion. And she told everyone present the story of how the Mpare had sent the girl to Mary to care for ten years earlier and had not since cared for or spent a shilling on her. Mary also frequently spoke of having searched for a secondary school place for the girl by herself with no help from either Wilfred or her mother.

One day in her millet store, Mary was telling the people present that she had been trying to reach *Mzee* in Nairobi by phone to have him arrange the daughter's confirmation there. She was upset by rumors that the Mpare was complaining that Mary had accused her of using witchcraft. According to the rumors, the Mpare was so shocked by such accusations that she had said she would not be able to take part in her own daughter's feast in Mayanka. Mary, for her part, acted as if this sort of claim was totally unfounded, and thus insulted, she wanted to talk with Wilfred about it.

The two women were thus effectively disputing through hearsay. These indirect, but ongoing disputes made setting a date for the feast quite difficult and it remained open until almost the eve of the confirmation. A feast was finally arranged for both children in Mayanka. Wilfred bore all the costs of the drinks, of which there was a wide variety available, from *mbege* and beer to the stronger Tanzanian *Konyagi*[30] and various kinds of imported alcohol, while Mary took care of the food. The Mpare was not present. She thus remained invisible to most of the people in Mayanka, and her nonappearance was seen as a concession to Mary's claim on place and authority.

## Household Economy

### Resources

The complaints about "the Mpare," the confirmation feast, and the children's needs in general were threads in the larger recurring theme in Mary's talk of how much economic and other responsibility Mary, the Mpare, and Wilfred carried for the "social whole." While at times Mary would complain about Wilfred's failure to provide support specifically, she more often emphasized her own excessive burden in taking care of the work and children, even the other woman's children, all alone.

I once asked Mary if Wilfred had sent any money to her from Nairobi, and she answered curtly, "I haven't seen any." Wilfred probably gave Mary some money when visiting her in Mayanka, but Mary once said, "If he gave me 10,000 TZS, how does it help me?" She said that the secondary school fees for her youngest child and the Mpare's were both 30,000 TZS. At another time, she told me that even if Wilfred gave her 20,000 TZS it wouldn't help much, adding, "*Mzee* says that 'you have your maize.'"

In addition to the home *kihamba*, there were four purchased *shamba* plots. Of these Mary would say, "I bought . . ." Upon further questioning, she would explain how she had added some money for the first *shamba* because Wilfred had said he did not have enough, and how the second *shamba* had been bought with Wilfred's money, while the other two *shambas* had been bought with her own money. She had managed the transaction in each case, regardless of whose money was used, Mary said. All the *shamba* plots were registered in Wilfred's name, however, she said. Had she bought a plot under her own name, it would have been taken as an indication that she was considering divorce. Being registered under Wilfred's name meant the plots would be inherited by his male children.

In years when the harvest was good, Mary could get a substantial amount of maize, forty or fifty sacks, from the *shamba* plots. Roughly three sacks would be used for family consumption, and Mary would sell the rest at market. The consumption of maize was low in Mary's family since they preferred bananas and rice. When bananas were scarce in the home *kihamba*, the family bought them at the market rather than eat *ugali* (maize porridge). This food preference indicates a difference in status and wealth, as many other families in Mayanka cannot afford such food purchases and have to eat *ugali* when bananas are scarce. At peak season, Mary's and Wilfred's *kihamba* produced enough bananas to sell some at the market. The farm plots also produced a few sacks of coffee in normal years. Unlike many other families where the income from coffee belongs to the husband, Mary arranged for the sale of their coffee and kept the money.

Regardless of recurrent references to her interest in "cultivation," Mary did no farming herself. She tried to delegate cultivation and as much of her household work as possible to her children and hired hands in order to devote her time to her main business of buying and selling millet. She rented a building for storing sacks of millet on the outskirts of the local marketplace. She typically had a steady supply all year round; when prices were low, she would hoard a larger amount of millet and sell it when prices rose. During ordinary times, the amount Mary could earn in a few days would equal a month's salary in the governmental or semigovernmental sector.

Opposite her millet store, Mary rented a modest building that accommodated her bar. In 1994, she could sell two cases of beer in one evening.[31] She liked to spend her time in the evenings and on Sundays in her bar, drinking beer and *Konyagi*, often mixed together. In doing so she was combining both economic effort and personal pleasure. As she conversed with people over drinks in her own bar, she kept her eye on the millet store at the same time and was ready to do business any time a customer appeared. The potential customer would also know that she was easily found in her bar.

Wilfred had given Mary two pickup trucks for use in the millet trade. Both of them had broken down, however, and were waiting for repair practically the entire time I was in Mayanka in 1994. By 1997, one of the trucks was occasionally in working order, and was mainly used for hauling fodder for Mary's three cows. Her newer business ventures included the purchase of one hundred chicks, for which she was preparing their old house by having it wired for electricity.

Wilfred had several businesses in Nairobi. He owned a workshop that produced furniture and was involved in buying and selling cars. He also had a four-story house under construction, the rooms in which would be for renting out.

## *Dependents*

There were six youngsters living with Mary in 1994. Two daughters who had finished secondary school were at home waiting for a chance to continue with their studies, meanwhile helping with the domestic and cultivation work. Two children were of primary school age; one was the last child of the Mpare, and the other was the child of Mary's first daughter. There was Mary's third child, a mentally retarded girl who could not take care of herself. There was also a boy from another region, hired to help in the home and the fields, and occasionally some girls hired for domestic work but who did not stay for long since Mary was not satisfied with their work. The two children who went through confirmation—Mary's youngest son and the Mpare's daughter—were attending boarding schools and stayed with Mary during vacation periods.

In addition to these dependents, a few young men helped Mary with handling the millet sacks, doing some cultivation work, serving in her bar, and doing occasional errands. Several of these men had once worked for her on salary, but she had "fired" them because they stole and drank. Since they had not found any other work, they would hang around and get tips from Mary when they worked. Mary never left her store in their hands, however, because she did not trust them. In fact, she was constantly arguing with the boy who took care of her bar, since he used to try to skim some money from the beer sales.

The two daughters who had completed secondary school expected Wilfred to arrange for them to continue their education. Like many other students, they had been advised to seek places at a college for teachers, but they were not the least bit interested. They wanted to take some of the more fashionable (and expensive) private courses. Their dreams came true in 1995, when they moved to Nairobi and lived with Wilfred for a year, attending day courses in both English and data-processing. Wilfred also arranged a private teacher for them in the evenings, and they finished the computer course at the head of the class. In 1997, the daughters were living with their older sister in a town in Tanzania and looking for employment.

Mary had four children living with her in 1997, and the house was quieter than it had been three years earlier. In addition to her mentally retarded daughter, there were a boy and a girl from another region who had been hired to help out. The fourth was Mary's sister's son, who helped with cultivation and other work. Mary was not happy with the girl she had employed and felt she did not work hard and left Mary with more of the duties than when her daughters had been at home. She could not fire the domestic helper, however, because her disabled child needed someone around while Mary was out.

Wilfred had three children living with him in Nairobi at the time. Mary's last child, the second boy, was being apprenticed for work there. The Mpare's last child, also a boy, and Mary's daughter's daughter were going to primary school in Nairobi. These children provided crucial domestic help for Wilfred, since he was not living with the Mpare any more.

## Material Resources, Affection, and Moral Fulfillment

An ongoing theme in Mary's talk was her disproportionate responsibility in providing for the family. At times, Mary said that however dissatisfied she was with her marriage, there was not much she could do to change the situation; she just had "to continue living with the man" and did so "only because of the children." Mary would also sometimes publicly complain about men in general, and how they seek female company in bars and leave their wives to "dry up" *(kukauka)*[32] at home. Even without the specific mention of Wilfred's name, people listening to her had no problem understanding the personal thrust of her complaints.

Mary seemed satisfied and proud, however, whenever Wilfred was visiting in Mayanka. He would usually arrive and leave without much advance notice. Once when we were sitting in Mary's bar, a man came in to tell her that Wilfred had just arrived and was having beer in another bar. Without knowing that the man was only teasing, Mary immediately became excited, alert, and restless. She started to fuss about where she would get meat at that time of the evening. Another time, Mary was telling another woman in the market about Wilfred and his plans to stay a few days more in Mayanka when a young man from her neighborhood told her he had just seen Wilfred leaving for Nairobi. Mary was surprised at this news and looked disappointed.

Mary usually sat in her bar until quite late in the evening, but she restricted her nights out when Wilfred was around. If Wilfred was staying at the house, Mary would not go out in the evening at all. More often, however, Wilfred would be drinking beer in the bars while visiting in Mayanka, and Mary would go to her bar and return home earlier than usual. She said she would then leave a meal waiting for Wilfred on the living room table and go to bed.

Despite her complaints of Wilfred "forgetting" her, Mary also seemed to enjoy the relative freedom and autonomy of living apart from her husband. Sometimes she would tell me how happy she was to be able to come and go whenever she wanted. If she came home in a good mood, she would turn on the radio or a video with Zairean (Congolese) music and dance in the night.

The provision and distribution of wealth and resources is certainly an emotional issue, as the above discussions show. In material terms, the issue was not only the present "place" and distribution of resources between the two wives and their children, but also about future prospects. As only male children usually inherit permanent property such as land, the main inheritors in this case would be Mary's two sons and the Mpare's one. As a rule, the home *kihamba* is divided between the eldest and youngest sons of the first wife—in this case Mary's two sons. Even though denying the shares of these two sons would likely raise objections in the extended family, a man can sometimes decide otherwise according to his personal preferences. He can, for instance, accommodate the son of another wife in the home *kihamba* if he so wishes. And every son who has inherited a piece of *kihamba* is allowed to bring his mother to live there.

With the increasing scarcity of land in Kilimanjaro, the definition of the order and legitimacy of a man's marriages and other unions is ever more crucial to the future of a woman and her children. The relevant matters that define a union are: the couple's cohabitation, their own and other people's understanding of the union, the payment or the promise of bridewealth, and possibly the confirmation of the marriage in church. However, as Comaroff and Roberts (1981, 150–51) have said about the Tswana, these factors are points of argument used to define or dispute the nature and status of a union rather than criteria that clearly define it.

The legitimacy of a union and the distribution of inheritance are thus always ultimately matters of negotiation and acknowledgement by the husband, the extended family, and the surrounding community. Mary's position as the first and legitimate wife could hardly be disputed. However, she did not exaggerate her need to accept Wilfred's decisions because "the place" was ultimately under his control and was therefore always ultimately susceptible to a potential shift in his preferences. What remained much more weakly defined, however, was Wilfred's union with the Mpare,[33] and Mary was busy trying to enforce her definition of it by attempting to convince both Wilfred and the surrounding community of her own superior moral authority and legitimacy to that of the Mpare.

Mary's discussions about her efforts to provide for the family, and about her work for the literal construction and development of "the place"—her house-building and land-buying—as well as her unfailing deference to Wilfred's authority, emphasized that she had worked hard, made sacrifices for and earned her position and "place." The struggle between the two women was also about the distribution of affection and the acknowledgement of their moral worth by Wilfred through his giving. In Mayanka, people call this dimension of sharing and distribution "mutual understanding" *(maelewano)* and "love" *(upendo)*. The competition between the two women was thus not simply over material resources, but also over moral recognition and emotional attachment as realized and made visible by Wilfred's material distribution and his presence.

## Categories for Discussing Moral Value

### Trust and Understanding

"Trustworthiness" *(uaminifu)* and "mutual understanding" *(maelewano)* were the key qualities of Mary's claim to moral value. Her talk emphasized her unfailing reliability and dependability, both as a wife and a mother who takes even the children of the other woman under her caring wing. I once asked Mary if she thought she might have been happier married to someone else. She said she believed Wilfred was a good choice because, "even though he went and married another woman, we have not quarreled or fought. . . . If there is no understanding [*maelewano*] at home, that's bad. There are houses where there is quarreling every day, and when the children see their father they run away. Quarrelling is very bad. We haven't quarreled or fought even one day. And I haven't suffered from hunger. Even with my father-and mother-in-law I did not quarrel. Even though my father-in-law was very severe, we did not quarrel."[34]

In Mary's reflections, the Mpare had ultimately failed to build such trust and mutual understanding in her relations with Wilfred. At the end of my time in Mayanka in 1995, Mary told me that Wilfred had moved away from the Mpare because they "don't understand each other" *(hawaelewani)*.[35] When I asked the reason behind that decision, Mary said that the Mpare had tried to kill Wilfred with "medicines" *(madawa)*. I asked how she did that, and Mary said that *Mzee* could not explain it; he just knew it. Wilfred came home from work one day and found "witch doctors" *(waganga)* the Mpare was trying to hide there. Wilfred realized that it was an attempt on his life and moved out. Mary said that the relationship had lacked "trust" for quite some time. One indication was the Mpare's nonattendance at her own daughter's confirmation feast. According to Mary, the Mpare would certainly have attended if her relationship with Wilfred had been good. Mary pointed out, "I mean, have I somehow offended her? No" *(Yaani, nimemkosea? Hapana)*.[36]

Wilfred's sister later confirmed that the Mpare had brought "witch doctors" to their house, causing Wilfred to run away. He fled to his large four-story house, which was still under construction. According to his sister's description, he quite literally ran. "He left, absolutely, and moved to that house of his which was not finished yet. He ran away, and left the woman there inside. He left her there inside. He left his clothes and everything when he ran away."[37]

### Motherhood and Witchcraft

In these conversations, the concepts of witchcraft and motherhood are used as opposing idioms for discussing moral value. Mary constantly emphasizes her wifely deference and motherly care against the image of Mpare as primarily relating to other people through occult powers. The Mpare is presented as a person who not only abandons her own children, but also "steals," "binds," and finally attempts to kill another woman's husband, and supposedly Mary, too. Motherhood and witchcraft are thus used as moral signs. In contrast to the essentially positive sociality, relatedness, and social generativeness of a "mother," a person involved in using witchcraft is antisocial, that is, socially destructive. The word "witch" therefore signifies an individualistic person, and thus an immoral one.

Mary's discussions about the Mpare and herself were often consciously public, even while seemingly spontaneous and fragmentary.[38] By means of these Mary was in indirect dialogue not only with Wilfred and the Mpare, but also with the surrounding rural community. However, while Mary was accusing the Mpare of using witchcraft medicines and failing to fulfill the responsibilities of motherhood, similar views of Mary were circulating in her neighborhood. What was at stake in the dialogue with the surrounding community was not only Mary's moral reputation in comparison to that of the Mpare, but also her status and value as a member of the community.

## Mary in the Community

Mary's controversial reputation soon became clear, as it was commonplace for different people to tell me, as the newcomer who aspired to understand life in Kilimanjaro, that Mary was "not an ideal Chagga woman." This summarized several aspects of her observed and supposed behavior. Mary's habit of spending time in the bars, drinking, and returning home late in the darkness was one issue that generated much criticism in her neighborhood. Gossip had it that she not only drank in her bar, but also met all her boyfriends (maboifrend; sing. boifrend). While some people were certain that she bought beer for her boyfriends, and in return they would have sex with her, others took the position that it was the boyfriends who had helped Mary become prosperous in her business.

A trading man was frequently mentioned as Mary's "boyfriend." Many asserted that Mary drank beer with him every night. One female neighbor said they were often together, drinking and "doing other things," especially when Mary's truck was still working and could be used for sexual liaisons. She said that such meetings would likely be more difficult since Mary's trucks were out of service, as taking man not her husband to her home would be inappropriate. Another woman said the man was very calm and hardly spoke, and although very rich, as far as she knew it was Mary who always bought beer for him and not vice versa. Interestingly, all four men in the same savings group with Mary were counted as her "boyfriends." Although any one person would mention one or two names, eventually each man in the savings group would be named.

It was also rumored that the father of one of Mary's daughters was not Wilfred, but another man from Mayanka. Occasionally, someone would tease that girl by greeting her with the lineage name of her alleged biological father, which was embarrassing to her. In the family's public presentation she was firmly considered to belong to Wilfred's lineage, and she had been raised as Wilfred's child. Usually a situation where a child lives in another man's house, on his land, is considered dangerous; the situation might bring mental or physical illness or a death among the children. Yet, even though one of Mary's daughters had long been suffering from a strange and, in people's minds, a frightening illness, never once did I hear this attributed to Mary's having an "illegitimate" child. It was widely believed instead that the girl's illness was caused by the witchcraft medicines Mary was allegedly involved with in her efforts to enhance her business.

Mary's ill daughter was said to have fits that sounded very much like epilepsy. Mary and others often told me how the girl would suddenly lose consciousness, fall to the ground, and begin to tremble and foam at the mouth. Even though people were generally aware of the disease called epilepsy, they were not usually willing to accept such an easy explanation for the girl's suffering. The girl was also mentally retarded, but there were very different views of for how long. Although Mary mentioned that the girl had been a sickly child for whom some sacrifices had been made during her infancy, she would usually emphasize that the girl was normal until she contracted the strange illness several years earlier. Some of the neighbors, however, recalled that the girl had been somewhat abnormal ever since she was a small child. But even these people did not think any simple medical factor could explain her condition.

The prevalent explanation for the girl's illness was that Mary had bought witchcraft "medicines" (madawa) or "spirits" (jini, pl. majini) to make her business flourish. This accusation is a serious one, since it entails an allegation of conscious choice to sacrifice her child for her own enrichment. The acquisition of such medicines is generally believed to require exchanging the health (and often the life) of a closely related person for business success.[39] Mary herself often said that the girl had put on weight. According to the gossip, however, the girl had become not only enormously fat, but was also becoming very hairy and starting to resemble an animal. She was thus allegedly losing her last vestiges of humanity and becoming a monstrous reminder of her mother's immoral choices and predilections.

This daughter was a source of constant worry for Mary, and she went to great length to find a cure for her. As if in answer to the general allegations that she had compromised her child—which were never discussed in Mary's presence—Mary often publicly complained that the sick daughter had "finished" her money, that she was already using her trading capital for cures. Sometimes the daughter was taken to stay with traditional healers *(waganga)*. Mary herself was open about relying mostly on specialists in traditional healing methods in her efforts to find a cure for her daughter. Other people, however, took that as another proof of her overall inclination to use "medicines."

Over the course of my stay in Mayanka, almost all possible kinds of witchcraft medicines were mentioned as being in Mary's secret arsenal, although those used to enhance trade were the most commonly named. She had allegedly acquired "medicines" for protecting herself and her property against physical and supernatural attacks by envious people, medicines for attracting men, for preventing conception and ending pregnancy, for preventing bleeding after abortion, and for "binding" people to herself. Some people suspected that she had made Wilfred "stupid" through medicines, a clear indication of which was seen in his apparent nonreaction to Mary's actions and in his overall mildness, which was often interpreted as his being under his wife's control.

My own impression of Mary was that she was a responsible person and mother. In contrast to the common Chagga stereotype of evil stepmothers, she seemed to take good care of the Mpare's children and they seemed comfortable with her. Whenever I visited Mary's home, there was a warm and cheerful atmosphere among the children and between Mary and the children. I often saw the ill daughter when I visited at their home. Mary did not in any way try to hide her or her state. The girl was silent, shy, and plump, but not enormously fat or in any way appalling.

In various ways, the talk about Mary's quality as a mother and a wife speak to her perceived masculinity. The images of her serving beer to men in the bar, with expectations of sex in exchange, and of her "entertaining" men in her vehicle, were like the ways wealthy men stereotypically courted women. The common characterization of both Wilfred and Mary's boyfriend as exceptionally calm and silent was an insinuation of their feminization in relation to Mary. Another gender reversal was Mary's alleged child out of wedlock, to which Wilfred apparently could not react other than to raise the child as his own. It is much more common for a Chagga man to have children out of wedlock and bring them to be raised at his home—as Wilfred did. Again, Mary's habit of drinking beer and eating meat in the bars on the market days and her overall lifestyle distinguished her from most of the other women. One woman, herself a trader, criticized Mary's late arrivals home and said that she was the only woman around who behaved in that fashion. She said that Mary did not care. "She's got used to that habit, like a man. When she comes home, she opens the door and finds the children sleeping."

## *Moral Economy*

NEIGHBORHOOD

The accusations that Mary had an extravagant lifestyle were related to complaints about her selfishness and stinginess. Many neighbors were not particularly sympathetic to Mary's complaints about her economic and other burdens. They felt she had no reason to complain because Wilfred had helped her a great deal. People mentioned the cars, the land, the cows, and the children's educations as his contributions. Wilfred's business ventures in Nairobi were also mentioned as family contributions, since all his wealth would eventually become inheritance for the children. While Mary constantly said she bore all the familial responsibilities, other people claimed that the wealth at home was primarily contributed by Wilfred and that Mary was more the caretaker of it.

One of Mary's neighbors used to wonder how Mary could perpetually expect Wilfred to support her, as the only food she had to buy was meat—everything else she could get from the land and cattle. Additionally, Mary's large business brought in cash to the extent that the neighbor emphatically wondered how Mary managed to use all that money. The neighbor said that at one point Mary had asked Wilfred to buy a brand-new car for her in Nairobi, for which she would give him the money. "Now, a person has that much money [as to] tell her husband to bring her a brand new car with it. Do you think the husband can keep on bringing you money like in the old days?" she asked.

The neighbors' and some relatives' comments about Mary's being "too fat" were also part of this moral discussion. The insinuation was that, rather than having put her own efforts into generating wealth, Mary had rather passively been "eating" what had been brought to her—worse still, that she had been "eating" it all quite alone and thus depriving others. Some people said that Mary was not cooperative in her neighborly relations. They said that both Mary and her children were proud and boastful *(wanaringa)*. For her neighbors, Mary's wealth was revealed in the conspicuous material goods in her house that many others lacked such as a television, videos, a refrigerator, and an inside toilet, and also in the aspirations and future prospects of Mary's children.

The people who frequented Mary's bar in the evenings formed perhaps her closest social network, more favorably disposed toward her than many of her neighbors. I never heard these people gossip about Mary in the same way. These were relatively well-off traders, some of them Mary's trade partners, including the members of a rather exclusive savings society that

Mary belonged to. This society consisted of four men and two women, each of whom contributed 2,000 TZS per week. The accumulated money was divided among the members once per year. That restricted membership to the relatively wealthy who could afford to save money for such a long period. At the time of the annual division, the amount each person received was quite large. The group, which Mary used to call *chama* (a club or society), used to mark that occasion with a feast at Mary's bar.

Over the course of several years, the *chama*'s feasts became more socially restricted. This development could be seen in the type of food and drink offered at the feast. A goat was slaughtered for the feast in 1994. Some of the meat was roasted for the *chama* members and the rest prepared as *machalare*[40] for the guests. *Mbege* was also prepared, and a couple of beers bought for each member. As is customary at any feast, many uninvited people gathered outside Mary's bar, expecting and receiving *mbege* from the feast. At the 1996 feast, the *chama* prepared four chickens and roasted bananas. Instead of *mbege*, there was only bottled beer. Chicken and roasted bananas are typical "bar food," less customary, domestic, or divisible than goat meat and *machalare*. Beer is a more individual and individualizing drink than *mbege*, which is usually shared by a group of people in a circle from a calabash passed around. Whereas the uninvited guests can hardly be denied *mbege*, drinking beer at the 1996 feast made it possible to avoid such requests for sharing, since nonmembers could not discern whether the *chama* members were buying their beers as usual or if they were being served. Indeed, by 1997, Mary was seldom even drinking *mbege* any more; she said she did not like its taste. Instead, she was mostly drinking beer and other bottled beverages. These consumption preferences also signify wealth and status.

The gossip and frequent direct requests for help, however, constantly reminded Mary of the expectations of the surrounding community. People would ask Mary for help both at her home and in the marketplace, sometimes seriously pleading for it, at other times making it a semi-joke. Her most common immediate answer to these requests was: "There's no business. I am finished [economically]" *(Hakuna biashara. Nimeishiwa)*. Depending on how serious and persistent the person was, Mary would offer other explanations to highlight her precarious situation. These explanations were usually connected to the constant and fairly excessive burdens and costs that her children caused her. In that kind of a situation, a serious questioner once said that it had not occurred to her that Mary would have any major problems because she seemed so well-off (referring to her fatness as an indication of well-being). Mary answered emphatically, "If you see me walking on the road, don't think that I'm living in peace and happiness; I am not at all at ease." Like many other relatively rich people, Mary did not usually admit to being comfortably well-off and stable.

Mary had to constantly seek a balance between helping other people and deflecting such expectations and claims. Sometimes she would help her neighbor, for instance, by giving 2,000 TZS or 5,000 TZS for a child's school fees. This money would, however, usually be called a loan, with the expectation of later repayment. Loans, whether small or large, are always risky in a place like Mayanka, where people's economic situations are precarious and can change unexpectedly. Some of these loans would tend in practice to turn into gifts, as the borrower would not be able to repay. The fact that the money had been called a loan, however, kept those people who did not pay it back feeling indebted to Mary.

THE TRADING COMMUNITY

By virtue of her business Mary was part of a larger trading community that consisted of people of quite differing economic means. In addition to the above-mentioned savings society, Mary also belonged to another group that included ten members, all of them quite ordinary market women. In 1994, each contributed 1,000 TZS a week, and each would get the 10,000 TZS every tenth week in rotation.

The one-day or several-day credit system[41] in the market also effectively linked Mary to wider "reciprocity networks," and, in practice, to some risk-sharing. Typically, the larger traders, the beer brewers, and the smaller retailers who bought millet from Mary would pay her only after they had completed their own business and received money for it. This involved risk, however. It was not uncommon at the end of the market day for a customer to come to Mary and complain that a sack she had bought from Mary had proved to contain a smaller amount of millet than usual. Because of this, the customer would typically ask if Mary would consent to reduce the agreed-on price of the millet sack, so that the customer could be left with at least the "bus fare" home. Sometimes Mary would do so, even though proving the customer's claim was impossible. The customers could also claim more significant losses. For instance, Mary had been regularly selling finger millet on credit to a few young men, which they paid for after selling the *mbege* made from it. At one point, they incurred a large loss and could not repay Mary. Thereafter, Mary would not sell to them on credit, even though they constantly pleaded for it. Instead, she urged them to try the maize business, which she felt was more profitable at the time, with her help and experience. Mary's condition was that part of the maize profit would belong to her as installments on their debt. That proved to be a good strategy, and Mary got at least some of her money back, but not all of it.

Mary's persistent talk about her responsibilities, combined with her downplaying of Wilfred's contributions, also has to be seen in this context of constant expectations and requests for support by the surrounding rural and trading community. Mary's public complaints included a message to the people around that she was already burdened with numerous dependents and thus could not meet all their expectations. Even though the claims that Mary was only the caretaker of Wilfred's wealth were exaggerated, because Mary really was an active creator of wealth and a creative actor, so too did Mary's complaints often understate Wilfred's contribution to the family wealth and the children's well-being.

Convincing others of her worries and responsibilities, and of herself as a respectable, caring, and social person, took constant effort on Mary's part. Her explanations and complaints were her way of making her positive moral value visible and public. And the people around Mary evaluated what she said in relation to what they observed: her fine house, her weight, her overall way of living. Mary complained sometimes that people had an unrealistic view of her situation because they could see her buy whole truckloads of millet at a time. Yet Mary, too, usually bought the loads on credit, and paid it back only after selling at least part of it. Mary explained that such a procedure was possible only because of her good and long-term relationship with the man who trucked in the millet from another region. According to Mary, the man would not so readily entrust his millet to another trader. Mary was thus arguing that it was not her accumulated money that enabled the large scale of her business but, again, it was more properly her moral quality of honesty and trustworthiness—like a "mother"—also as a trader.

## Moral Agency, Gender, and Economy

Regardless of all the criticism that depicted Mary as less than "an ideal Chagga woman," in many ways her social behavior was in fact "ideal." Mary was a very social, good-spirited, and agreeable person who behaved respectfully towards other people. Even though she could admonish her dependents for their misbehavior harshly, she carefully and calmly avoided quarrelling with people, be they kin or in-laws, neighbors, customers, or other traders. Mary was also careful in choosing her words when talking about other people, and in general was not openly critical of other people. She was a clever gossiper, and would offer a short and quite neutral hint about somebody's affairs without explanations, and then it was up to the interlocutor to add something to it. Or she would typically criticize through indirection by dressing her opinions about a certain person in a more general statement, for instance, by talking about men who leave their wives to "dry up" at home, or of women "who talk too many words." Even her public critique of the Mpare woman was often, if not always, couched in general comments about the "Pare people."

Mary's public behavior was also "ideal" in the sense that she showed the necessary respect towards her husband and other men and to her elders. Although she always had a clear opinion on how any domestic problem should be solved, she would usually call her husband in Nairobi before taking any action and ask for his opinion. At the feast of their *chama*, Mary made sure that the women of the group, when they had prepared the food, first served it to the male members and male guests and only afterwards to themselves and female guests. I once asked Mary why one local woman was "fired" from the *chama*, and Mary said it was because "she was being bold. She thinks she knows better than the men do."

Thus, Mary's public demeanor often complied with the expectations of good social and womanly behavior. Even her criticism of others and her own violation of ideals and expectations were usually so artfully and indirectly conducted that she rarely became involved in open conflicts. Consequently, criticism of her was most often expressed in gossip, typically used to reveal "secrets" lying underneath appearances. Many of the gossipers were Mary's neighbors. Ogden (1996) discusses the different dimensions of female "respect" and argues that in a poor Kampala suburb good neighborly behavior has become an important source for judging a woman's "respect," mitigating the importance of sexual behavior as the primary basis for moral judgment. In Mary's case, the rather conventional attributes— sexual behavior and "proper" wifehood and motherhood—are used to evaluate Mary's moral quality, both by her neighbors and by Mary herself. However, rather than indications of persistent, conventional values, these attributes are better understood as more inclusive moral signs that are used to talk about Mary's person—and Mary used the very same categories to discuss the Mpare's moral value. The categories signify a moral opposition between a person's social orientation and an individualistic orientation.

Mary's roles as a wife, a prominent trader, and a distinctively well-off person intertwine in her neighbors' evaluation of her moral quality. Gossip about her is prompted both by her lifestyle and her accumulated wealth in comparison to most of the other people around her. The gossip further distinguishes Mary from the others, but is simultaneously a call for her to share, and thus an attempt to be included in her prosperity.

Mary's case shows how moral reputation is a continuous social process of mutual persuasion, claims, and counterclaims. Mary cannot in the end distinguish herself from the people around her and their views, because she is dependent on them for moral acceptance and recognition. It takes constant effort by Mary to construct her own positive public image and to convince others of her moral quality, not only in her practices of giving, but also in mundane conversations where she constructs the meaning and value of what she does and does not do.

In all this, the discussions are polemical and political, but should not be reduced to mere politics or to individually managed political instruments. The witchcraft accusations and other gossip about Mary are not simply purposefully strategic and manipulative—people really do tend to believe that she uses "medicines"—but in themselves speak of Mary's exceptional standing. So exceptional are Mary's accomplishments that something both earthly but unnatural (her "masculinity") and occult forces are ascribed to her. Even the prevalent interpretation of her child's illness as having been caused by witchcraft medicine or bought spirits (and not by her illegitimate child) links Mary to suspicions typically related to successful men's current ways of enrichment.

In discussing Mary's moral value, people are simultaneously discussing and processing more general cultural expectations and ideas about gender. They are discussing what it means to be a woman, a wife, a mother, and a trader, and constituting ideas of appropriate gendered spheres of action as well as gendered forms of wealth and control. Mary provides an exceptional example of someone who has stretched the limits of gendered behavior to the extent that she resembles a man socially.

This case reveals how agency is relational, how women's agency is a social accomplishment, conditioned both by the agency of men, and the surrounding community. It shows how an individual's "voice" and personal narratives are embedded in her social surroundings and entwined into a dialogue with it. This dialogue also reveals how economic activities and decision-making are inevitably sociocultural and moral issues. It shows that "economy" significantly includes a moral economy and a political economy that span the limits of the household. As much as it is about money, income, material resources, and consumption, economy is about distribution, affection, and gender within and without the house.

## 4

# From Captured Wives to Bound Men

## Rethinking Female Respect

In addition to their market rhetoric, the market women take part in discussions of female respect in their recollections of their marriages by capture, which this chapter examines. I suggest that in collective memory wife-capture marriages have come to represent and exemplify gender relations as they used to be. For many middle-aged and elderly people, this idealized and homogenized picture also represents certain pivotal values and gender qualities that today are seen to be going increasingly awry. The contemporary situation is reflected upon through the notions of men "bound" by women (from the verbs *kufunga/kufuga*) and "roaming/loose" women (sing. *mhuni/mzururaji/mzungukaji*). I will examine the market women's recollections of their marriage by capture as a cultural text that both reproduces the dominant ideas and values about gender relations and critically comments on them (cf. Boddy 1989, 148–49).

In several ways, the accounts indicate and are about women's agency, artfulness, and pragmatic wisdom in their self-presentation and interpersonal relations. The middle-aged women who tell about their capture are actively constructing an honorable portrait of themselves by, paradoxically, emphasizing their youthful non-activeness as well as their later submission to the wifely and motherly roles. The stories about "loose" women and "binding" women are expressly about female agency, yet an agency that is represented morally by the narrators as manipulative and socially destructive. The description of such agency as immoral and "unrespectable" derives from its seeming shameless negation or reversal of the cultural ideals of marriage and marital relations. The question is not, however, about the simple labeling of different forms of activity or women as morally good or bad, but about an ongoing discussion and mutual persuasion regarding moral value, both of particular women specifically and present-day women in general. The accounts presented here are thus part of the larger discussion about changing gender relations and social formations and the ongoing definition and redefinition of what is "respectable."

## Captured Wives

In Kiswahili, wife-capture is called "to carry" *(kubeba)*, "to carry by force" *(kubeba kwa nguvu)*, "to carry on the shoulders" *(kubeba mabegani)*, or "to carry high up" *(kubeba juu)*. In Kichagga I heard it called *iiro* (to carry) or *iiro ko ngufu* (to carry by force). Gutmann (1926, 130) uses a Kichagga term for it: *iira mana ndzien*, "the lifting up of the girl on the way."

People frequently talked about wife-capture marriage as belonging to "matters of the past" *(mambo ya zamani)* or to Chagga traditions *(mila)*. Elderly and middle-aged men and women often mentioned wife capture with a nostalgic tone. For instance, one fifty-year-old woman who had not herself been abducted explained to me that girls had to be married by force earlier, because they were so "settled" *(walikuwa wametulia sana)* and had respect and modesty *(heshima)*. On the other hand, it was also common to hear that only young women up to twenty-one years of age, and of "good habits" *(tabia nzuri)*, were abducted. This indicates that not all girls were considered chaste and simultaneously, that the chaste ones were especially desirable.

One man of about fifty noted that it was common in the past to hear noise and cries from the road indicating a case of wife-capture, but that one does not hear it any more. He said that it also used to be common to see pregnant women walking on the road, but that today one never sees pregnant women. His lumping together of wife-capture, biological reproduction, and the past was not idiosyncratic. Neither was his view of the road as the site where female "respect" was manifested, both in decent girls and prospective mothers.

Nowadays the association between roads and women more often connotes unsettledness and lack of respect. Elopements and informal and occasional unions are conceptualized as affairs negotiated "on the road," and they are probably more frequent and more openly exercised today than they used to be.[1] During my time in Mayanka, I never actually witnessed an instance of wife-capture, but I did hear of a few cases and several other attempts. Today they mostly take place during the Christmas season, when Chagga men who work in other regions and countries come home, some of them with plans to get a Chagga wife, by abduction if need be, after one of the many feasts.

Both elopement and wife-capture are called "short-cut marriages." What differentiates these from "proper marriages" is the absence of negotiations and initial bridewealth exchanges between the two families before the marriage. This is the situation with wife-capture, when the abduction comes as a surprise to both the girl and her parents. Yet the difference is not always so clear. In some cases of wife-capture, at least incipient negotiations and bridewealth exchanges have taken place. Sometimes the capture is planned in advance by the boy and the girl or by their parents, in which latter case the girl may not know about it. In the views of many older Chagga, the crucial difference between today's shortcut marriages—elopements and temporary unions—and those of yesterday—wife-capture—is that the latter is a more social and public way of marrying, whereas the former are usually secret decisions by two individuals. This includes a view of the girl's differential agency and initiative in the two forms of marriage, as I will discuss later.

When a woman says that she was married by capture, it is difficult to know the actual situation without further questioning. For instance, Mama Njau used to say she was captured to become a wife. This is fitting in the sense that her transition to new home and status included the elements of some coercion by her husband-to-be, torn clothes, threatened violence, and finally, the absence of wedding ceremonies. Yet it was still a very subtle and negotiated capture in comparison to many others. Compared to the six other market women who said they had been captured, Mama Njau's experience was certainly the least aggressive.

Two of the six women said they had never before seen the man who "carried" them and thus became their husband. Two women knew the men who captured them, but had had no intentions of marrying them. In one of these cases, the man had been the girl's schoolmate. In the other case, the man had brought the girl presents for some time, supposedly from his brother, who wanted to woo her. Only when the ostensible messenger captured her did the girl realize that the presents had in fact been from him. The fifth woman had known the man for some time before he suddenly "carried" her; she said she had chatted with him several times "on the road," and replied to his proposals of marriage by saying that she did not yet want to marry because she needed to finish her education. The sixth woman had only known her man for a week when he captured her, although the respective families had already agreed on the marriage.

The following is based on the accounts of these six market women about their own capture. The women interviewed were all between thirty and fifty years old. For this description I have merged the women's accounts because of the similarities and repetitions of expressions and themes. However, I have quoted a few individual comments to highlight the narrators' tones and emotions.

### Wife-Capture Accounts

The capture is planned in advance by a man with his male friends or relatives. Perhaps in its purest form and most commonly, the girl is walking on the road in the middle of the day when she is suddenly set upon by the men, who had been hiding in the bush. First the men cover her mouth with their hands and tell her she should not make noise nor fight back because "we have taken you from within" *(tumekutoa ndani)*. She is then "carried" to the man's home or that of his relatives. Before their arrival, all the girl's clothes are usually torn to pieces so that she is completely naked. "Even the underpants, even the shoes" *(mpaka chupi, mpaka viatu)* were ripped off, the women emphasized.[2] If the girl struggles while she is being carried, the men hit her and admonish her to be calm. One woman said she was hit so badly by her future neighbor that even today, after more than ten years, she glares at him angrily whenever she sees him.

The capture does not always take place on the road. In some cases, the capturer asks a close friend of the girl to help him. The friend then persuades the girl to go somewhere with her, to visit someone's home, for instance. There the girl is kidnapped and carried to the boy's home. In some cases, the same house is both the place of capture and where she is to be kept secluded, and no actual carrying takes place. For instance, one woman described how she was "deceived" *(nilidanganywa)* by her girlfriend to go for *pombe* in a bar; after a couple of drinks, she found herself locked inside the bar with an older man. She explained her reactions: "I told him that I will hit him until he opens the door, or otherwise I will die. We fought and fought, starting from seven in the evening until three in the night . . . eeh. . . . By three I don't have any clothes left, not even one, I am completely naked; no dress, no underwear, no nothing. And my face has become like this [swollen]. That is indeed how I was married."[3]

It is expected that sexual intercourse will take place on the day of capture and that the girl will get pregnant a short time later. She is subsequently given some clothes to replace those that had been torn off her. But
if the girl continues to show signs of opposing the marriage and wanting to
escape, she can be kept inside the house for a week or so. She may be given
only some maize gruel *(uji)* through the window, and she is not allowed to
go out—as one woman said: "To urinate? No. To go to the toilet? No" *(Ku-
kojoa? Hakuna. Kwenda choo? Hakuna)*.[4] A small cup for her to urinate in is
passed through the window. If opposition is anticipated, the girl is often
taken to a place farther away, like a town from which it would not be easy
for her to find her way back home.

Most of the women said that they had wanted to escape after being captured, but that returning home was practically impossible. They all stressed
that their clothes had been torn off, which hindered their escape. But the
main reason that kept them from running away was, in all of their minds,
the inescapable "shame" *(aibu)* that the capture caused, and which returning to home would only have increased. Having spent the night inside the
house with the man meant that the girl had become married, no matter
what her own wishes were. Whether the capture took place on the road or
at a social gathering, the news of the girl's having become married spread
and soon became public knowledge. The women explained that should a
captured girl have returned home, not only would her parents have been
angry with her, but her peers would also mock her by saying, "She is not a
girl any more; she has become a mother" *(sio msichana tena, amekuwa
mama)*.[5] One of the women explained: "In the past, if you just went to a
man, and you were with your girlfriends . . . if they only saw that you were
locked inside, they would go and immediately announce that so-and-so has
been married. Even if you were following behind them at that very moment, they would keep announcing that that one has been married. And
you would not have a girlfriend any more to eat with or to walk with, 'You
were there inside.' People call you *mama*, eeh, *limama*."[6]

Another recurring comment was: "How would you return home? You
have been damaged" *(Unarudije? Umeshaharibiwa)*.[7] One woman said that
she was kept inside for six months without even being allowed to "glance at
the road" in order to prevent her from fleeing. She said that before her abduction "I had not seen a thing" *(nilikuwa sijaona kitu)*, and pointing to a
small building made of mud and wood she continued, "I was split [lost my
virginity] here" *(nilipasuliwa hapa)*.[8]

Should the abducted girl stubbornly oppose the sudden marriage while
at the boy's relatives' house, the boy's mother and other elderly female relatives will do their best in order to persuade her to accept the situation. As a
last resort, the abducted girl might be given a small child to hold on her lap.

She is warned that should she leave, she would never be able to have a child or that her child would develop problems and die.

When the girl has submitted to the marriage, she is confined for three months at the boy's home, during which time she is fed good food and is not expected to work. After those three months the woman[9] "comes out" (anatoka); she is given a new dress and a new pair of shoes in which to appear in public. She should be fat by now because she has been well fed, but also as an indication that she is pregnant.

Asked whether they liked the men who had captured them, all the women answered that they had no alternative after the event. One woman said, "How can you abandon the person who has spoiled you and who has become your husband?"[10] After having accepted the situation, most of the women described as their greatest sorrow the realization that they had to abandon their own plans for their futures. One woman explained that she had been working in the office of the local church and had wanted to stay. "I just wanted to stay with my pastor, I just wanted to work there, I just wanted to study in the Bible School and attend the Holy Communion,"[11] she said, but she had to leave work after being captured. Another woman described how she had been accepted at a nursing school in Dar es Salaam, and how her father had promised to help her buy the mattress, pillow, and clothes she needed for the school. She explained, "But as I had these plans, that one [her husband] came and carried me. . . . [I realized that] I have been married, to go there [to the school] would only be shameful. It is better to stay here."[12] Yet another woman said she was about to be sent to Nairobi for a job. She was to travel there in May, but was "married by force" in January. She explained that her teachers even tried to persuade the man to let her go to Nairobi first, but he refused because "he needed a woman to make food and wash clothes at home."[13]

Another woman explained that her father had planned to take her to live with him in Nairobi so she could attend a typing school. Her father had prepared all the things—clothes and mattress—needed for the trip that was to take place on 19 January. All these plans were shattered when she was "carried by force" a week before that date.[14] One woman who was "carried" by her boyfriend when the negotiations between the families for the marriage had already begun also explained how disappointed she was because "you have not planned . . . you know, if you are being courted, you start planning, you plan in your head. But now he . . . one has not planned; isn't it very difficult to start that kind of life?"[15]

### The Values of Wholeness

The accounts include an abundance of cultural imagery and ideas about the wished-for qualities in a young girl and bride, as well as about the gender and social relations under construction in marriage. The desired quality of a young girl is conceptualized as "wholeness" *(uzima)*. Most basically it refers to intact virginity. After losing her virginity, a girl is said to have become "damaged/spoiled/injured" *(ameharibiwa)* or, as one of the women mentioned above put it, "split" *(amepasuliwa)*. I frequently heard complaints of how contemporary girls "damage/spoil themselves" *(wanajiharibu)* by "going/walking" *(kutembea)* with boys without getting married. I once asked a woman if the same word could be used for a boy who "walks with" girls but does not get married. The woman did not remember having heard it used for boys, but as she considered the question totally logical she proceeded to ask her husband. He immediately explained that the expression means that a girl has been "going with boys to the extent that she has become deflowered" *(ametembea na wavulana mpaka amevunjwa bikira)* and that the expression cannot be used for boys because they do not have a hymen.

A young girl's "wholeness" is expressed also in her public behavior. Shy conduct is judged to indicate her "respect" *(heshima)*, "shame" *(aibu)*, and "settledness" *(ametulia)*. Respectable young girls even avoid looking boys and older men and women in the eye, because it is considered a sign of assertiveness and, in relation to men, suggestiveness. As a young bride, and especially in marriage ceremonies, the girl instead is the object of other people's gazes (cf. Weiss 1996, 123). The secluded bride usually remains in the innermost room of the house and farthest from the road, and like any good girl avoids meeting the eyes of her visitors. "Respect" and "shame" are thus both social and sexual attributes; being shown in and judged by a girl's social behavior, they simultaneously connote her sexual chastity. Therefore, one woman's comment that she "had not seen a thing" before her abduction referred both to her general ignorance of worldly affairs and her sexual purity.

The quality of "wholeness" is furthermore supposedly indicated by a girl's skin.[16] It is customary that in the bridal send-off party, the lineage brother who "gives the girl" *(anamkabidhi msichana)* to the groom's representative utters the following: "Look at this sister of mine and the way she is. She has no mark *(alama)* on her. I am giving her to you now to take good care of. In the case that you cannot do so, return her and do not hit her." While saying this, the brother lowers the upper *kanga* on the head of the girl to display that she has no "mark" on her. Instead of saying she has no "mark" *(alama)*, the brother can also say she is "well/whole" *(mzima)*, which also means a virgin.

This reveals the value of "wholeness" as a social virtue. A bride's shining and flawless appearance represents the protective care that she has received in her natal home. Her physical and social integrity is expressed as a social product, and it subsequently brings "respect" to all those who have participated in producing it, especially the girl's mother and paternal aunts.

In a send-off ceremony the bride is first led in front of the guests fully covered in a *kanga*.

The lineage brother lowers the bride's *kanga* when handing her to the bridegroom's representative.

Moreover, it brings "respect" to her husband and his kin. A virgin thus embodies the value of an unruptured potential for reproduction, in both its physical and social terms (cf. Weiss 1997, 356 –57). In her overall, seemingly immaculate "wholeness," a young bride is an embodiment of sociocultural value. A bride's or a young girl's "wholeness" denotes not only her bodily intactness but also the "wholeness" of her person as constituted by and containing social relations and cultural value.[17]

## Recreating Wholeness—Rearranging Social and Gender Relations

The images of "wholeness" and being "enclosed" do not apply to a virgin bride only. They are recurring themes in a woman's marital life cycle and are reproduced on the bodily and spatial planes, for instance, through the practices of clothing and seclusion. These start at the time of betrothal, when the boy gives presents of clothes and decorations to the girl. In the first half of the twentieth century, a girl wearing a necklace given her by a boy signified engagement. By the 1960s, girls in Mayanka were given wristwatches and gowns as engagement presents. Nowadays, a girl is often given a ring as a sign of engagement, of which it is said that the boy "dresses her with a ring" *(anamvalisha pete)*. Thus, even though the type of present has undergone changes over the course of the time, the idea of binding and enclosure has remained in that they are all things to be bound to a girl's body or limb. The periods of seclusion repeat the theme; confinement of the new bride inside a house ideally also takes place in ordinary marriages, and again after each child she delivers. After a period of seclusion, the woman emerges "enclosed" in new clothes provided by her husband. "Wholeness," both natural (virginity) and as recreated by these bodily and spatial enclosures, is considered important for safe and ordered reproduction and for the reconstruction of social relations and personhood. The shifts between bodily and spatial exposures and enclosures are as meaningful in the event of wife-capture as in other forms of marriage.

In wife-capture the girl is "taken from the inside" of her natal home. Her exposure takes place spatially on the road, and bodily when her clothes are ripped off and her "wholeness" is "damaged." The re-enclosure again takes place on both the spatial and bodily levels: seclusion entails keeping her bodily secretions (urine) inside and feeding her inside the house. During the three months' seclusion that follows, it is said that the woman "sits inside" *(anakaa ndani)*. When her seclusion is over, she comes out but remains enclosed—in the new clothes provided by the husband and his family and by her physical state of pregnancy, which again is to be "closed" (in Kichagga, *nakufungie*).[18]

These exposures and re-enclosures reconstruct the girl's social personhood. The spatial practices, her "sitting in" *(anakaa ndani)* the house of seclusion without even a "glance at the road," are to make her an insider in her
husband's home.[19] The idea of placing and "planting" the girl in the husband's home is also clearly shown in Gutmann's (1926, 130) description of a
captured girl who is stripped stark naked and carried, "the head in front,
like a beam," to the suitor's mother's home.

Through the enclosing and feeding practices, the woman is thus "placed
in" *(kuweka ndani)* and "settled down" in her husband's *kihamba* and lineage. "Settling down" refers also to transformations in the woman's sexual
and reproductive powers. The purpose is to affect certain temperature ad-
justments and transformations in the woman's body through which, for instance, a girl's sexuality is transformed and directed into generative power,
and the energies of the postparturient woman are renewed and replen-
ished. A married woman is expected to become sexually settled even if she
had been wild in her youth. As mentioned earlier in the market context,
female sexual and spatial mobility is conceptualized as excessive "heat"
*(moto)* that endangers fertility and reproduction.

Equally importantly, feeding, clothing, and seclusion practices constitute the social context for legitimate reproduction.[20] These practices establish the husband and his lineage as the providers for the wife and the
children she subsequently produces, which is also the basis for the male emphasis in kinship reckoning.[21] The processes of putting the wife into seclusion, feeding her, and clothing her after the seclusion are repeated after each
childbirth. By these practices, the complementary spheres of gender are
also created. The wife's task of providing her family with food every day is
culturally circumscribed by her husband's and his extended family's provision of the basic structures within which the wife's and mother's role as a
"feeder" takes place.

The wife-capture accounts build and reinforce this kind of a dominant—
and idealized—picture of past gender qualities and relations. It offers a
picture of a girl who has remained in her natal home secure, intact, and
well-guarded, in both her physical and social person until she is moved by
her future husband and quite against her will to the different but equally
"bounded" bodily state and social identity of wife and mother in her
husband's lineage. What makes the circle of transference complete, flawless,
and ideal is starting with a state of virginity, a state of "wholeness" that immediately after capture results in pregnancy, another state of "closedness." It
is no coincidence that virginity and pregnancy are such central themes in
the wife-capture accounts. They are respectively the most respectable and
ideal states of a girl and a woman in Chagga society. The "boundedness" of

a virgin or a pregnant woman and mother means that their social belonging and value are unambiguous.

These wife-capture accounts do more than construct ideal female persons, however; they also build an image of a most masculine man, for what is more manly than to capture a virgin and immediately make her pregnant? The picture of wife-capture as it is described entails the dramatization of certain wished-for gender relations and attributes. Such issues as sexual desire, physical strength, power, determination, innocence, and activeness are played out in public and become constructed as gendered attributes and, at least for the moment appear as "natural" gender relations. So even if the girl was not virginal and the boy not very masculine and able, wife-capture as a performance and as a rite recalled presents the ideal as if it were real and as if the girls did not want to get married and had to be taken by force by the man. In this way, wife-capture is a cultural performance and text of the dominant gender relations among the Chagga.

## Rhetorical Art in the Recollections

In recounting their captures, the women reproduce and employ these ideal images. Allusions to virginity and innocence were prevalent in their recollections. Some of the women who told about their capture remembered having been younger than they actually were at the time. And apparently not all of these captured women were virgins. By stressing their youth, innocence, and ignorance at the time of abduction, however, the women emphasized their "wholeness" as young girls. In this way they employed the ideas of proper gender and social relations to present themselves and emphasize their moral value (cf. Lindisfarne 1994, 87, 94).

Without exception, the wife-capture accounts were related to reflections on the contemporary situation and how times had changed. The narrators compared their own histories to the alleged "shamelessness," freedom, and options of contemporary girls. It is important to note that their understanding of the past and the present was mutually constitutive; the view of the contemporary girls' freedoms served as the basis for these women's reflections on their own lack of alternatives in their own youths. Here lies the double message of the wife-capture accounts; the narrators draw moral value from their exemplary virtue and fulfillment of social ideals and expectations—for indeed having been the very embodiment of those values—and criticize contemporary girls for failing to meet those expectations. At the same time, however, this is their basis for critical commentary on the dominant values entailed in wife-capture event and accounts.

The very detailed reporting and the grieving tone evident when the women describe the abruptness and the pain of their capture and their lack of alternatives vividly express their criticism and anger. They recount that there was no place for their own agency, will, or desire. Instead, their plans were shattered and their futures dictated by the actions of other people. These include the men and their friends who captured them, the female relatives of those men, the women's own parents, who would not accept them back, and their own peer groups. Even though the women probably were somewhat exaggerating the viability of their more ambitious plans and how close they were to realizing them, this emphasis in their accounts is significant. It reveals their awareness of the socially constricting side of the highly valued chastity and shame of a young bride-to-be—of being such an objectification and embodiment of cultural value. Thus, while their capture is ultimately a source of pride and indication of moral value, the women also lamented the subjection of their persons and plans to the concerns of the larger social whole, and especially to authority of the husband and his mother.

## Roaming Girls

In contrast to the submissiveness, chastity, and shyness of girls in the past, present-day girls are often depicted as selfish persons who decide for themselves and change their minds as their desires and feelings change. They are said to be so easily available to men that there is no need to capture them. Furthermore, even if they are captured it is believed they would not hesitate to escape because they "have become used to it" *(wamezoea)*. This expression refers to the perception that spending a night with a man without any social consequences or feelings of shame is now common, unlike "in the past." Furthermore, this alleged selfishness and lack of shame and respect imply an active, determinate, and desirous agency quite in contrast to how girls of earlier times were supposed to behave. It was common to hear people assert that, whereas earlier it was boys who wooed girls, now it is "like you do in Europe;" girls woo boys, and if they do not like a boy's home, they look for another.[22]

Certain socioeconomic and attitudinal changes form the context for contemporary girls' and boys' behavior and the discussions about them. The marital age of young men has risen because most of them aspire to establish themselves economically by studying and/or working before marriage. They are involved in occasional relationships but delay marriage itself. Thus, they can live with a girl and even have children, but decide not to actually marry the girl. Regardless of the continuing emphasis on marriage and the idea that it is not appropriate for a girl or a woman to give birth and live in her natal home, such cases are common today. In the neighborhood where I was living there were unmarried girls with children in almost every house. While some young girls say that they do not want a conventional marriage, many others do not get "properly" married even though they want to. These cases vary from girls refused by men to others who have children with men who would like to marry them, but lack the economic means to provide a house or other necessities.

In spite of the diversity of situations and the constraints of the socio-economic circumstances, in the predominant way of thinking a woman not attached to a husband is prone to be seen as a "loose woman" *(mhuni/mzururaji/mzungukaji)*. As an indication of her status, an unmarried girl with a child is not usually called by the honorable title *mama*. Such girls are more often either called by their first maiden name, or more bluntly "children who give birth to children" or girls/women who "wander on the roads" *(kuzurura/kuzunguka barabarani)*. The latter designation can also be attached to women who separate from their husbands and return to their natal homes.[23]

As in the case of the married women, spatial idioms (looseness, roads, and roaming) refer not only to the perceived sexual looseness of unattached women, but also to the vagueness of their social and gender identity and their seeming disregard for social values. Having "damaged themselves" *(kujiharibu)*, and in their subsequent "unboundedness," their persons are perceived as unable to contain social relations and values. Such mobility and the "heat" that it involves is thought to endanger the continuity of life (cf. Comaroff 1985, 67, 116; Weiss 1996, 184, 200–201). Older people in Mayanka often expressed the value of "slowness" and "coolness." For instance, one old woman explained to me that the number of deaths has increased due to increased "fornication" *(uasherati)*, for which she blamed both men and women. She added, "But if you remain [at one place], you will live" *(lakini ukikaa, unaishi)*.[24] Another old woman took my hand in hers after I visited her home and gave me the following blessing: "God bless you so that you would walk slowly on this earth."[25]

Like the older people, many young girls regard wife-capture marriage as a thing of "the past" *(ya zamani)*. The tenor of their comments reflected their dislike for the model of gender relations that wife-capture represents rather than any sense of nostalgia, however. Some of the young girls referred to the threatening consequences of wife-capture as the culture of the "old women." One unmarried girl had heard that, if one does not agree to the marriage after capture, "The old women come and lay out their customs. They tell you that it's shameful, shameful" *(wabibi wazee wanakuja, wanatoa mila zao; wanakuambia ni aibu, aibu)*. This statement reminds us that the potential conflict in wife-capture is not simply that between the man and the woman, but that the older women are important and interested actors in attempts to capture a girl with "good habits" for the family. However, even while describing the imputation of shame as a preoccupation of "old women," the young girl did not mean that considerations of "shame" would not touch her. Indeed, the possibility of capture as well as the subsequent "shame" remain part of the awareness of the young girls, even if not always considered to be their destiny in the same way it was in previous times.

Before and during the Christmas season, wife-capture becomes a subject that engenders both serious precautions and humorous warnings. As I was coming home at dusk with a girl one evening before Christmas, a woman we passed warned us that if we were not more careful we would be carried during the coming Christmas. Before and after Christmas and New Year's, several young girls said that they would "just stay inside" (*kukaa ndani tu*) for fear of being abducted, and even if this is somewhat exaggerated, it was not usually said as a joke. After Christmas reports would circulate about abductions that had been successfully accomplished, as well as of other failed attempts and plans.

So, we see that wife-capture does still take place. Today, however, some girls will escape from the boy's home if their capture was an unpleasant surprise. Even though it is unusual to take a capture case to court, I did read about one such case in the local court records that had been filed by a captured girl against her capturer in 1994. The local judge told me that a wife-capture case is to be handled like a rape, for which the sentence is seven years. No such sentences have been handed down by that court, however, since even the very rare cases that are taken there are usually withdrawn to be discussed between the families, as happened with this particular case, too. According to the judge, with whom I spoke, this case did not end in marriage after the family discussions. I also heard of other girls who had escaped shortly after their captures, which suggests that today a potential curse[26] is not invariably believed to threaten a girl's ability to bear children in the future.

Nevertheless, feelings of "shame" tend to accompany capture even today, although the content and manifestations of those feelings may differ from those of the earlier times. These days, a girl who escapes from a boy's home after abduction may feel her reputation has been damaged to the extent that she will not stay at her natal home, and will move to some other place, often to a town. A study done at the large Kiboriloni marketplace near Moshi town in 1992 (Sawayael 1993, 18) found that three of the sixty market women interviewed had fled their home area after, and because of, being captured against their will. I know a girl who moved away from her home after being captured in 1993. In her case, her father agreed to her fleeing the boy's home because he did not consider the marriage to be a satisfactory one. This girl moved first to Moshi town and later to Dar es Salaam. However, she suspects that her escape caused her to suffer permanent misfortune; she regards her repeated bad luck in trading ventures as evidence of this.

I will now turn my discussion to girls and women who are alleged to use different means to "bind" *(kufunga/kufuga)* men. This and the moral connotations have been raised in earlier chapters, but I will now elaborate the meanings.

## Bound Men

The idea of enclosing and binding a woman is a repetitive feature of a normal marital life cycle, as discussed above. Gutmann (1926, 77) describes an engagement in which the *mngari* (the bridegroom's representative) and the bridegroom's sister go to the girl's home early in the morning while the house is still closed, grab the girl by force and put ornaments on her. The bridegroom's sister slides a leaden ring on the girl's arm, and pearl necklaces around her neck, and shouts out joyously, "Today I [have] bound my cow." Women are customarily and honorably equated with and called "cows," especially in ceremonies related to marriage and reproduction (see Gutmann 1926, 9, 67, 95, 105).[27]

The binding of a man is always considered unnatural. I will henceforth use the term "binding" for certain situations of gender-reversal where the man seems to have become obedient and his mobility restricted in spatial, social, physical, and often also intellectual terms, while the woman freely moves about and/or amasses money and wealth. Because of the similarity in the results, I will use the term "bound" in reference to men even though, strictly speaking, two different Kiswahili verbs are used, depending on how the condition is believed to have been produced. In cases where witchcraft "medicine" *(madawa)* is believed to have been involved, the word "bind" *(kufunga)* is used. In other cases, such as those produced by more "domestic" means and female devices, the term *kufuga ndani* is used—this meaning "to keep inside," which in its most common usage refers to domesticating animals, such as stall-fed cattle.

When the expression *kufuga ndani* is applied to human beings, it most often refers to an illegitimate relationship between a married man and an unmarried woman and can be used to refer to either person. Thus, a woman can be said to "domesticate" another woman's husband, or the man to "domesticate" the woman. Although both expressions are disparaging, the "domestication" of a man humiliates and emasculates the man, whereas the "domestication" of a woman refers to her being so well cared-for that she does not need to go out to seek a livelihood. Marriage being understood as a kind of self-evident domestication of a wife is shown by the fact that a man cannot be said to "domesticate" his wife or another man's wife, but only an unmarried woman. But, a wife who seems to control her husband's movements and activities is said to have "domesticated" him.

In addition to "domesticating" or "binding" a man, when a wife seems to be more mobile and/or economically stronger than her husband, and therefore seems to have control over him, it can be said that "she has married her husband" *(amemwoa)* and not vice versa,[28] the way it should be, or that she "sits on him" (in Kiswahili *anamkalia;* in Kichagga *uramilia*) or "milks him" *(anamkamua).* All of these expressions refer to the immobilization and "feminization" of the husband.

## Outside Women (Hawara)

Sometimes a married man can secretly maintain another woman, typically in town, and the signs of this are a lack of support for the rural wife and the man's constant absences from home. In such cases, the "outside woman" *(mke wa nje)* is often believed to have "bound" the man, causing him to "forget" *(anasahau)* his rural home and legitimate wife or girlfriend. Comparably, a man's perpetual absence from home is readily interpreted as his having become "bound" by someone in town. If a married man builds a house or rents a flat for an outside woman without having children with her, she is called a *hawara.* Such women are often believed to "bind" the man either by "medicine" or by feminine wiles taken to such extremes that they hold an almost supernatural sway over the man.

The latter type of entrapment is described in one girl's account of how her long-term boyfriend, who was to be her husband, had been "stolen" by a Swahili woman. She was certain that the woman had used a special method that coastal women are believed to use. According to the girl, the woman had invited the man for a meal at her home, for which she had bought meat. In preparing the meal, she would have taken one piece of the meat and placed it in her vagina as she cooked the rest of it. When the man arrived, she would have seated him at the table and fed him first the piece of meat that had been inside her, while slowly saying, "Welcome," *(karibu)* in the sweetest and most alluring voice possible. After that first bite, the man could not forget the woman, the embittered ex-girlfriend said.

A quality that seductive women are believed to make full use of is a persuasive and supplicant manner of speaking, *kubembeleza,* which was described in the market context. Although part of the ordinary behavior "kit" of any woman, those designated as *hawara* or high-class "prostitutes" *(malaya)* are believed to be especially skilled in this kind of talk. One man described a woman who was so seductive and beautiful that a prominent local man built her a house on a plot of land that the man had skillfully "deceived" *(kudanganya)* from her brother. Living in that house, she gave birth to several children: some children were this man's, and some children were fathered by another prominent man. The man who told me this burst out as he described her: "Large! Light! Very beautiful! And the way she talked!"

The man imitated her smooth and seductive voice and said: "She talked VERY NICELY!" These women were thought to have such verbal skills that it was as if they held some knowledge of a kind of speaking magic.

A *hawara* is expected not only to be attractive but also to be ready to entertain a man with food, sex, sweet talk, and her overall lovely presence whenever he comes to visit. A *hawara* thus makes use of the most ordinary and "natural" feminine means—food, sex, general attractiveness, and respectful talk—to "bind" a man. Even though any wife is expected to show her husband this kind of deference, it does not always materialize as rural wives often face much harsher realities in their daily chores. In return for her ideal femininity, the man gives a *hawara* expensive presents, rents her a flat or builds her a house, takes her out to fancy places, and may even send her children to school abroad. These exchanges resemble those of a marital relationship, yet there are significant differences in the two kinds of unions.[29]

In marriage the mutual bond is children; a wife in effect "ties" the husband through fertility/children, food, domestic services, and the showing of respect. In a *hawara* relationship the bond is thought to be plainly sexual, and although she may act like a wife, a *hawara* is understood to control the man's desires and finances, whereas in marriage a man is expected to be the stronger partner and to control both his money and his wife's desires. How the illegitimate binding of a man by a woman involves mixing the domestic and the sexual is made clear in the above account of the meat fed to the man. The apparent "cooking" of the meat—not in the hearth provided by the husband, but in the woman's vagina—also suggests the woman's own "heat," itself connoting her dangerous, undomesticated sexuality.[30] Thus, regardless of her apparent obedience and the "enclosing" of the woman by the man, it is more accurately the *hawara* who has strategically tied the man, since he is understood to be under her control. The resulting emasculation involves the man losing both his male qualities and male wealth.

There are many stories of women who are believed to have built a career out of "binding," often with the further help of acquired "medicines." First, by binding a man with love medicine, a woman is said to make the man forget all his other obligations and obediently bring his money to her. After the man has labored to amass wealth, the woman—now often his wife—can proceed with her own plans by using medicine to destroy his mind and intelligence. This makes the man unable to look after his own wealth, and the wife takes over the management role. This stage is often believed to involve some kind of physical immobilization, which restricts the man's movements and makes him ever more homebound.[31] The woman can then complete her plans by killing the man with medicines in order to take all his wealth under her control.

That these kinds of images about "natural" and "unnatural" gendered forms of control have a broader historical and regional resonance is implied by some details of the vampire stories from Eastern Africa in the 1920s and 1930s (White 2000). These stories depict both African men and women as victims of the colonial regime, but the effects of, for instance, colonial drugs (especially of anesthesia) were gender-specific. Anesthesia was believed to affect men's intellect by making them stupid, whereas women more typically lost their speech (ibid., 116–17). These concerns reveal what were considered the qualities valuable to each gender. A comparable image of economically strong women's agency to that of binding is relayed in the stories of house-owning prostitutes in early Nairobi. These women were believed to cooperate with the colonial regime in imprisoning African men and women in pits in their houses, where they were kept like "dairy cattle" for blood-sucking purposes (ibid., 167). These gendered qualities and forms of agency resemble the ones described above for today's Kilimanjaro where women are believed to use both the "natural" female skills of talking and "unnatural" means of medicines to capture men and male forms of wealth; as an indication of such control men become stupid and immobilized.

In Kilimanjaro, the stories give a contrasting view of female agency: whereas the girls of the wife-capture accounts and "times" are portrayed as complying with the concerns and "plans" of the larger social group, "binding" women are depicted as bold and strategizing actors, who are fulfilling their own selfish plans.

### Self-directedness

Selfishness is often related to both "loose" and "binding" women, and specific terms that emphasize self-direction, are used for them. They are often blamed for being preoccupied with "rubbing creams on their skin" (*anajipakapaka*). *Anajipakapaka* ("she rubs and rubs cream on her skin") refers to women's habit of applying makeup and lotions on their skin to both make it shiny and chemically whiten it. This accords with the customary assumption that a girl's flawless skin signifies the quality of her person, and echoes the habit of anointing the bride. Fairness of skin being also one desired result of the seclusion periods, the women's search for light skin thus repeats the customary beauty ideal. The moral message implicit in the expression *"anajipakapaka"* is, however, that whereas in earlier times a girl's glowing appearance demonstrated the care of others, today's girls use chemical lotions to create that glow by and for themselves. In so doing they are perceived as negating the traditional domestic and reproductive values that are produced by and for the larger social grouping. They are creating their beauty themselves instead, and supposedly for selfish purposes.

A negation of the customary values is found also in women's quest for "European-type" *(Kizungu)* clothing, straightened hair, and slenderness. The wish to be relatively slim is a rejection of the customary beauty ideal of being plump, which connotes fertility and is the expected result of the seclusion periods. Self-direction is also indicated by the earlier mentioned verbs that are frequently used for "loose" women, such as *anajiharibu* and *anajipoteza* ("she spoils/loses herself"). Through these expressions the moral blame for her situation is put on the woman herself; it is thought of as self-induced.

## Discussing Female Agency and Moral Value

Through these concepts and their usage people in Mayanka discuss their understanding of a historical change in gender relations, and especially of women's increased agency in regard to their own lives. Although the expressed focus is on changed women, the accounts indirectly reflect on contemporary men as well. The accounts of "bound" men often include a critical commentary on the failure of present-day men to fulfill their responsibilities. On one hand, there are those rural men, allegedly "bound" by their wives, passively "staying at home like an idiot." On the other hand, there are those urban men, who in their persistent absence have "forgotten" their home folks and instead direct their energies to illegitimate liaisons. In comparison to the idealized vigorous men of the wife-capture era, these present-day men appear sexually, socially, and economically emasculated.

It is noteworthy, however, that by accusations of "binding" it is the women who are blamed for distracting men from their duties and not the men themselves. I never heard of any case where a man was believed to have used medicines in order to "bind" a woman. When I asked people in Mayanka if this was possible, many acknowledged that it was theoretically possible and "must happen in town," but no one could recall any such instance. In contrast, men among some of the other African peoples are occupied with matters involving love magic in an effort to enchant women (see e.g., Caplan 1997, 162–63). This indicates that a Chagga man's "settledness" always calls for explanation. The tendency to blame an "outside" woman for a man's failure to provide for his family, and the overall feminine bias in "binding" agency, reveal that men are considered worth capturing. Wealthy men are especially sought-after, and they can find women willing to attach themselves to them with relative ease.

The above discussions reflect on the diverse forms of women's attachment to men and their differing moral value. The way of commenting on the present gender relations through an idealized past much resembles the one Cornwall (2001) describes for Ado-Odo, a small Yoruba town. Contemporary women there are seen as wayward, rude, and disobedient, and the men as useless. As in Kilimanjaro, the wider economic changes form an important background for the state of the conjugal relations, especially in the enhanced economic potential for trading that women have enjoyed in Ado-Odo since the 1940s. The seeking of personal autonomy by women seems to have gone further in Ado-Odo, however. This is evident in that many women have become economically independent from their husbands and built their own houses (Cornwall 2001, 78). Although unattached women engender moral commentary as in Kilimanjaro, Cornwall observes a decline in women's willingness to marry or remarry, because women are able to provide for themselves (ibid., 80). In Kilimanjaro in the late 1990s, marriage remained the most respectable basis for a woman's identity and material security. I once asked a market woman who had a large business and teenage children what she thought were the most important issues in life. She answered immediately, "First, you have to get a husband [*Lazima upate mume kwanza*], then everything else will follow."

Despite claims to the contrary, most women in Kilimanjaro do not strive for total independence from men, not even economically strong women. Such independence would be difficult on purely material grounds, as men continue to control land and other important resources. Material concerns are not the only reasons for women's willingness to remain in relationships with men, however. One prominent market woman who became the second wife of a relatively wealthy businessman after separating from her first husband explained her motives for the new union: "You know, as an adult person you have desires. . . . It flows well within your body. . . . You cannot retire. You can rest a little bit, but to leave it totally? An adult person cannot." She hurried to explain, however, that she had decided to "remain" *(kukaa)* with that one man and not to "go recklessly with this one and that one" *(kutembeatembea ovyo na huyu na huyu na huyu)*.[32] Another market woman with several adult children and who was living at her natal home after separating from her husband said that she definitely did not want to "be married and to live with a man any more" *(kuolewa na kukaa na mume tena sitaki)* But she did say that she might occasionally involve herself with someone whom she "meets on the road" *(kumkuta barabarani)*.[33] The situation of both these women was backed by their good relations with their natal homes and the fact that they each had several children born in wedlock. The first woman's wealthy husband helped her materially, while the second woman's sons had legitimate claims to their father's land. These relations ensured the women the necessary material security, alternative social networks, and the respect of legitimate motherhood.

Middle-aged market women who tell about their capture draw moral value from their fulfillment of social expectations throughout their lives. These same women emphasize their feeding efforts in the market. By emphasizing their youthful chasteness, respectable motherhood, and their feeding endeavors, these women emphasize their enduring social value, relatedness, and positive generativity. They present themselves as women who have fully fulfilled their duties as daughters, wives, and mothers. Their described personal histories, filled with endurance, submission, and responsibility, is the very basis for their sense of, and claims for, moral value and respect.

Yet their views are not simply a recitation of conventional ideas. As in their emphatic talk about feeding, their critique of dominant ideas more often takes the form of indirection—or more properly redirection—than open dissent or resistance. The women express their critique within familiar cultural categories by extending, reinterpreting, and shifting their meanings. In their recollections they celebrate their young girl's chastity as the expression of a highly valued sociomoral quality, while at the same time bringing out their own experiences of its restrictiveness—their lack of options and painful submission to the actions of others. Furthermore, what complicates their position is the fact that, as the grandmothers of children born to unwed mothers, many of these women face the moral dilemma in their own homes.

The situations and attitudes of younger women vary. Some girls openly criticize the conventional marital relationship. A twenty-four-year-old woman, born in Mayanka but living and doing business in town, explained that she would not want to get married in the usual way because it would mean working like a slave and being under male control. As to her future, she said, "If I only got a man to close me in [anifuge]; I would be like a hawara." She said she would not want a husband of her own, but a "husband of somebody" (mume wa mtu), because in that way she would have more freedom to go out in the evenings and "exchange ideas" (kubadilishana mawazo) with other people and thus to become "more clever" (mjanja zaidi). Yet there are other girls who want to get married in the conventional way, but find themselves unable to do so.

Regardless of the reasons for a girl's unmarried status, moral blame for her situation tends to be put on her. In everyday language, mama is a sociomoral label and signifier that is not applied to girls with children born outside of a marriage. The notions of mother and virgin denote the fulfillment of concerns for the continuity and reproduction of the larger group, and arguments about the negation of such concerns—that is, the seeking of individual and selfish fulfillment by "roaming" or "binding" women—are comparable to witchcraft accusations. These discussions show that notions of the person as individualistic extend well beyond economic issues and material exchange that have been the primary focus of the recent ethnography of witchcraft in Africa.[34]

The popular assigning of blame to women by depicting their agency as destructive and antisocial can be used as an example of how women, and especially young women, tend to become scapegoats (Hodgson and McCurdy 2001; Schuster 1979, 140–69), and their bodies moral icons (Apter 1993, 122–23; Boddy 1989, 9), in situations of socioeconomic change that have much wider roots. Women are not simply passive victims of the historical tale, however, as indicated by the wife-capture narrators' participation in the very creation of it. Nor do the young women's views remain "muted" (Ardener 1975) or evasive. In addition to the open criticism of marriage by some girls, others set out to redefine the favorable qualities of a young girl and bride. They maintain that a child born to an unmarried girl is evidence that the girl's fertility has not been harmed by abortion or contraceptives. Furthermore, they assert that the healthiness of the small child attests to its mother not being infected with HIV/AIDS. This view redefines notions of proper and improper motherhood by suggesting that nowadays it is childless girls who arouse suspicion as potential wives when it comes to the prospects for reproduction.

Even while they are considered reprehensible, the increasing number of "unattached" women and children born outside marriage forces people to rethink the notions of "respectability." As in a poor Kampala suburb (Ogden 1996) or in 1920s Nairobi (White 1990, 59–60), in Kilimanjaro as well a girl's and a woman's sociomoral reputation includes other aspects than the purely sexual, aspects such as polite and respectful behavior and industriousness. Considerate and calm behavior certainly helps to repair a once-damaged reputation, although in rural Kilimanjaro it can hardly substitute for the respect that accrues from marriage.

These discussions show how women in Kilimanjaro not only respond to moral labeling by others, but also participate in defining and redefining female moral value and "respect" in the face of changing socioeconomic and conjugal circumstances. In this, women do not speak with one voice but argue with each other from different perspectives. Moreover, the understanding of these differences affects how women evaluate their own lives and the lives of others. Thus, while the once-captured, now middle-aged market women draw value from their own personal histories of compliance, their reflections on the contemporary girls' alleged assertiveness include an element of bitterness and regret for the lack of options in their own youth.

*Part 2*

# Men

# 5

# Urban Men
# in Their Home Lineages

For a number of decades, reproduction and enrichment have required increased mobility of Chagga men, as well. Men's sources of and places to acquire wealth underwent changes in the twentieth century. During the 1920s, coffee, which was introduced to the area by Catholic missionaries, the Holy Ghost Fathers in the 1890s, started to spread among the ordinary families. As a perennial plant and valuable monetarily, it came to be identified as a crop and source of income for men. Coffee was mostly planted interspersed among the banana trees on the *kihamba*. Due to the increasing population and the booming interest in coffee cultivation, settlements and agriculture began to expand into areas formerly unoccupied. By the 1950s, practically all the available land in the highlands had been turned into coffee-banana farms, and permanent settlements had spread to lower areas that had previously been regarded as marginal and used only for cultivating such annual crops as maize, eleusine (finger millet) and beans. Areas earlier used for grazing were taken over as well, with the consequence that the number of cattle decreased markedly and became stall-fed (Maro 1975, 24–25). The most valued forms of resources and wealth were changing, as land and money were replacing cattle in importance, and education opened new avenues to salaried work, initially for young men.

Even though coffee prices fluctuated over the years, coffee was generally a significant generator of cash for households until the 1960s. Its importance has declined for many families since then, however. By the early 1980s, bananas and maize had become important cash crops, replacing the cash importance of coffee.[1] In 1994, coffee prices increased due to the failure of the coffee harvest in Brazil and the presence of private buyers in Kilimanjaro as a result of trade liberalization. Relatively few in Mayanka could benefit significantly from the higher prices, however, because many had neglected their coffee trees. The fact that banana trees had been taken better care of than coffee reflects the labor and cash constraints that many households faced; coffee is a labor-intensive crop, fertilizers are relatively expensive and at times difficult to obtain. Even while coffee trees usually still grew on *kihamba*, in the mid-1990s many of the younger households were prioritizing the growing of bananas, vegetables, and fodder for cows on *kihamba*. This shift sometimes involved generational and/or gender politics, since coffee is still considered a man's—and increasingly an old man's—crop and source of income, whereas income from milk, bananas, and vegetables usually belongs to women.

Today there is hardly any vacant land left in the fertile mountain areas. The *vihamba* land plots are divided among male heirs, and over the generations many of the plots have become smaller than is sufficient for subsistence.[2] It has become common for men to leave home in search of work in order to earn enough money. Some young Chagga men were seeking employment on European-owned estates on Mount Kilimanjaro as early as the 1920s. In the late 1920s and 1930s, enterprising men made their way to Mombasa and Nairobi, where they often worked for wages or found different forms of self-employment. Some of these men began to import cloth from Kenya and sell it at home. The overall numbers of men moving away from home were initially low. According to Setel (1996, 1172), a trend of young men departing from and paying an annual visit to their rural homes emerged in the 1950s and had solidified by the 1970s.[3]

Some men moved to find and take formal jobs and salaried employment in the public sector, and this developed into an important source of income and status for educated men during the colonial period. It was typical even for the salary-earning Chagga men living outside their home areas to augment their incomes with different kinds of business activities. By the mid-1990s, business ventures had become an increasingly important means of support and enrichment for men in various localities. At the same time,

Chagga men who live in Dar es Salaam gathered for a feast there.

personnel layoffs and low real wages had decreased the importance of the formal wage sector. Some men had returned to their rural homes, others stayed in town clinging to the non-wage benefits of their jobs or moving into business altogether.[4]

Wherever they find their means and places of enrichment, few Chagga men are willing to give up their tiny inherited *vihamba* plots on the mountain. Some men leave their wives and children at their rural *kihamba*, while they themselves live and work elsewhere. Others take their wives (especially those with younger wives) to live with them in town, and visit their rural home only every so often. Such a man might build a house at his home *kihamba*, to where he expects to retire in his old age, and he will ultimately be buried in his *kihamba*. Prosperous Chagga men today want to establish themselves in more than one place, preferably in their home villages and in town, in each place marking their presence by building one or more houses. At the same time, some poor men are unable even to build one house and may have to give up their lineage land altogether and look for land or other means to live on in other regions. So, while the classic texts claim that access to land depends on lineage membership and position (e.g., Bohannan 1963; Colson 1971; Gluckman 1972 [1965]), holding a piece of land in Kilimanjaro now signifies effective membership in the lineage and locality. This status every man wishes to retain, but some are unable to because of their economic situation.

Lineage theories have been criticized for portraying lineage as a corporate-like group and lineage ideology as the lived reality, and for ignoring other important principles of forming relationships. Lineage theories have thus been blamed for attributing a false or exaggerated orderliness to people's lives and relationships. Some critics do not accept the concept at all (e.g., Kuper 1982). Yet in Kilimanjaro people talk about "lineages" *(ukoo,* pl. *koo)* so frequently and so emphatically that it is safe to claim that lineage membership serves as an important source of identity. Lineage "laws" *(sheria)*, which do exist in written form in some lineages, are frequently called upon in the judging and justifying of one's own or others' behavior both in lineage meetings and in less formal contexts. Acknowledging the existence of patrilineages and their "rules" does not, however, mean acceptance of a corporate model or a rule-guided model, whether by the anthropologist or the members of the lineages. The "rules" and structure always contain ambiguity and conflict and are continually being redefined to adjust to new situations (see S. F. Moore 1986).

The relatively wealthy urban-based men have become important actors in the local lineages of Kilimanjaro. While making significant contributions to their extended families and lineages by means of the customary forms of giving and feasting, wealthy men are also shaping lineage relations and emphasizing their positions in their lineages. These actions by urban men and the motives behind them spark evaluative and critical discussion in their rural home areas. This chapter addresses the strategies of men in regard to land access and other forms of presence in the local lineage, along with the challenges and conflicts that sometimes ensue from their endeavors to establish themselves more prominently at home. The chapter sets a basis for the subsequent chapter's examination of how the moral value of ambitious men is discussed and constructed.

## Changing Practices in Land Inheritance

*Kihamba* land is transferred from father to sons. Distinctions are made between the sons according to their birth order whereby the quantity but also the value and significance of the property given to different sons vary. Customarily, the first and last male children are distinguished as primary patrilineal stewards who are to remain on the core lineage land and inherit most of the other property. The first-born son is typically given a *kihamba* next to or near his father's house where he builds his own house. After his father dies, the first-born son assumes the position of head and guardian of the extended family. The eldest son is thus most closely associated with his father and his grandfather.[5]

Women singing hymns in a funeral at a deceased's grave in his *kihamba*.

The last-born son typically inherits the father's house and *kihamba* surrounding it. The youngest son also used to inherit the mother's house, all the livestock included with it, and any private property his mother had (Gutmann 1926, 23). Today the old mother's house—if a separate house exists—and such personal belongings as clothes are usually given to the last son's wife. With his wife, the youngest son is also expected to take care of his parents in their old age. Through these practices, the last-born son is customarily associated with the maternal (female) spheres and spaces as contrasted with the paternal (male) spheres associated primarily with the first-born son. In his relative immobility, the last-born son resembles his mother and her expected "settling down" in her husband's *kihamba*. He is associated with the practices of maintaining and caring for his parents, which in the domestic group is seen as the responsibility of the wife. At the same time, he is associated with the patrilineage more than any other brother in that he is responsible for caring for the ancestral graves in the *kihamba*.[6] In the role and space accorded to him the youngest son can be said to have customarily symbolized lineage locality and permanence.

Middle sons were expected to move out of the homestead land and clear their own plots (Gutmann 1926, 22, 27). In the early twentieth century this was still generally easy, as vacant land was still available. As land has become

*Matanga* meeting, where men sit in a circle in the yard and women outside the circle.

Women sharing *mbege* amongst themselves after the inheritance discussions in a *matanga*.

less and less available, however, this inheritance practice has changed. Nowadays, many fathers try to give some land to all of their sons. The lesser position of middle sons is indicated by the trend towards purchasing a plot of "outside" land for them, while the core lineage land is still ideally reserved for the first and last-born sons. But many fathers cannot afford to buy new plots of land. For these men, the common solution has been to divide their home *kihamba* between all of their sons. The uncertainty of the middle brothers' position tends to linger, however. For instance, a middle son living in Dar es Salaam explained to me during a visit to Mayanka that he did "not actually belong here" (meaning in his home village), but that his generous father had been able to buy a *kihamba* for him, for which he was extremely grateful.

These inheritance practices ensure that land on the mountain remains a predominantly male resource.[7] Land and other lineage issues are indeed characteristically male concerns. In the *matanga* meetings, where inheritance issues are discussed after each burial, this is reflected in spatial arrangements: men occupy center stage, usually sitting on chairs or benches in a circle in the front yard of the house of the deceased, while women attend the meeting sitting on the ground outside the circle on the fringes of the *kihamba*. Although a woman can speak in *matanga,* it is often thought of as a men's meeting. This was shown when I asked one woman about the inheritance decisions made at a *matanga* she had attended with many other women. She began by saying, "The men sat and decided. . . ." The case described next reveals certain subtleties and changes in people's practices and lives, however.

### Interventions by the Old Mother and the Middle Son: Simon's Land

Simon was the first-born of the three sons of a man called Petro. Petro was the elder of his mother's two sons. His father Lyatonga had five wives, each of whom had a house and a plot of land on which they lived with their children. The following land history was related to me by Simon.

Petro's mother was living on a plot of land that would be divided between her two sons, with an adjacent, as yet uncultivated, piece of land to be annexed to it later on. Lyatonga, who died in the 1930s, had been strongly opposed to planting any coffee on this land. Like many other men of his generation, Lyatonga was afraid that Europeans would take over the land if there were coffee trees on it. When Lyatonga died, his first-born son Petro did not hesitate to plant coffee trees on both his late father's *kihamba*—a large part of which was now his own—and on the open land next to it that was to be part of his younger brother's *kihamba*.

Petro's brother died young, however, in the 1950s. His land went to Petro because there were no other full brothers and because he had planted the coffee trees on it. As a perennial, coffee was effective in marking the planter's control over the land.[8] During the 1950s, Petro also built a house on the newer part of the *kihamba*, which, as another permanent structure, marked the land as being under his control.

In the early 1960s, Petro's mother advised him to give his late brother's *kihamba* to Simon. The old mother argued that Simon, as the eldest son of her eldest son Petro, was equal to her late husband Lyatonga. In appealing to her late husband's and her own authority, the old mother drew on hierarchy, which made it difficult for Petro to refuse. The old mother's activity in the *kihamba* transference did not end there. She also showed the borders of the *kihamba* by walking them, followed by Petro and Simon behind him. Simon told me that he could not say that he had gotten his *kihamba* from his grandmother, since Chagga women do not hold land, but he could say that it was given to him by his father and his grandmother. He explained that the grandmother had walked the borders because she was the one who knew them best and wanted to remind the others of them. Today, Petro shares his *kihamba* with his youngest son.

The transfer of the *kihamba* and establishment of its borders were made effective by having the men of the greater lineage section gather together to drink *mbege*. By so doing, Simon thanked his father for the land and had its boundaries confirmed. If any dispute later arose, the men of the lineage would affirm having witnessed the division and the boundaries of the *kihamba*.

Simon attempted to sell part of his *kihamba* to his lineage cousin in the 1990s. I first heard of Simon's land sale through gossip by several of his neighbors. It was only at the very end of my stay that Simon told me about it himself. I will first report the events as Simon described them to me, and then I will present the neighbors' interpretations.

The buyer was Simon's affluent lineage cousin Henry, a grandson of one of Lyatonga's wives. Living in Dar es Salaam and newly retired, Henry had begun to establish himself more prominently on Kilimanjaro. He wanted to establish a business enterprise there. Considering the location of Simon's land most suitable for his purposes, Henry approached Simon with his proposal. A man should not dispose of his land without first seeking his agnates' consent and ascertaining their possible interest in buying the land (see S. F. Moore 1986, 267). According to Simon, he did not decide to sell his land before asking the opinions of his father, the youngest brother at home, and his own wife and children. By letter, Simon also asked the opinion of Justin, his younger brother (Petro's middle son) who lives in Dar es Salaam. As no one objected to the transaction, Simon proceeded with it. Henry paid Simon 3.5 million TZS for part of the *kihamba*. Simon explained that he was thinking of his sons' future; this arrangement would enable him to

divide his home *kihamba* only among a few of them while the rest could be
accommodated on a new plot of land on Western Kilimanjaro that Simon
planned to buy with the money.

Simon explained that Justin came home from Dar es Salaam later on,
saying that he wanted the sale cancelled. Simon objected that it was too late,
as Henry had already started building a large cement house for his enterprise on the land. Furthermore, Simon could not afford to return the sale
price plus building costs to Henry. Justin was unyielding, however. He discussed the matter with Henry and finally cancelled the transaction by reim-
bursing him for the land and the building costs. According to Simon, Justin
never explained why he wanted to cancel the transaction, but he suspected
that Justin had discussed it with some close kin living in Dar es Salaam.
Simon believed that part of the money for canceling the sale had come
from their sister's family in Dar es Salaam, who were relatively well off. Although they had never directly discussed it, Simon felt he should return the
money Justin had paid to cancel the transaction, part of which Simon had
already paid back.

Some of the neighbors had slightly different interpretations. One
woman said that, in addition to the 3.5 million TZS, Henry had given
Simon a land plot in another region and a promise to build him a house
there. The woman saw Justin's intervention as motivated simply by jealousy
*(wivu)* over the favorable transaction made by his brother and the large
amount of money he had received. Another neighbor (not related to the
people involved) said that Simon had been swayed by Henry and his ample
servings of *pombe*. She explained that Henry had been searching for land
for his enterprise a long time before he started to work on his cousin. It took
several weeks and a lot of *mbege*, beer, and meat before Simon agreed. According to this neighbor, Justin had asked Simon after the transaction why
he had not told him about his plans—that he, as Simon's brother, would
have been willing to buy the plot because his own plot was not in an area
with good soil. This neighbor's interpretation was that the plot of land now
in effect belonged to Justin, because he had paid for it.

In this case history, the power to act did not follow the formal lineage
hierarchy. The initial land division and the timing of it shows the power
that an old widow can exert even in such a quintessentially male concern as
the division of land. In this case, the lineage men's role was primarily to
confirm publicly the decision initiated and propelled by the old mother.

Furthermore, Simon's attempted land sale was an example of the power
that a middle brother and other relatives—all with money and living in
town away from the mountain—can exert despite the customary lineage
ideology. It is difficult to know whether Simon really asked Justin's consent
beforehand, as he was expected to do and as he said he had done. It is

equally difficult to know what Justin's motives were. As a middle brother, Justin had been bought a land plot by his father from a less fertile area than his brothers' *vihamba*. It is likely that the sister in Dar es Salaam was also involved, as Simon believed, even though she did not have any direct interest in the land. As a sibling, she was related to the matter and the people. What makes her involvement plausible is the fact that she considered Henry boastful, and would probably have been willing to help her brother get Henry off the land. Without the necessary money, neither Simon nor his father had much say as to the outcome. This story ended with Simon, the first-born son, failing in his plans to provide his own sons with adequate land and feeling humiliated by and indebted to his younger brother.

Simon's case is an example of how reality is often more complex than ideology and the official and public dimensions of lineage affairs. His case also speaks of certain subtle changes in inheritance practices and subsequently in lineage structure. In the past, because of their unfavorable position in traditional inheritance practices, middle sons were more prone to move away than the first or last-born sons. Even though nowadays it is not only the middle sons who leave, there seems to be a continuing trend for the last-born son to remain at home (or close to it), or to return home, or at least to send his wife to live there when the parents grow old. Today, middle brothers living outside—and urban men in general—are often much more affluent than their rural brothers. With their money and their willingness to use it at their natal home, the middle brothers are able to make themselves more of the insiders in the lineage and family issues than they used to be.[9]

Another shift in inheritance practices seems to be the increased prominence of widows. According to the literature (Gutmann 1926, 39–40; S. F. Moore 1986, 237), the brother of a deceased man used to be appointed guardian of the surviving dependents—the deceased's wife and children—and trustee of the property until the sons of the deceased reached marrying age. Nowadays, however, it is more often the widowed wife who becomes the trustee. The brother is still usually appointed as the successor of the man if his sons are not married, but the brother's position is reduced to that of a guardian alone. This means that he gives advice and mediates in any problems or disputes at his late brother's home, but he no longer controls the property of the deceased.

Thus, in addition to their acknowledged spiritual power and the maneuvering behind the scenes—as in the case of Simon's grandmother—the old widows can today quite openly control their late husband's land holdings. This does not give the widow the power to dispose of the land to an outsider; she takes care of the land on behalf of her sons until they marry. In some cases there was, however, uncertainty about how long and how

A grandmother next to her house. Her grandson decided to hold his school exercise book in the picture.

thoroughly the widow should exercise control over land. In one such case, a father died when his sons were young. The father's brother was appointed guardian of his home and his widow trustee of the property. The two sons eventually married and built their houses on the *kihamba*. It was only the younger son who was given a part of the *kihamba* by his mother, however.

The mother was only willing to give the older son the less fertile part of the plot. As the older brother was not satisfied with this division, he had no cultivable land at all in the *kihamba*. According to the neighbors, the old mother was being difficult because she did not like the elder son's wife. The dead man's brother, the guardian of the family, felt the *kihamba* should be divided equally between the sons so that each would have half of the better area and half of the less productive area. This division was not possible, however, in the face of the widow's opposition. When I was in Mayanka in 1994, this situation had being going on for years and was a constant cause of tension in the family. By 1997, however, a satisfactory agreement was reached after several lineage meetings and the *kihamba* was divided between the two brothers.

The practice of making a widow a trustee is today quite common in Mayanka. This shift may be linked to the decrease in "widow inheritance"; the leviratic practice of a brother inheriting the widow of the deceased brother has become quite rare. Christianity had an impact on this change; a Christian inheritor was supposed to act as the widow's guardian but not to have sexual access to her (S. F. Moore, 1986, 284). In the field, many people explained the practice of naming the widow as trustee by the need to ensure that the deceased's brother does not misuse the property before the sons get it—and many could cite several earlier cases in which this had happened.[10]

## Instances of Unity and Distinction

Real life thus often produces strife between people who should be closest to one another, as with relationships between siblings, fathers and sons, and sometimes even between mothers and sons. Rather than being self-evident fact, the unity and the shared interests within an extended family and lineage is something that continuously needs working on. Lineage meetings and the ceremonies where meat and *mbege* are distributed—their distribution still being a delicate and controlled process—are instances for reproducing, formalizing, and reinvigorating the lineage structure. The *matanga* meetings where inheritance decisions are made, for instance, are just as importantly situations where all conflicts between people related to the deceased's household are discussed and resolved.

Moments that should work for unity can, however, turn into instances where distinctions among lineage members are made and displayed. S. F. Moore (1986) has written about the ability of wealthy Chagga men to meet the customary expectations of feasting and sharing more than poorer men can. Moore reports that this kind of social reproduction has become a luxury that only the rich can afford, yet the rich tend to translate the poverty of their lineage mates into a moral failure to share (see also Howard and

Millard 1997). In what follows, I will describe how part of the distinguishing strategies of the wealthy is not only following and fulfilling "customs" (*mila*), but also their subtle and continual attempts to reform customs through innovations and new fashions. The examples that follow show how fulfilling the usual expectations of a Chagga man, such as burying his father and building a house, can become a claim to social status and how that is evaluated by his neighbors and lineage members.

### Henry and His Father's Burial

Henry, who had attempted to buy Simon's land, was a very affluent man by local standards. He was the first-born son of a relatively poor household, but by means of studies in Tanzania and abroad, subsequent employment in positions with links to Europe, and different entrepreneurial activities, Henry had become very prosperous. His prosperity far exceeded that of his father and the younger brother at home. Although he was frequently elsewhere, he had made his position visible by building houses at home and giving support to his close lineage members.

At home he had built a large concrete house that included a bedroom for him and his wife, another for his mother, a big living room, a kitchen, and a bathroom. Another wing of the house was reserved for his children's use, when they came home on vacations from their schools abroad. Henry's mother was the matron of the house when her son was away in Dar es Salaam, where he lived with his wife. The old mother controlled all the keys and the use of the telephone inside the house. So strict was she that some people in the lineage and the neighborhood regarded her as stingy and arrogant. Her pride was seen as the product of her son's wealth and his tendency to pamper her by bringing her anything she might possibly need, and more.

Henry's lineage mates considered the large house in effect to be the old mother's house, as Henry had built another house for his father next door. The father's house was also made of concrete, but it was significantly smaller than the "mother's house," and had a small living space and a sleeping room. Next to the father's house, Henry had also provided his younger brother Arnold with a house, this one a little bit bigger than his father's, but built of cheaper materials. The lineage mates commented on Henry's housing arrangements by saying that "He loves his mother too much," by way of suggesting that his father's house was too humble in comparison to hers. Additionally, some also considered Arnold's house of disproportionate size and quality compared to the large house, and that altogether the differences among the houses were too great. The differences were read as deliberate statements regarding the relative position and importance of the three men—as ordered by Henry.

Arnold was considered a lazy person. He was said to have dropped out of all the schools that he had been sent to, and had spent all his money on "eating and drinking." This is a common and highly moral idiom expressing the image of a selfish and lazy person who consumes anything of value without an effort to create, share, or transform it into more lasting wealth. Out of brotherly responsibility, Henry had given Arnold several "projects" (miradi) and the capital to start different trading ventures, but every time Arnold had allegedly "eaten it all," always ending up empty-handed before the enterprise had properly begun. Henry was also known to pay the secondary school fees for Arnold's children. Thus, the difference between the uprightness of the two brothers was apparent and a topic of common mockery. Yet the situation was also favorable for Henry; it was his brother's lack of moral backbone that made Henry's public image shine ever more. Every time Henry gave his brother any support or starting capital for another project (amounts that were often not very significant for Henry), he would do so publicly, arrogantly, and admonishingly, thus humiliating his brother and stressing his own righteousness and generosity. It was clear that whomever Henry helped, he did so publicly and expected some kind of reciprocity. In this way he bound people to himself as dependents.

Since Henry had retired from his job, he now had the time and desire to establish himself more vigorously in his rural home. He was active and visible in the rural villages in several ways. He used to cruise around in his car and was known as a man who "loves" women. Many women were attracted to him and the glimpses of the luxurious life that he could offer. He was one of the most eager and visible advocates for multiparty politics and a certain new party in Mayanka. Henry's ambitions were to become the elected representative of the new party in the district government and the leader of the local KNCU (Kilimanjaro Native Cooperative Union), and his generosity with beer in the local bars, as well as other support that he publicly gave to people, were intended to further those ambitions. In that respect, his behavior resembled that of any "big man" or chief, and was part of the "straddling strategies" (Cowen 1981) of modern East African men, who combine resources and relations from both the urban and rural sectors.

Henry's father died while I was in the field. As the first-born son, Henry took a managerial role in arranging his father's funeral, which was an exceptionally big occasion. Before the burial, as the neighbors and kin were following the preparations for it, there was a lot of gossip about the coming event. As one woman aptly put it, "The whole road is talking about it." Henry wanted his father's funeral to be memorable. People asked each other disapprovingly whether the son was making a feast (sherehe) out of his father's death and funeral, when it should be a day of sorrow. The arrangements were thought to be too complicated and too lavish, and the main reason was believed to be Henry's desire to show off his wealth.

There were plenty of issues to talk about, starting with the actual digging of the grave. Henry did not want any simple grave; the bottom and the walls of it were to be lined with stones. To ensure enough time for the grave to be readied, Henry wanted the digging to start a day before the funeral. The lineage elders intervened and sharply prohibited that, however, because they claimed death would come to yet another member of the lineage if the grave were prepared a day before and waited empty until the burial. Henry yielded to these elders' pressure and started the digging immediately after midnight on the funeral day.

The burial ceremony itself was not usual, either. In most cases such a ceremony is conducted at the homestead and *kihamba* of the deceased, but this time the arrangements were more complicated. The coffin was first brought to the house of the deceased and the people in attendance were told over loudspeakers that only close relatives were to go inside to view the deceased; others would have that opportunity at the church. The coffin was later carried to the church, followed by a huge crowd of people. Instead of the old smaller church building, which was used for Sunday services, the very big one, which was still under construction, was used for this funeral to ensure that all the people in attendance would fit inside. As the church building was still without a roof, large sheets of plastic were spread above to protect the people from any possible rain or the hot sun. Microphones and loudspeakers were used in the church.[11] Although the building was enormous, the crowd attending the funeral was so large that not everyone could find a place to sit down.

The coffin was placed in front of the altar and the priests. Men and women then proceeded, as instructed, row by row to the front to view the deceased one last time. The coffin itself was of a better quality than usual with a window of glass over the deceased's face. The number of priests and church choirs invited for the ceremony were also more than was usual. A group of three men with trumpets were invited to play in the church. This aroused some disapproving comments about making the funeral into a celebration; trumpet music is usually played at such occasions as weddings and send-off ceremonies for a bride-to-be.

After the church ceremony, the coffin was carried back to the homestead and *kihamba* of the deceased. As it was anticipated that not all of the large crowd would be able to get close to the grave, a few loudspeakers had been set up around the *kihamba*. A relative was given the task of informing people of the coming events through a microphone. After the blessing of the deceased for the last time by the priest at the graveside and throwing some soil into the grave, the grave was closed with a hard cover instead of being filled with soil. A lineage member commented on this solution—and the lining of the grave with stones—by saying that Henry did not want soil to touch his father.

The usual procession of people bringing flowers and wreaths to the grave followed. What was unusual was the microphone used to announce the names and the order of the people (men first) in the procession. After the long procession, the venue for the ceremony moved to the front yard of the house complex where all the people present sang hymns. A short life history of the deceased was read aloud, after which some of the grand-daughters presented a touching song they had composed as a farewell to their grandfather. Also, a telex sent by two of Henry's children, who were studying abroad, was read aloud. It was written in English, read aloud in English, and then translated into Kiswahili.

For the funeral the widow, Henry, his wife, and his sisters were dressed in black. Wearing black is not usual for Chagga funerals, and was adopted from the European manner of dressing.[12] Also against tradition, food and drinks were served on both the funeral day and the day after, at the *matanga,* and not only on the *matanga* day as usual. Many people found this inappropriate; again, in their opinion it made the funeral seem more like a feast. The servings were lavish, the usual *machalare* being only one among many sorts of foods.

On the *matanga* day, a large crowd of people gathered at the deceased's house since, among other things, they knew that food would be plentiful. After the meeting, the guests were organized into spatially different sections. Local men and women sat in their own groups: the men in the front yard, the women close to the kitchen building and in front of the deceased's house. The widow stayed inside her house with her close relatives and some neighbors. The guests, both men and women, who had traveled from farther away, sat in a closed yard between two buildings. These guests were served both *mbege* and different varieties of bottled beer, whereas the local people were only served *mbege.* Local women were not happy with what they considered discrimination, however, and started to slip, one by one, to the "VIP" section in order to get beer. Drinking *mbege* at the deceased's house had begun already at the news of his death. *Mbege* and beer lasted for one week after the burial; each day there were people visiting the house and drinking. Some guests, mostly wealthy friends of Henry, came with cases of beer. Henry also made sure that they would not run out of beverages.

An old woman of the same lineage died a few weeks later. She was the wife of a full brother of Henry's father, and thus equivalent to his mother. Her funeral and *matanga* arrangements were brief and very modest. When I asked the lineage members if this was because she was a woman or because the dead man had been an exceptionally important person, I was told that neither of these was the actual reason. The main difference was said to be Henry's wealth and his willingness to display it. People also reminded me that Henry, having traveled a lot, had friends in many places, not only in Tanzania, but also in Kenya and Europe, and that these friends of his had come to the funeral. In contrast, only relatives and neighbors attended the old woman's funeral. How could she have gathered a crowd of friends when she had just stayed home all her life, they asked.

The gossip during the burial revealed the reservations that many neighbors and lineage members harbored about Henry. In diverse ways it spoke of Henry's perceived inclination to sidestep the importance and authority of his father. The comment about Henry not wanting the earth to touch his father hinted that, in isolating his father's remains from the ancestral earth, Henry did not want his father to become an ancestor in the proper way. The comments about his turning the sorrow of his father's death into a joyous celebration and an opportunity to show off his wealth expressed the understanding that he was "feasting" on his father's death, as he now came to replace him as the head of the extended family. The comments about his houses and his too-pronounced love for his mother hinted at his perceived willingness to outdo his father even while he was still alive. Henry's generosity in funeral arrangements appeared thus to be more for the enhancement of his own prestige and distinction than his concern for his father and the other relatives.[13] It is difficult to judge Henry's motives and intentions; for instance, the "isolating" of his father's body in the stony grave can also be interpreted as an attempt to make the father distinctive as well. It is meaningful, however, that such views were widely held among his kin and neighbors. They criticized what they perceived as Henry's arrogance and his lack of regard for the customary authorities and Chagga "customs."[14]

### City House in the Countryside

Regardless of official monogamy, many wealthy men aspire to maintain relations with women besides their legitimate wife. Where poor men often have trouble building just one house, wealthier men can build houses for several women, just as prosperous men at the beginning of the twentieth century did. Houses, women, and cars mark the status and prestige of a man and his person. It is not only their number but, just as importantly, their style and elegance that is significant.

One day I witnessed a situation where three wealthy men, all born in Mayanka but living in Dar es Salaam, were discussing the building of a house for one of them in Mayanka. The man, Gifti, had planned the house with his architect friend, who arrived at the building site in his white Mercedes Benz. The house was still under construction and had no furniture inside, but the major part of the outside building and the inside trimmings were already completed. One could see that the house would be beautiful and refined, and also that it represented a different style from other modern houses in the area. It was different in its architecture, materials, the arrangement of its surroundings, and its size; it was smaller than many other almost monumental houses of prosperous men in the area. This was not a decision based on economic reasons, since Gifti did not lack money and was in fact a thriving businessman. Rather, his house was to present "a new idea of a house."

The building materials were impressive; the outer walls were made of white stones, the front wall was decorated with stones projecting out. The ridge roof was made of red Spanish tiles. In its shape the whole front of the house formed a round curve, made of glass between a few columns, and enclosing a veranda. A surveillance camera perched on one of the stone walls next to the veranda. The tops of all the windows were curved to form an arch. The steps leading to the veranda, the floor of the veranda, and most of the floors inside the house were covered with light-colored tiles. The ceilings in the house were done with wood panels. The first room was a living room with very large windows and a big chandelier hanging from the ceiling. To the right, a few steps higher than the living room, was the dining area, from which a door led to the kitchen. In the middle of the house were two rooms for children, and in between them a bathroom and a separate shower room, both with white enamel sinks. At the inner core of the house was a large master bedroom with a big lamp hanging from the ceiling. One wall was reserved for a dressing table that would cover it entirely. A door led from the bedroom to a sizeable bathroom with a large bathtub, toilet and sink, all of white enamel.

One of the men was admiring the careful construction work, especially the unusual veranda and roof. This man said he wanted to build a similar house in Moshi town. Gifti said that at the end of each month he had to have 200,000 TZS on hand for the costs of the house, and one of the men added in a carefree manner, "And one just searches for money for that."[15]

As he emerged from the house, one of the men said joyously, "New house, new wife!" (Nyumba mpya, mke mpya!) There seemed to be a mutual assumption that the house would be for the owner's favorite girlfriend who was living in Dar es Salaam. Gifti said, however, that "somebody" (either this girlfriend or his wife) had already complained that the house was not good enough, as it did not have enough rooms. One of the men said that person had not understood "the present idea of a house," the most important parts of a house being the living room, dining room, and bedroom.

At some point, a fourth man appeared at the building site. This was a professional gardener who had planned the cozy gardens of the two local

guest houses where these and other well-off men liked to gather for entertainment. Interest turned to the surroundings. The men shared the opinion
that there should be a vast, soft and flat lawn around the house. To make the
ground flat, some earth would need to be moved away. Because of the construction work, most of the soil around the house had already been turned,
yet there were still some of the usual banana and coffee trees at the side of
the house. The gardener asked if any of those trees would be left there. One
of the men exclaimed that if he wanted to spoil the whole garden, then he
should just leave that "rubbish" *(takataka)* there. Cooling down, he continued that not a single banana or coffee tree was to be left. "What we want is a
city house in the countryside [*tunachotaka ni sitihaus mgombani*]," he said.
The other men agreed. One man remarked that it would be good for the
children to have an inspiring view from their windows.

Instead of the customary "shaggy" *masale* fence that surrounds a *kihamba*, a tidy living hedge would surround this garden. It was emphasized
to the gardener that the fence should be of such a height that no one could
see into the living room. The gate should be placed so that it would lead
straight to the main door. The gardener was told to take extreme care to see
that the hedge was absolutely straight on all sides; the corners were to be
slightly curved, however. Another plain and private gate would be made on
the side of the back yard for Gifti's father. The father, a round-shouldered,
weary old man, was living in a small modest house next to this house.
When we set off, one of the men cheerfully said again, "The younger wife
will live here." As we sat in the car, another man laughingly explained to me
that Gifti actually had six wives.

The style of the house and the garden were thus planned to be distinct
from both the customary Chagga homestead and other "modern" houses of
the area. The spatial and architectural arrangements were also intended to
arrange social relations inside and outside the house. It was after all the garden that would be the most different and novel in its large size and style.
The removal of the banana and coffee trees—the most crucial signs of a *kihamba* that surround even the modern houses in this area—was effective in
creating an image of a "city house" and one of its owner as a modern man.
While Gifti set himself apart from "customs" by these arrangements, the
private gate for his father was Gifti's way to signify his desire to maintain his
relationship with his father.

The remarkable size of the garden and its orderly comfort reflected
Gifti's intention to entertain a rather large but select circle of people. The
other markers that distinguished Gifti from the larger social surroundings
were the fence and the surveillance camera: they gave Gifti the power to
monitor his surroundings while ensuring his and his selected guests' pri-
vacy from public scrutiny.

Both the fence and the house are enclosures, yet they demarcate different kinds of spaces. The garden is a semipublic, male—Gifti's—space, while the house would more properly belong to his ("new") wife's sphere. The strictly linear shape of the fence would be a sign of Gifti's modernity, whereas the repeated circular forms in the house (the front, the windows) invoked the rounded shapes[16] of the traditional Chagga house. The garden was thus more innovative than the house, which still shared something with traditional forms; this difference between them was intended to express and arrange the relative positions and modernity of Gifti and his "wife."

## Lineage, Locality, and "Big Men"

The scarcity of land and the discrepancy in economic potential between rural and urban areas influence the current points of tension in the lineage structure and reality as lived and experienced. They have impacted the structure of opportunity between men located in different areas, enabling middle brothers and other urban men to strengthen their position in their home patrilineage.

Among the Chagga, the ascriptive criteria of birth order, seniority, and gender coexist with the acknowledged value of personal achievement and the quest for "self-realization" and "singularity." These terms come from Guyer (1993). She uses them to describe the process of becoming a person in Equatorial Africa in pre-colonial times, but I also find these terms useful for thinking about contemporary Kilimanjaro. Guyer says (ibid, 255) that becoming a real person—a person recognized as being dimensional in his or her own singular or unique fashion—involved a succession of ordeals and achievements, a husbanding and protection of personal power and repeated demonstrations of it.[17]

Singularity does not mean individuality. A man's person consists of his social relations (Strathern 1991). In order to extend their social relations and thus their persons, prosperous Chagga men use such conventional methods as distributing riches by patronage and feasting, achieving spatial control in the form of land, houses and cars, and having many "wives."

Henry, for example, was quick to realize the possibilities for position and power in local institutions opened up by the political liberalization policies. His ambition was to become a prominent figure in the reestablishment of older institutions, the KNCU and the District Council, as well as in the new political party.

The way prosperous men typically extend their patronage is by giving out presents, arranging scarce services for others, and providing people with beverages like beer and *mbege,* and also food (especially meat). Frustrated by an affluent relative's refusal to give him a loan, one man explained to me that he could not understand why giving out even a few coins was so difficult for rich men, when they could easily and unexpectedly bring you a case of beer. By turning money into presents, affluent men bind people into a reciprocal patronage relationship. It is not only the number but also the quality—the singularity—of the persons related to a man that is important. The huge crowd of people who attended Henry's father's funeral—many of them distinguished people from Tanzania and abroad—was more a manifestation of Henry's relations and personhood than those of his deceased father, as was emphasized.

The spatial control inherent in possessing land and houses is a form of presence and marks a man's belonging and relations to a locale, neighborhood, and lineage. At the same time, they objectify and make visible a man's capability and his social personhood; establishing houses in several places is a way of extending the person. A house and its style display a man's capacities as a male and his uniqueness. They also arrange and rearrange both male-male and male-female relations at the same time.

Both Henry and Gifti fit into the category of "big men" (Godelier 1986 [1982], 170–75) as a "concentration of characteristics, making visible what other men might be" (Strathern 1991, 197). As such, they "present men to themselves in an exaggerated, masculine form" (ibid., 198). Yet while affluent men frequently transform material resources into "symbolic capital" (Bourdieu 1977, 177–80), reputation cannot be built up by the simple logic of accumulation. Status depends on the acknowledgement of a man's person by others around him. This was shown in Henry's case. Henry might have done everything expected of a "big man," but it did not guarantee him such recognition because people had reservations about his moral quality. Henry's individualism and self-centeredness were summarized in an expression I frequently heard people use in reference to him: "He really likes himself!" *(anajipenda kweli)*. This self-reflexive verb resembles those verbs used to criticize the persons of contemporary women for their perceived self-direction (see previous chapter). Henry's perceived individualist aspirations kept him from being recognized as a "big man," as someone who in his person and in his use of wealth is expected to be capable of instantiating and representing the interests of a larger social whole. Genuine "big men" are not individuals but "fractal persons", composed of social relationships, and capable of "collecting" and enacting many wills in their will (Strathern 1991; Wagner 1991).

Lineages and families have different histories and different reputations. Yet it is unlikely that Henry's modest family background shaped the common portrayal of him as an upstart. The men of chiefly lineages were not generally held in high regard, but were stereotyped and mocked as lazy and as heavy drinkers, the common explanation being that because of their chiefly background they lacked the experience and ability to work. For instance, only one of the sons of a former chief was recognized by many as earning the name *mangi,* or "chief." One man explained that he was the only one who knew to talk nicely with different people, who always behaved respectfully, and was generous. He did not mention that the man was also a significantly rich man who had made his way in the outside world, and not always in honest ways. Yet the man's description summarized the characteristics that are expected from an affluent man in order for his status and person to be acknowledged: recognized singularity and achievement are not only of value to the person concerned, but also an "asset, the pool of wealth" for the wider group (Guyer 1993, 253).

However, as with Mama Njau, rather than fixed positions, Henry's situation has to be seen as a constant process of negotiation in which Henry attempts to achieve recognition while the people around him evaluate those attempts and his person. Some of the ambiguity of the situation was conveyed by the fact that, regardless of all the criticism around Henry's funeral arrangements, people were attracted to participate in the funeral, both out of curiosity and because they expected ample servings of food and drink.

Locality, as acknowledged in Polynesian and New Guinea studies,[18] is important for identity formation in Kilimanjaro as well. The peculiarity of Kilimanjaro is that the value of locality is often combined with frequent absences of the wealthiest landholders and the owners of distinguished houses. While the houses are becoming ever more conspicuous, the land plots they occupy are shrinking. This is a change in the proportion of different types of manifest property, with the land being more social in nature, while houses are the primary signs of personal distinction and advancement. The changes in the forms and proportions of riches, in the locations of enrichment, and in the categories of people with access to them, create discussion and struggle in contemporary Kilimanjaro. Debates swirl around the line between what is considered a healthy quest for distinction and what exaggerates it, what belongs to distributable riches and what to personal wealth, and who the people are with whom a man should share his wealth. The next chapter considers how the moral value of ambitious men is discussed by interpreting the reasons for their fates.

# 6

# **Making Sense of Failure**

## Stories of Businessmen and Wealth

This chapter deals with stories that people in Mayanka tell about business-men who were unable to transform their riches into enduring wealth. Such men also failed to attain full personhood. The stories are typically discussed in informal circles when a man either dies young or experiences misfortune in his prime. They are in fact interpreted life histories, since they probe the reasons for the man's fate by reviewing his life trajectory. They are moral stories in that the reason for a man's downfall is found in the moral quality of his person and acts. Here I will compare stories about past and present-day businessmen whose unhappy fates were believed to be caused by the il-legitimate means of enrichment these men pursued. I heard many such sto-ries, but here I will present a few cases as representatives of different story types. This is because the stories were seldom idiosyncratic, except in their details; instead they followed certain quite schematic patterns. Examining these stories and their narrative idioms enables us to see how ambitious men's moral value is discussed and how understanding of the contempo-rary life is constructed.

The stories reveal that regardless of the Chagga people's long familiarity with trading, even in the case of men is business often considered a more morally suspicious way of advancement than, for instance, education. The changing forms of men's labor and enrichment form a background for these views. In the 1970s and the beginning of the 1980s educated and salaried men were the most influential people in the lineages after the elders (S. F. Moore 1986, 216, 250, 289 –90, 305). In the mid-1990s, however, a widespread understanding was that the influence of uneducated men who engaged in business had become greater than that of educated and older men. Nevertheless, the fact that morally suspect propensities were also ascribed to earlier businessmen complicates the stories' relationship to the present. Rather than simply looking at these as stories that reflect political and economic changes, I will here analyze the moral and symbolic aspects of the narratives.

Interpreted life histories are ways to problematize the social status and local influence of newly rich men. The stories are political insofar as they try to control changes in the status hierarchies and the actions of ambitious men. However, they should not be reduced to mere politics. Recurring concepts in the stories such as "staying" and "vanishing," as well as "bought spirits" and "businessmen," are also used idiomatically to discuss the broader consequences of the changing possibilities of wealth-making for social continuity. The imaginative and the fantastic in the stories have to be given full significance as ways of expressing feelings and concerns and of interpreting present-day events by creatively applying and expounding older concepts and metaphors.

Success stories about men were hardly ever told, even though I occasionally tried to solicit them. Failures seemed to offer much more raw material for moral reflection on present-day men. On the event of a sudden and unexpected death, the stories that emerge are in tension with and counter to the official, formalistic, and nondramatic life histories that are publicly read at funerals. These official histories are respectful and respectable. They attempt to deflect any speculation about possible abnormalities in the deceased's life—and at the same time to ensure the deceased a restful sleep in the family grave and a respectable position in the home lineage. But the informal life histories unsettle the official truths. Any sudden advancement or affluence invites suspicions and speculation, but it seems that death or a reversal in fortunes confirms that there really had been something hidden or unseen worthy of speculation. Such events become moments when appearances fail and hidden realities become interpreted and reinterpreted through gossip. The informal stories keep histories alive and in motion; with new events, the life histories once told and put aside become discussed and reinterpreted anew.

Whereas the stories about men were often clear (even logical), chronologically sequenced, or progressive accounts that were often told to me without any prompting, such stories were not told about women. When I tried to get people to tell stories about the fates of women, those stories would be much more fragmented and less clear than the interpreted life histories of men. This difference must arise from the expectations and real-ities of gendered processes of wealth-making. The relatively linear and lucid stories about men reflect the expectations of a male life course, which in-volves advancement, accumulation, and the display of wealth. Like men's lives and careers themselves, stories told about them are much more public and conspicuous than those about women.

Some of the life histories that follow were told to me as entire chrono-logical stories, others I have compiled from several sources of gossip. But both types of narrative were gathered in informal discussions and gather-ings. Some of the stories were told by the men's kinfolk, but most came from other villagers not closely related to the men concerned.

## Stories about Short-Cut Means to Success

Men's ambitions to succeed and distinguish themselves are culturally ex-pected and thus considered natural, as was discussed in the previous chap-ter. Some men are believed to have such an unmitigated desire (tamaa) for success and riches, however, that they use short-cut means to achieve their ends. Setel (1996, 1174) has noted that an excess of tamaa is an aspect of personhood with a negative connotation and is made manifest in the qual-ity of one's actions towards others. It is seen as formative in an amoral, profligate lifestyle. In the following stories such tamaa is revealed in a man's appropriative tendencies towards other people.

All the stories tell of men who amass their initial riches outside the local community. Taking place far away, these men's means of enrichment re-main invisible to the people at home, and for that reason cause speculation among them. The illegitimacy of such men's means is finally revealed, how-ever, when they fail to stabilize their riches—to convert them into lasting wealth—at home. In the older stories, the appropriative acts take the form of stealing and killing. Such illegitimate means are acknowledged to have a long history and some of contemporary men are believed to use them, too. An increasingly used newer method is thought to be "buying a spirit," how-ever. All the various illegitimate means depicted in the stories are shown to result in downfall and destruction, but we find important differences in the interpreted forms and the social and spatial consequences between the older and newer methods.

### Stolen Money and a Curse: Ruben

Ruben used to be one of the most remarkable and affluent men in Mayanka. He was among the first—according to some people, the very first—who began importing cloth from Mombasa and selling it in Mayanka in the 1930s. He opened quite a large shop where he sold a range of goods. He bought several vehicles later on, among them trucks and buses that he used for a transportation business. He opened another shop, built a few houses (two of them in town), and opened a gasoline station that is still the only one in Mayanka. Although Ruben died long ago, his accomplishments and memory live on. The place where he had his gas station and shop is still popularly referred to as "Ruben's place" *(kwa Ruben)*, even though they are under different ownership now.

Ruben was described as a very fat and good-spirited man who used to sit in his shop from day after day, drinking *mbege*. So keen on his business was he said to have been that he would not close his shop even for the funerals of close relatives. People said that he began to lose his wealth towards the end of his life, however. Some people claimed that he died virtually empty-handed. Although this was an exaggeration, the assertion brought out the common conviction that his fortunes and fate had turned at some point, which was considered a logical consequence of his actions.

Several people unrelated to Ruben told me he had built his wealth on stolen money. As a young man he lived in Mombasa, where his agnatic relative asked Ruben to help him to hide money that he had stolen from an Indian man. The man himself was caught for the robbery and imprisoned for several years. Meanwhile, Ruben came home to Mayanka and, according to the people relating the events, established his businesses with that stolen money. When the imprisoned man was set free, he returned to Mayanka and asked Ruben for the money. Ruben denied he had ever received money from him, however. The man was said to still be alive, but very poor; it was said that he went around "hardly owning even shoes."

Dwindling riches were only one of the conceived outcomes of Ruben's immoral deed. Ruben died some time after the agnatic relative had appeared in Mayanka. And a little bit later, one of his sons died. Another son left his job in Dar es Salaam in order to return to Mayanka and take care of his late father's property, having inherited the gas station, a shop, a truck, and a house in Moshi town. Shortly afterwards, the son sold the gas station and shop; the truck had not been used ever since the father's death and was run down and useless. These acts of selling and the decrepit truck were interpreted to imply that the son was bankrupt *(amefilisika)*.

Ruben's third son inherited a pickup truck and a house in Moshi town. He sold the house, and with the money built another house in a smaller town and bought a truck to start a transportation business. An unrelated man questioned whether this transaction was wise. The house in Moshi was rented out, this man claimed, and would have been more profitable and stable than the uncertain trucking business. The man took these decisions as signs of this son also being on a path to bankruptcy. Another unrelated man commented in 1994 that the sons had no more money and that their father's property had vanished *(imepotea)*. He considered this "vanishing" a natural and expected outcome of the father's immoral means of acquiring the money to start with.

By 1997, this history had been augmented. Ruben's second son had died. Several people from the same village remarked that now only one son remained, but he was not quite sane. One indication was his constant restlessness. For instance, he would travel to town daily, but nobody knew what he was doing there and it was simply suspected that he had no proper reason to go there.

In 1997, two alternative explanations for the fate of the sons and the wealth were circulating among the villagers. One was that these outcomes were because the money had been stolen and because of the curse the agnatic relative had pronounced against Ruben. The other explanation was also based on the wrongful appropriation of property, but by Ruben's sons. According to this version of the story, Ruben had had a business partner, Filipo, who took care of Ruben's other shop. Before dying, Ruben called a meeting with Filipo, Filipo's wife, and a prominent neighboring businessman to witness his last will, according to which Filipo was to receive half of Ruben's property. After he died, however, Ruben's sons allegedly denied the meeting and claimed that Filipo was just their father's employee and thus not entitled to any part of the property. As Filipo himself was already elderly and weak enough that he was unable to properly look after his rights, his wife called the only outside witness to Ruben's last will, the businessman, to a meeting. The businessman claimed that he had not heard Ruben utter such words; people believed that he had been bribed by Ruben's sons to so claim. Such lying was all the more serious and risky because Filipo's wife was a categorical patrilineal aunt to this businessman.

Some time after Ruben's second son died. Filipo's wife was said to have cursed the son, saying that if the son had lied, "food will not enter his throat"; instead it would turn up "in one side of his body." People recalled that the son was sick long before he died. He ended up being taken to the hospital because of stomach aches, and an operation determined that one side of his stomach was blocked with excrement. He died shortly after the operation. The other traitorous witness, the businessman, died at approximately the same time in a car accident. He was driving home from a feast with one of his sons in the passenger seat. For some unknown reason, his car ran off the road into a ditch. The man was killed instantly, while his son was badly injured. The son eventually recovered from the accident, and the fact that he survived made many people think that the father's death was predetermined or fated. Thus, the other explanation had it that the fate of

Ruben's son and the outside witness as well as the vanishing of the inherited property was due to the curse laid by Filipo's wife.

Even though the fate of the people and property involved was described in both explanations as being the result of a curse, there was also a sense that the very acts of stealing and building wealth on stolen money had made Ruben's and his sons' future precarious. It was not simply that stealing made Ruben corrupt; stealing also revealed Ruben's dishonest and appropriative tendencies and the immoral quality of his person. That he prized his own comfort and business interests higher than the people close to him was also expressed in the villagers' assertion that he kept his shop open even during the funerals of relatives. The two acts of theft were not equally significant in terms of social relations: although the money had originally been stolen from an Indian man, it was clearly much more weighty, immoral, and fatal that loss was caused to an agnatic relative.

### Killing and Spiritual Affliction: Isak

At the beginning of the twentieth century, butchers were among the wealthiest local men. They usually acquired their cattle from outside the local area. They used to walk to western Kilimanjaro, buy one or two head of cattle at an auction and walk them back home. There the cattle would be slaughtered for their meat and hides to sell. These men aroused admiration and fear, because they were not afraid of exposing themselves to the risk of attack and robbery along the way.

The following is the story of a butcher called Isak, a story from the 1960s or 1970s, when it was more common to drive long distances rather than walk them. The story is pieced together from what people not related to him said.

Isak was said to have been a "very bad person" (mtu mbaya sana) who "desired money a lot" (alikuwa na tamaa ya pesa sana). Most often he bought cattle from Maasai sellers. It was believed that after he paid for the animals Isak would sometimes offer the Maasai seller a lift in his truck, with the intention of killing him and taking home both the money and the cattle.

Isak had five wives and he lived with one of them in a building that also accommodated his bar. This wife had a lover, another butcher, who visited her every so often. A jealous man, Isak wanted to kill this lover and saw an opportunity one day while driving down the local road. Isak saw a man he took to be his wife's lover and knocked the man over with his truck. Only too late did he realize that it had not been the man he thought it was.

The wife's lover had been walking along the road with Isak's brother when—"matters of God" (mambo ya Mungu), as one local woman put it—Isak's brother had admired the butcher's white coat and the man had taken it off and given it to the brother to wear. Isak had run over and killed his own brother.

Isak fled from the spot and drove to the next former chiefdom, where he hid his truck and then returned to Mayanka on foot. Before dying, his brother was reported to have said, "You killed me, but you will not stay long either." After this incident, Isak was often seen walking along the local road and talking to himself.

One day, Isak prepared *mbege* for sale the next day and went to bed. The next morning someone came to call him but found Isak lying dead on the floor with clenched fists. This dying position was believed to reveal what had happened during the night. His raised fists in death, and his recalled habit of talking to himself along the road as if fighting with a spirit, were seen as indicative that the spirit he was battling had killed him. It was believed it was his dead brother's spirit that had tormented him and finally caused his death, although it was considered possible that the spirits of the Maasai men were persecuting him as well.

Three of Isak's sons died young. One died in Dar es Salaam after being struck by a car while riding his bicycle. Another had just returned to Dar es Salaam from this brother's burial at home when a car knocked him off his motorbike. The fact that a passenger riding with him on the motorbike was not injured made the accident more meaningful in people's recounting of the incident. The third son died of some illness. There is only one son left, but he is said to have "bad habits" *(tabia mbaya):* smoking hashish *(bangi)* and making his living by stealing. This son did not want to live at his home after the deaths of his brothers, and moved out without any permanent place to stay. The home house is now empty and the *kihamba* uncared-for.

The dying man's curse thus caused more than the early death of Isak himself. None of his male progeny would continue his lineage line, and thus his life. The way the two sons died in car accidents was a reflection and kind of replay of Isak's brother's death. Like the last son of Ruben, who was described as mentally confused, Isak's only remaining son was not considered able to assume the status of an adult person and continue the lineage. Their fate was shown in their restlessness and unsettled way of life.

Here again, even though the final demise comes through an agnatic relative's curse and harassment by his spirit, the implication by the storytellers was that the curse was not the only reason for these outcomes. The immorality of Isak's person and his unmitigated desire for riches were believed to have led to his tragic demise, as well as that of his close agnatic relatives. Killing was Isak's means to enrichment and control, but as recounted in the story it also described his overall impatience, and acquisitive tendencies.

## Majini: *Bought Spirits*

The stories about bought spirits *(jini;* pl. *majini)* also tell of attempts to internalize value from outside the familiar context, attempts that are finally incompatible with and end up destroying such lasting value as family and kin. Buying a spirit for enrichment is considered a relatively new development. Many figure such practices to have begun in the 1980s.[1] This is regarded as a form of witchcraft acquired from off the mountain, and the most powerful of the spirits are believed to originate in the coastal Islamic regions. These stories usually involve such signs of individual success as cars and houses, as the following examples show.

## ANASELI'S PICKUP TRUCK

An unrelated girl who lives close to Anaseli's home explained to me that his pickup truck was so feared by many people that they would rather walk than accept a lift in his truck. The fears and suspicions had developed after Anaseli's brother's son had an accident on his motorbike and died. Later, as the dead boy's mother was consulting a diviner to find out the reason for his death, Anaseli started to scream inside his home, saying that he had killed the boy.

According to the girl who told me this story, Anaseli had bought a spirit from Sumbawanga (a town in western Tanzania) because he wanted to become rich, and the spirit required his brother's son's blood as its food. Before the boy's death, Anaseli ran a shop that was not particularly successful. After the death, he closed the shop, acquired a pickup truck and opened a bar that prospered. It seemed, however, that Anaseli was failing to take proper care of the purchased spirit and meet its requirements. As some time later Anaseli's own son died, people were convinced that the spirit had gotten loose. People began to think that Anaseli's pickup truck was dangerous and bound to kill people because of the spirit's thirst for blood; in effect, the spirit was thought to be driving the truck.

## A BOUGHT SPIRIT CONFRONTS JESUS

A woman called Upendo told me about a house in her neighborhood where there was a spirit (jini). She explained it to me as follows:

> There is a spirit there, it lives there, there is a person who has bound his spirit in there (amefunga jini lake hapo). Once someone asked me how it is possible that I wake up every day even though it is known that there are powers of darkness (nguvu za giza) that frighten people here. I told her that I have not seen them, because when I wake up, I wake up with Jesus in my soul, and when I go, I sing [hymns] in my heart. Well, one day I went, I don't know, it wanted to try me, I went. Tsah! I saw a loooong thing . . . aah! It was that giant that I have been told of, that's what it was. I said, "I tell you, vanish, in the name of Jesus," just like that, "Vanish, in the name of Jesus." . . . I did not see it here, it turned there, and when I looked [again], it had moved to my back. It said that "the one on my back, you will die, absolutely." I told it, "Vanish." I walked away. Looking back I did not see anything.

I arrived and called my friend, we go [to the market], and I tell her: "I see. Today I have been tried! People have been telling me that there is a giant there, and me, I have denied it, but today I have seen it." She asked me why I did not run away. I said that I did not run because I was with Jesus, I did not even get frightened, only a bit to see it, to . . . throw the blood of Jesus at it; it was finished *(liliisha)*, it turned away, and it vanished to that side, and I continued walking ahead. Now until this day I have not seen it again, and when I pass there, I say that it is Jesus who passes by here, and may all let me pass here, and nobody pass me.

But later that thing turned into a snake. . . . I tell you, Jesus is surprising! The day before yesterday I was going to the market. I woke up at quarter to five in the morning. I went here to the front [of the house], and I jumped up! There is a thing that comes towards me, it's a snake, a snake, aaah! It's night, I almost stepped on it, I said, "Jesus, Jesus help me." I jumped, and it passed there, there, there [going away], a big snake.[2]

Upendo showed me the place where people used to meet the spirit. It was a spot on the nearby path lined with tall grass. She said that her husband encountered the spirit every day at that place, especially if he was coming home somewhat late. In order to avoid the spirit, the husband often chose to take a longer way. I asked Upendo what the danger was in meeting with such a spirit. "It can enter you," she said, "and you can go crazy." Upendo said that she always reminds her husband that a strong faith in God protected one from such things as witchcraft and spirits. "For if you love Jesus absolutely, absolutely there is nothing that can enter you, absolutely," she assured me.[3]

According to Upendo, this spirit was originally acquired by one person in the neighborhood in order to "bring him property" *(alilileta ili limwingizie mali).* She continued: "It made property enter, but [it also] destroys his things, his children are not nice. It only strolls around. He cannot return it any more . . . it only rambles there on the road."[4] Upendo said that this person is "only a young man [*kijana tu*]; he has five children."[5] He used to be employed by a company in Nairobi, but had returned to live in his house in Mayanka. There the spirit started to harass him *(kumsumbua)* and he had to flee to Nairobi, where, however, the spirit increasingly persecuted him.

In another story, the old motif of Chagga men killing Maasai is blended with this newer means of acquiring wealth. A woman told about a man who had bought a spirit to enhance his business in Nairobi. The spirit also helped the man kill Maasai so that he could take their cattle and sell the skins. Having become rich, the man donated 300,000 TZS to his home church in Mayanka. After this donation, a strange apparition began to appear in the church, however; each morning the church caretaker saw a Maasai man with a rifle there. Seconds later the vision would disappear. As this continued, the priest decided to return the money to its donor.

The woman who told me about this said that since then the donor "has become totally lost, he does not have a house, no money, not even clothes, and his wife . . . their condition is bad; they will die."[6] I asked the woman what she meant by this, and she explained that the couple was somewhere in Nairobi, the man had lost all his money, the house in Mayanka was closed down and its surroundings were overgrown with grass. Nobody can sleep in their house in Mayanka because the spirits make an awful noise inside.

## CONDITIONS OF THE SPIRIT PACT

The relation of a man to a purchased spirit imitates the reciprocal relations between man and his wife. As a man "places his wife in" a house, so can a man "close a spirit in the house" or "domesticate" it. Yet, as it is a spiritual force expected to bring protection or prosperity, a bought spirit is also like an ancestor. As a man is to "feed" his wife and his ancestors in return for domestic continuity and prosperity, so he is to "feed" a bought spirit regularly. The crucial difference is that a spirit is only satisfied with human blood. Acquiring a spirit is believed to require a conscious pact to sacrifice closely related people's blood and life for the success of the one that acquired it.

After an initial success, however, a spirit pact is always described as developing into a disaster. According to the stories, in the beginning a bought spirit is content with the blood of more distant relatives, but gradually starts to demand the blood of people ever more closely related to its owner. Characteristically, cooperation between the spirit and its owner ends as the spirit begins to insist on getting the blood of the man's first-born son. As any man finds consenting to this demand impossible, the spirit becomes furious; it "turns against" *(linageuka)* its owner and starts to destroy his life. The lesson of the stories is that even though they imitate the forms and value of the marital and ancestral relationships, bought spirits are ultimately incompatible with and antagonistic to them.

A Chagga girl gave me a telling summary of the process, requirements, and outcome of the spirit business. She told me the story of two men who traveled to the coastal town of Tanga because they wanted to buy a spirit and become rich. The anonymous and insubstantial character of the seller, the location, and the whole transaction process as described in the girl's account reveal the sense of an abstract and asocial power that purchased spirits are about.

As the two men arrived at the address in Tanga that had been given to them, they found a large, empty, and dim room; without seeing anyone, they heard a macabre voice (the girl lowered her voice to a dark and ominous tone when explaining this) echoing in the room, asking each of them separately, "Young man, do you want riches?" *(Kijana, unataka utajiri?)* The voice repeated the question a few times and required the men to answer each time, as if to confirm their seriousness. Since the men had answered in the positive, the voice proceeded to give instructions. "Kill your child, or your wife, or your father, or your mother, or your agnatic relative," it commanded. Hearing this, one of the men retreated from his plan, while the other one went ahead with his own. He killed one of his brother's children and became very rich. Finally the man could not fulfill the spirit's further demands, however, for which "the spirit beat him badly and that man has really been tormented."[7] The girl told how the man fell to the ground as the spirit beat him, leaving him so crippled he was unable to walk anymore.

## Mobility and Stability in a Man's Lifecycle

### Mobility and Obstacles to It

The stories related above reflect the desires and failures inherent in Chagga men "straddling" (Cowen 1981) their home community and the outside world. These desires and failures are expressed by the recurring notions of mobility and what I will term "blockage," and the notions of staying and vanishing. These are not simply fixed oppositions; they are linked to the entire male life trajectory and the process of attaining full personhood. Mobility is desirable for young and middle-aged men, but in his old age a man should become more stable. The death, illness, or impoverishment of a man who should be at the height of his advancement is an unwanted blockage and hampers his potential for self-realization and achieving the final state of stability—that of a man who has achieved wealth and respect in his old age, and final rest in the family grave.[8]

Any restriction on a man's actual physical mobility is frequently considered to signal a broader limitation on his possibilities for self-realization. The deterioration of a man's feet or legs and his capacity to walk is often interpreted to be the effect of external agency. The suspected agent in such a situation can be a woman seeking to control the man and his wealth, or perhaps an envious man who wants to stop another's advancement, or even a dissatisfied spirit, as the above account described.

The different forms of physical mobility in the stories also symbolize men's differing possibilities for advancement. It has been customary that when a person comes home to visit after being away, the relatives ask for a present by saying, "Let's lick your shoe [clean]."[9] A woman translated that to mean, "Let's wipe off the dust that came with you." A man explained that it implied a request to share in any success a person had achieved with the shoes that enabled him to go away. Today, however, "shoes" and "walking" often represent poverty and failed self-realization in comparison to "cars," the modern way of moving about. Thus a man's indigent condition is frequently expressed by saying that "he walks," or worse still, that he does not even own shoes.

The accounts of a prosperous man's life history often include the telling of how he gained and lost cars, where the changing number, model, and condition of those cars indicate his rising or declining success. In their capacity for embodying a biography and epitomizing social identities and inequalities, cars can be likened to what the Comaroffs (1992) have described as the fetishized or commodity nature of cattle. Yet cars are also different in that they are seen as a more fleeting and individual form of wealth than cattle, thus sharing characteristics associated with money.

The symbolic capacity of motor vehicles to condense power and social difference between men is seen in Isak's story. Isak's truck made him feel mighty and enabled him to realize his plans or intentions to kill his "lesser" that "walks"—the Maasai men and his wife's lover. Right after he hits and kills his brother with his truck, Isak abandons the vehicle. After that there is no mention of it or of his cattle business in the accounts; he turns into a pitiful and miserable man whose downfall and turning-inward is evinced by his walking on the local roads talking to himself, and fighting with invisible forces. Having turned inward and to the spirit world, Isak was no longer a fully able social person related to the surrounding world.

Cars also frequently appear as mediators of death. Car accidents are common in real life, but in narratives they also symbolize the vulnerability of a man's success or the illegitimacy of it. For instance, the way in which the outside witness of Ruben's will, the affluent businessman, had died in a sudden car accident was seen as a metaphor of his history. As he was driving home from a lavish party, full of high spirits and on the move—advancing and dynamic like his career—his car suddenly went off the road, ended up in a ditch and he was killed. That was the abrupt end of his mobility and life; as the driver—or as the bribed witness who selfishly valued money more than the rights of other people?—he was the agent of his own death.

In addition to the deterioration of physical mobility, the decline of a man's intellectual and verbal abilities is often interpreted as a sign that his advancement in life is impeded. Because a person's mind is an important asset that makes his advancement possible in the first place, destroying his intelligence—making a man "stupid" (mjinga)—necessarily leads to his decline. Such is often thought to be the outcome of a woman "binding" a man, as discussed previously.

Even more than feet, mind, and ability to speak, the typical targets of those wishing to do a man ill from afar, the stomach serves as an overall metaphor for the nature and quality of a man's social relations. Problems in relating to others are typically expressed as digestive defects. Instead of a tranquil blending of the inner and outer substances bringing about nurturance and growth, food or drink in problem cases creates disturbances, such as vomiting or blockage in the intestines. Just as sharing food is a sign of an intimate and trustworthy relationship, succumbing to poisoned food or drink indicates the victim's mistaken trust in the one he eats or drinks with.[10] The symptoms, as they are interpreted, replicate in the body the specific nature of the problem in the victim's social relations. Whereas poisoned food or drink is typically believed to cause lesions in the intestines (utumbo umekatika), the cause for an intestinal blockage is more likely found in a curse. The image of intestines full of small lesions indicates how the soundness and the bounded wholeness (uzima) of the inside of the body has been destroyed by outside forces, and reproduces on the physical plane the dangers of betrayal by another person. On the other hand, a blockage in the intestines indicates a man's too restricted flows, his unwillingness to help or support someone else, which has brought about the deprived person's curse, a counter-blockage.

Eating, thinking, talking, and walking or driving are all among the ways a person interacts with the outside world. If any of these linkages is disrupted, it causes the negative binding and immobilization of a man, in other words, a blockage. In losing his ability to relate properly and to move about, a man also loses essential aspects of his masculinity. Affluent, successful men strive to publicly display their wealth, which often most effectively takes place on roads and in public places. An untimely retreat to home by a once-affluent man reveals his shameful position and his loss of status. Indeed, the expression siku hizi anakaa nyumbani tu, or, "nowadays he only stays at home," summarizes the deep humiliation of a once-prosperous and well-known man, who should still be in his prime.

### Staying and Vanishing

As he enters old age, a man ideally settles down and is able to transform his riches into more enduring wealth. At the same time, his dynamism and ability to move and relate tend to become inner qualities, indeed they become part of his person, as through his accrued wisdom, experience, and knowledge he begins to mediate the problems of the wider community. It is usual for an old Chagga man to sit daily on a chair in front of his house, his face motionless and firm, leaning on his walking stick. In becoming such a focal point that attracts other people to him, he has already started to resemble the respected immobility of the ancestors and the patrilineal land[11]—and Mount Kibo (see e.g., Gutmann 1926, 571).[12] This positive immobility is expressed by the notions of staying, remaining, and living (kukaa/kuishi); it is revealed in "cool" peacefulness, and is the prerequisite for fertility and continuity.[13]

According to the stories, such stability is unobtainable when illegitimate means of enrichment are used. In those cases, a man is instead doomed to restlessness and endless mobility, consumption rather than generation, which finally leads to his destruction, vanishing and dying away *(kupotea/ kuishia)*[14] as well as that of his descendants. In the older stories his downfall results from the curse or the spirit of the wronged person (as in the stories of Ruben and Isak and their sons, for example). Bought spirits are believed to lead to comparable restlessness.

The stories about bought spirits often emphasize the difficulty of sleeping in a house that was built with money acquired with spirit help. These stories parallel older stories about uninhabitable land. Both the young and the old in Mayanka know to tell about certain *vihamba* that are taboo *(mwiko)*. They have been acquired by fraud, depriving *(kurusha)*[15] the rightful owner, usually an agnatic relative. The deprived person "leaves certain words" *(anaacha maneno fulani)*—a curse, in other words—typically by saying "This *shamba* will grow millet." It means the land is cultivable, but no one can live on it. Should anyone try to sleep in a house on that land, that person will either find himself sleeping outside in the middle of the night, or he will be beaten badly *(anapigwa)* during the night. Any animal or human who tries to sleep there will eventually die. The form of the curse expresses the wish for restlessness and mobility. Already the naming of the plot as *shamba* and not patrilineal *kihamba* land refers to its unstable character. Accordingly, instead of the customary perennial trees of the *kihamba*— bananas and coffee—the curse states the wish for only the typical *shamba* crop, millet, to be cultivated on the land.[16] Millet, as a key ingredient of *mbege,* is an important part of customary exchanges and thus represents mobility in and of itself.

Contemporary stories about the turmoil that purchased spirits can cause in a house seem imaginative applications of the stories about uninhabitable land.[17] As opposed to such a collective and inheritable asset as land, bought spirits are believed to reside in the primary manifestations of individual accomplishment, such as a house or car. While meant to display a man's success and enhance his status, these possessions can thus escape his control and come to reveal the immoral quality of his person and actions in the outside world. Through the interpreted events, a house and the ancestral grave are likened to each other, with the grave only a more permanent structure, the very final resting or sleeping place, and the house a kind of preceding form and another expression of the stability that the grave symbolizes. Restful sleeping in a house serves as a sign of both the quality of the homeowner's past deeds and of his future lying in the grave. In this light, a house is a kind of junction in time.

There are certain differences in the forms and outcomes of the different means of illegitimate enrichment, however. While appropriation of land, stealing, and killing require the manipulation of personal relations—that is, these acts require some kind of interaction or contact between the actual people involved—acquiring a spirit takes place by means of a more abstract and impersonal monetary transaction. Even though initially easier, buying a spirit is even more immoral than other means because it entails a conscious and calculated deal to sacrifice the lives of closely related people for one's own success.

A further difference is found in the various forms of "vanishing." In older stories vanishing takes the form of untimely death, insanity, life by theft, and an overall, yet relatively local, restlessness, whereas in the bought-spirit stories a man's family vanishes to the place where the riches were first illegitimately acquired, like Nairobi or Dar es Salaam. They thus become invisible to their home community in Kilimanjaro. Local people get only occasional reports about them, that they have been seen somewhere. The reports typically describe how the family was only fleetingly seen, passing by some place, and usually in a miserable condition. In town they are believed not to have any proper and permanent work or place to live; instead, they are said to wander around, "lost" *(wamepotea)*. These accounts thus produce an image of how these people's presence and corporeality have turned into vulnerable, shadowlike flickering, and ceaseless mobility. In their restless wandering and ethereal being, they have begun to resemble the tormented spirits of the dead people who did not die properly and thus did not become ancestors either, but instead stay hovering among the living. On the other hand, they also resemble the passing and abstract character and value of money.

There is thus a distinction between the older and newer stories in the material, social, and spatial "boundedness" of the means and outcomes of wrongful acquisition. Buying a spirit is an attempt to create value and spiritual protection from outside the familiar context; with new means, but transformed into customary forms of wealth. The new means and the outcomes remain more invisible and abstract than in the older cases of stealing, killing, and land appropriation.

## Money, Markets, and Sociality

### Spirits, Curses, and Poisoning

Both the older means of illegitimate enrichment—land appropriation, stealing, and killing—and the newer one—buying a spirit—are comparable in that they ultimately harm not only the wrongdoer himself, but also his close, most often his agnatic, relatives. In the stories, these agnatic relatives are either the very people the man deprives of rights or property (Ruben's case and land appropriation cases), or they come to share the disastrous outcomes of the man's immoral deeds, however unwittingly (Isak's case and bought-spirit cases). Even an individualistic man's person is thus entangled with those of his close relatives. There are, however, important differences in these older and newer forms of entanglement, especially in the conceived possibilities for action and the correction of people involved.

In cases of stealing, killing, and land appropriation, the wrongdoer's demise is caused by his agnatic relative's curse or a spiritual affliction. This kind of agency by a wronged person is considered rightful retaliation. In cases of bought spirits, by contrast, the people involved do not finally have any possibility for action, either correction or retribution. After consuming the more distant relatives' blood, the spirit finally destroys its owner and his male children. And the damage often affects a wider circle of people than the close agnatic relatives, as also the spirit-acquirer's wife and innocent neighbors are caused to suffer by the voracious spirit lurking along their paths.

One woman aptly described this difference when she said that acquiring *majini* always turns out to be a losing proposition because they are not human beings *(binadamu);* for this reason one cannot negotiate with them, and can only acquiesce to their demands or else suffer persecution at their spiritual hands. The nonnegotiable and unconditional quality of communication with a purchased spirit is conveyed in the term used for its demands: such a spirit is said to present its "stipulations" *(masharti)*. In its uncompromising demands and reactions, a bought spirit contrasts with the afflicting powers of the curses and the spirits of the people who have been wronged.

Unlike the pact with a bought spirit, a curse is not usually absolutely unconditional; it is rather a threat or a sanction. In the lineage I know best it is even written as a "law" *(sheria)* that a person should not curse someone else secretly but should do so publicly amongst relatives in order to give that person the possibility of making amends before it is too late—that is, after the death of the person who uttered the curse (see also S. F. Moore 1986, 369). In that sense, a curse or spiritual affliction, adjudged by one human being and caused by the action of another human being, is dependent on the actions, discretion, and reflection of the people involved—their very humanity.

There is also a moral difference between curses and witchcraft. While a curse is considered a public and legitimate form of exerting power, witchcraft is seen as secretive and illegitimate. Indeed, using witchcraft is frequently considered a sign of a lack of civilization and development *(maendeleo)*, belonging to the "matters of darkness" *(mambo ya giza)*. As such, it can be ascribed to any areas or people regarded as less developed, and often it is used to draw a moral distinction between themselves and other ethnic groups, especially the Islamic people on the coast.[18] Thus, while pronouncing curses is considered the major supernatural force used by the Chagga themselves in Kilimanjaro, witchcraft is believed to be the main force used off the mountain, among certain other ethnic groups, and especially in the

Islamic world. Indeed, the new bought spirits, *majini,* were invariably believed to be acquired from off the mountain, and it was common for people to claim that all of them were of Islamic or Arabic origin.

In addition to the curse, the other customary way to harm another person in Kilimanjaro is through the use of poison in food or drink. In comparison to bought spirits, cursing and poisoning are socially more restricted forms of power. Poison necessitates physical proximity. A curse is often generational and hierarchical in that typically an older person utters it against his or her junior.[19] Finally, the affliction that a curse, human spirit, or poisoning causes does not usually extend beyond the target and his or her descendants, whereas an infuriated bought spirit is ultimately dangerous for anyone it encounters.

In her research in Kilimanjaro in the 1970s, Swantz (1985, 88–91) found an interesting shift in the explanations of illness and misfortune. This was a move from curse to the use of harmful medicines, and as the newest innovation, a type of sorcery called *mafusa.* This form of spell-casting requires the sorcerer to acquire some of the victim's hair, urine, excrement, or a piece of clothing belonging to that person. Since *mafusa* is a more individualized way of affliction than the older forms, Swantz interprets the shift as an expression of social structural changes, such as increasing individualization, on the one hand, and growing importance of nuclear families, on the other. I will return to this issue later. Based on her fieldwork in Kilimanjaro from the end of the 1960s until the mid-1980s, S. F. Moore (1986, 299) also mentions that the methods of supernatural vengeance usually require some form of contact with the victim. *Majini* are different in this respect, expressing a more abstract and socially unbounded kind of power.

Not only generalized in their ultimate threat to the larger community, *majini* are beyond sociospatial boundaries in that anyone—even "young" men (as Upendo described her neighbor)—with money and means can acquire them and subsequently send them to afflict a victim. In addition to purposes of enrichment, it is held that a spirit can be bought in order to torment someone, which is accomplished by "sending" *(kutuma)* it to the targeted person. The transmission can supposedly be done with a glance, from a distance, at the victim. Yet, there are accounts where even this relative physical closeness is not required; a person can allegedly buy a "spirit," say, in Mwanza and "send" it immediately to afflict someone else in Dar es Salaam, hundreds of kilometers away. The amazing speed and invisibility of the spirit's transfer and the overall immateriality that is associated with such spirits expresses the sense of omnipotent, capricious, and antisocial power. *Majini,* as things bought with money and capable of transforming their material form, and taking on a life of their own, seem to represent the quintessence of an alienated commodity.

## Money and Individualism

The stories about bought spirits tell thus of power that is unconstrained by customary social considerations and boundaries. They convey a vision of a world where both success and affliction—the means to attain and destroy the highest ambitions of a Chagga man—can be bought with money. Studies from different parts of Africa have noted capitalist overtones in current witchcraft discourses. Whereas a "customary" witch or sorcerer aims to completely consume ("eat") his or her victim, newer witches are said, for instance, to change their victims into zombies that work for them in plantations, or go to the "market of sorcery," or sell their victims or their blood.[20] Writers such as Comaroff and Comaroff (1993) and Geschiere (2000 [1997]) have suggested that conceptions of witchcraft and sorcery in contemporary Africa are invoked to interpret new inequalities, new forms of power and their drastic consequences for local relations. With their obvious emphasis on individual accumulation, the discussions are readily related to increasing individualism, a capitalist worldview, and the immoral economy of modernity (e.g., Comaroff and Comaroff 1993, xxv; Swantz 1985, 88 – 91). Such stories are not necessarily a recent innovation, however. The older legacy of such images is revealed, for instance, by the "vampire stories" that arose in East and Central Africa during colonial times (White 2000).[21] For this reason, and because they are narratives, it is difficult to regard such stories as a direct window on increasing capitalism, individualism, or postcolonial modernity.

Other scholars have emphasized that money and other outside forces are rather subsumed to the local social order and cultural understandings (e.g., Parry and Bloch 1989; Englund 1996; Green 1997). Interestingly, even though the Chagga are famous for their early and easy acceptance of money and the "Protestant spirit" preached by the missionaries, money and its particular qualities certainly play an important role in the imaginings revealed by these stories. In Kilimanjaro, the present perceptions of money seem indeed more controversial than the relatively easy acceptance and convertibility described, for instance, for the Bemba (Moore and Vaughan 1994, 156 –64) or the Dedza villagers in Malawi (Englund 1996). Among the Chagga, money is clearly seen as a potentially individual, individualizing, and fluid resource—in both its real and social value.[22] More frequently than not, money forms a "domain of contestation" (Ferguson, 1985, 656 –57).

It is the invisibility and unpredictable value of money that contributes to the creation of the stories and their concerns. Yet this should not be confused with the "invisible hand" of money and markets. Money and commodities are acted on and their meanings are continuously defined and transformed through different means of conceptual and semantic conversions (cf. Werbner 1989, 69). For instance, money and commodities are frequently converted into gifts, because they are seen as connecting people in a way that money cannot. If money is given instead of gift item, people still frequently conceptually convert the money into a giftlike thing by naming the purpose for which it is intended when they give it.

Another example of such semantic conversion of money to more socially acceptable purposes is the current reasoning for selling a domestic animal such as a cow. S. F. Moore (1986, 215) reports a strong expectation that animals are to be kept for sharing meat and not for the purpose of selling them. In the mid-1990s, it was quite widely accepted that animals provided a form of property that could be turned into money, but the sense persisted that that was appropriate only in order to meet necessary or urgent family needs, such as children's school fees and clothes, or to cover the expenses of hospital treatments or a customary feast. Meat-sharing expectations are nowadays often met by the distribution of small portions of meat to the closest relatives after taking a cow to a butcher and receiving the bulk of its value back in cash with only a few kilos of meat. Although this had become quite the usual practice, people still felt the need to explain the reason for turning livestock into money. The most common and legitimate reason—children's school fees—is already a socially more restricted purpose than the meat needs and rights of an extended family or a larger lineage. Furthermore, quite diverse requirements could be included in the category of urgent and necessary needs; for instance, livestock might be sold to replenish trading capital.

It would therefore be wrong to separate gift and commodity logics as Taylor (1992, 6) does, for instance, when writing: "Visible hands manipulate gifts; an 'invisible hand,' the market, manipulates money and commodities." Instead, there is a constant conversion and conversation about the meaning of money and the morality of its use. Even though part of the conceptual conversion is a matter of rhetoric, it is significant that explanations for money and its use are persistently expected and given. Together with fancy houses, cars, and other commodities, money is often experienced as a different and socially more ambiguous resource than, for instance, land, cattle, and food.[23]

There is a dimension of gender-specificity in the need for conversion of individually earned money into more social assets, however. It is considered more natural for men to possess even relatively large sums of money, and displaying their riches by means of consumption, redistribution, and different forms of immobilization is a crucial part of how men build their status. In contrast, women are not expected to hold significant sums of money, and if they do, they generally keep it more concealed than do men. The market women's conversations and their persistent conceptual conversion of money, profit, capital, and trading into social assets and goals speak also of this relative unacceptability of women's accumulation of money compared to men. The somewhat problematic relation between women and "loose" money was once expressed by a three-year-old girl known for her wittiness and expressiveness who suddenly jumped up in the middle of a meal, and made a small performance, saying that if she only saw money, she would immediately hide it (embracing the fictitious money with her arms), and repeating this notion by saying that if she managed to find some money, she would conceal it at once (carrying make-believe money into a cupboard and closing it tightly).

Because of the increased importance of money in comparison to the more customary forms of assets in Kilimanjaro, the world may indeed seem to have become less predictable and less stable. The interpreted life histories emphasize and reiterate the human agency involved in the processes of making and using money, however. The moral accountability in the stories about bought spirits and other forms of illegitimate enrichment derives from the fact that a man is thought to make critical decisions about how he acquires and uses his money. The stories warn that a man who fails to control his desires and possessions—and his women—ends up becoming controlled and consumed by them. The above stories are finally more about men imagined as commoditized and alienated rather than about money and commodities per se. These men become blinded by their desire for success and its trappings, to the extent that they come to identify with and ultimately vanish along with those mere outward indications. They become as antisocial, programmed, and mechanical as bought spirits or any "alienated" commodity.

Because of the acknowledged human responsibility, the crucial question is therefore not only the inherent moral quality of the means, money, or modern commodities in and of themselves, but about ambitious men's relations to these things and to other people. What is experienced as dangerous and threatening on the communal level is the power of those with money to transform and disrupt the basic conditions of life and its continuation. For instance, the hungry spirit's ability to go anywhere, to "enter anyone it happens to like," and to torment whomever happens to get in its way can be read as an imaginative expression of the overall power that rich men can exert both in the local world and elsewhere. An affluent man's power is often expressed as his ability to pick up any woman who appears in his line of sight and whom he happens to like.[24] And his withdrawal of support from a former dependent can cause major problems in that person's life.

## "Businessmen" and Sociability

The stories I heard in Mayanka often portrayed "businessmen" as especially prone to use immoral means of enrichment, while "educated men" were more often portrayed as adequate in their moral quality. Whereas stories about businessmen depicted their various downfalls as often having been self-induced, stories about educated men portrayed them more often as victims of other people's jealousies and manipulations.

Setel (1996, 1174) also notes the prevalent, disparaging opinions of businessmen in Kilimanjaro. In the area where he did his research, men's productive labor fit into a moral hierarchy where the activity with the highest social value was farming, and the lowest was business. He relates these views to the changing base of productive life in Kilimanjaro—basically the lack of land that forces young men to move away to town. By doing so they become stigmatized, seen as people not engaged in proper work, as people wasting their energy in sexual excess and subsequently spreading the HIV virus on the mountain.

The relative lack of local means for enrichment certainly forms part of the larger context for these attitudes. However, the shortage of land and the need to search for ways to earn a living outside the rural area are not recent phenomena and cannot thus alone account for the rather heated moral discussions that businessmen often arouse. The older stories in this chapter also indicate that negative attitudes towards businessmen have a longer history. As for opinions about contemporary businessmen, the era of liberalization and its consequences also play a part.

There are different strands in attitudes towards "businessmen" that, even though based on perceptions of certain similar dishonest and impatient tendencies, relate to the different scales of business and wealth. In the case of young men who come and go restlessly on the mountain, explaining vaguely that they are "busy" with their businesses, the disparaging tone used by others expresses the suspicion that such people are not occupied with anything respectable and are using "business" as a cover for obscure activities. When used disparagingly of a relatively established, prosperous man who lives in one of the major towns, the term "businessman" refers to differences in relative wealth between Chagga men, which is often simultaneously a spatial distinction between rural and urban.

The economic and political liberalization measures were started after the election of a new leader, President Ali Hassan Mwinyi, in 1985. Due to the liberalization policies, Ali Hassan Mwinyi was soon nicknamed "Mr. Permit" (Mzee Ruksa) among the Tanzanian people. Ten years after, aside from the enhanced opportunities, the era of liberalization was considered a time when corruption and individual profit-making had become increasingly reckless and blessed by the regime.[25] A Chagga man in Mayanka exclaimed in 1994 that, "During the Mwinyi time EVERYTHING became permissible!" Another local man explained that rich Chagga people in the 1990s, especially those living in Dar es Salaam, started to arrange big feasts and ceremonies in order to compete in "prestige" *(fahari)*, because they had earned money through improper means *(njia zisizofaa)* and did not know how else to use all that amassed wealth. Other frequent comments like "all those who have been able to build a modern house are thieves," or, "the rich think only of themselves," are internal criticisms of those Chagga men who were able to amass and consume money during the Mwinyi era.

In addition to businesspeople in general, Muslims *(waislamu)* in Tanzania were believed to have benefited under the Mwinyi regime. This was an attitude shared by many Christians in Tanzania beyond Kilimanjaro; as a Zanzibari and a Muslim himself, the president was believed to favor Muslims. Antagonistic attitudes towards Muslims gained momentum especially after Zanzibar's controversial accession to the Organization of the Islamic Conference in 1993. The membership was eventually declared illegal under the Tanzanian constitution, but the incident widened the religious rift between Christians and Muslims in the country. Being a strongly Christian area, the religious antagonism is of longer standing in Kilimanjaro, yet it did become more emphasized there during the Mwinyi era also (see e.g., Samoff 1974, 48–49, 166–68). In the mid-1990s, there were rumors circulating the mountain about alleged sabotage attempts by Muslims against some Roman Catholic and Lutheran schools and churches.[26] It was also common for preachers in their church services to illuminate Christian conduct and values by didactic stories where more or less fictive Muslims served as antagonists to those values.

As mentioned earlier, in Kilimanjaro bought spirits were most often considered to be of Islamic or Arabic origin, and people were believed to acquire them from the Islamic areas in Tanzania in particular. Many people related the appearance of *majini* to the mid-1980s, that is, to the liberalization era. The stories about bought spirits combine thus several phenomena perceived as threatening contemporary life and order; the liberalization era, the corruptly rich Chagga, and the increasing Islamic influence. The stories express an image of contemporary Chagga businessmen interacting with occult forces on the Islamic coast. In allying themselves with the outside, and with what for many Chagga represents the utmost other—the Islamic world—these men are depicted as becoming strangers dangerous to their home communities and values. Rather than the Islamic influence itself, the most profound concern here is about the seeming alienation of the rich Chagga men from their home communities and values. Indeed, the stories do not simply reflect the prevailing political and economic situation. In what follows, I will deal with the symbolic and political dimensions of the stories and their idioms.

## The Morality of Enrichment

### Forms of Enrichment as Moral Categories

More than starkly distinguishing what is proper labor and what is not, such terms as "businessmen," "education," and "cultivation" are also moral categories that are used to discuss the morally differing ways of life and relationships that ultimately embrace more than the factual contents of "business" or "cultivation."

In Mayanka, there was often a discrepancy between the reality and the statements about "cultivation." As discussed earlier, women often preferred to call themselves "cultivators" rather than "traders." In fact, cultivation had not been an ideal form of male labor for quite some time; in my census of a hundred households only the old men—in addition to women—named "cultivation" as their primary occupation. The respectability of cultivation is related to the symbolic value of the continuity of land and lineage, however, and involves a generational and gendered order. As a moral category, "cultivation" refers to the mutual fostering and reciprocity that creates lasting value among both agnatic and affinal relatives. Like cultivation, education requires a person's patient effort and is a slow form of advancement.

The moral ordering of different kinds of labor in Kilimanjaro echoes both Christian ethics and some of the government rhetoric of the socialist era. After the Arusha Declaration of 1967,[27] the government emphasized agricultural work as truly productive labor. This culminated in two government campaigns during 1983 and 1984 called "The War Against Economic Sabotage" and "The Human Resources Deployment Act," also known as *Nguvu Kazi* ("Hard Work"). While the former was intended to prevent black market entrepreneurs from hoarding currency and goods, the latter aimed to relocate the urban unemployed—many of whom were active in the informal sector—back to the rural areas (Kerner 1988). On the national level, these campaigns and their rhetoric was about the competition over labor and the government's attempt to harness and secure labor for cash-crop production. Comparably, in the Kilimanjaro area the moral ordering of different kinds of labor is employed in managing local gendered and generational relations. The ideas and notions are intertwined with Chagga moral imagination about what is generative, however.

Both cultivation and education are thought to require and foster certain morally positive qualities in a person. I once asked two men why education continues to be valued even though it did not necessarily bring either employment or riches anymore. After a thoughtful silence, one said that educated people are often really not affluent, giving as contrasting examples a few educated, but relatively poor men and several uneducated, but prosperous businessmen. The second man said that education brings intelligence (*akili*) rather than profit (*faida*). Both men went on to explain that an educated person understands how to clothe his or her children well, and see that they are clean and eat properly. This comment emphasizes the moral distinction between profit (*faida*), money, and business, on the one hand, to education, intellect, and children's well-being, on the other.

The intelligence (*akili*) required for illegitimate forms of enrichment is thought to be different from that entailed in cultivation and education. Instead of fostering the well-being of surrounding people, the intellect needed in illegitimate forms of activity takes advantage of other people's lives and efforts. In the stories, such activities included stealing, killing, the appropriation of another person's land, and acquiring spirits for enrichment. The terms "business" and "businessmen" in themselves have come to include connotations of such illegitimate tendencies. Already the word "profit" (*faida*)—which market women do not like to use—carries the implication of making use of other people.

Interestingly, part of the disparagement of "businessmen" derives from the sense that these men, even though affluent, were neither intelligent nor patient enough to continue with their studies. Thus, even though the popular criticism of both trading women and businessmen is based on their allegedly appropriative tendencies, there are differences in the conceived forms of appropriation. Whereas any success in trading by women is thought to require cunning and an accumulation of knowledge, such qualities are not similarly ascribed to businessmen. Men's illegitimate means of enrichment do not require the indirect, clever, and circumspect ways that are seen as characteristic of the illegitimate means used by female traders, but are based on quite straightforward acts of appropriation: stealing, killing, and buying (a spirit). This distinction is also evident in the popular conceptualization that likens women's trading to attending school, whereas "businessmen" are characterized by their very lack of education and sophisticated knowledge. This distinction reflects in part the fact that women, whose positions in society often still depend on their relationships to men, have to negotiate and seek out less direct ways of achieving economic success than men do.

What is common for such categories as "thief," "killer," and the current notion of "businessmen" is the idea that instead of creating, generating, and redistributing value, these types of persons destroy other people's real value. In that respect, these categories become similar to the category of "witch." Taylor (1992, 13) has remarked that the "commodity system's maximizing individualist is the gift system's witch" (see also Englund 1996, Piot 1999). Individual accumulation is indeed conceptualized as a form of blockage to its social surroundings and is contrasted with processes of composite growth (cf. Guyer and Belinga 1995, 108), as represented by the categories of cultivation and education in the case of Chagga men. It is, however, important to realize the moral nature of the categories and stories; it would be too easy to say that the stories testify to a clash between two different economic logics in which the gift system is giving way to the commodity system.

## Moral Economy in the Era of Liberalization

Geschiere (2000 [1997]) could well be describing Kilimanjaro instead of Cameroon when he says that occult forces are considered not only the weapon of the poor, but also the secret reason for the success of the newly rich. It is for this reason that witchcraft and sorcery continue to serve so well as idioms for the increasing disparities in wealth. Geschiere discovered a persistent link between witchcraft and kin in the Cameroonian cases that he studied. Even though in Kilimanjaro the concerns of agnatic relatives particularly seem to prevail and are conveyed in the stories, there is also a sense of an increased impersonality and the inability of kin to contain the new forces that the *majini* stories tell about.

A sense of increasingly reckless individualism and escape from the social conventions by ambitious men permeates conversations in Kilimanjaro. The fact that current forms of illegitimate enrichment are believed to be exposed in the primary expressions of personal success (such as cars and houses) reinforces this perception. Indeed, conceptions such as *majini* and "businessmen" include connotations that seem quintessentially to be about commoditization, individualization, and capitalist attitudes. However, stories cannot be understood as direct reflections of such processes; rather storytellers attempt to interpret and manage developments that are more complex and local than global capitalism, commoditization, or modernity. The stories deal with the repercussions of the increased mobility and liberties on sociability, social order, and the continuation of life and lineage on the mountain.

The life stories told and retold in small circles reflect on and try to reveal the secret means of the rich—"secret" in that they are being undertaken outside the rural home, are in monetary form, and often allegedly involve witchcraft. The stories are also attempts to control and contain the processes of making and displaying wealth by bringing them into semipublic contemplation. By reminding others that selfish accumulation and negligence are by necessity short-lived, the stories are attempts to persuade ambitious men to domesticate and share their flows of wealth.

Equally as important, the stories are about status. The persistent moral ordering of "education" above "business" reminds us that status hierarchies do not simply follow changing economic hierarchies. Economic prosperity is not directly translated into acknowledged social position and status; "businessmen" might have money, but they must still convince their home communities of their moral worth. Even labeling the acquirers of *majini* as *vijana* ("youth") is a way of subordinating them to the generational order, of calling them "minors." Furthermore, the threatening power of the curse has not withered away, even though bought spirits and acquired witchcraft in general are believed to have become more prevalent than ever before. People of very different ages and means share a rather strong belief in the force of the elders' curse. An old mother's curse is particularly feared, often enough so to make a prosperous Chagga man move back to his rural home, or at least to send his wife there when the old need assistance.

Terms such as "education," "cultivation," *"tamaa,"* "thief," "killer," "businessman," and *"majini"* formed the language for constructing moral reputation and value in Kilimanjaro in the 1990s. These categories are used as signs, which are applied to the prevailing situation and to particular men, but they have their roots in a historically older moral imagination. Claims of individualistic aspirations and appropriative tendencies are used to denote an inversion of moral value. In this way, the categories can be compared to those of "mother," "feeding," "cultivation," "witch," "virginity," "loose women," and "binding women," the idioms that are used to discuss and construct Chagga women's moral reputation and value.

# Conclusion

Listening to gossip and other informal conversations in the mid-1990s in Kilimanjaro, one easily got the impression that the cause of moral upheaval is in the increasing importance of markets and individualistic profit-seeking attitudes—precisely the issues propelled by neoliberal policies. Much of the moral discussion revolves around the market women and businessmen and their imputed impatient and asocial urge to get rich and keep the returns to themselves. However, rather than as reflections of reality, these views are more properly seen as arguments in an ongoing moral dialogue about the nature of markets, market women, and businessmen—and about contemporary women and men more generally. The background for the current debate is to be found in the changing economy, which has led to shifts in the relations of autonomy and dependence within families and local communities. It is, however, only through the cultural debate and conceptualization of such shifts in the moral dialogue that socioeconomic transformations are ultimately made real.

In popular discussion traders and businessmen are criticized of the vices of privatization and individualism, which are often conceptualized as some kind of concealment. This is shown, for instance, in the persistent suspicion that market trading is a secretive profit-seeking exercise, and in the belief that modern houses and other extravagant signs of a man's success veil dubious or far worse means of enrichment. The controversial quality most often associated with market women is *ujanja* (cunning), which connotes circumspect and "disguised" means that women use as they generate profits from trade. These involve persuasive, seductive, and deceptive skills, expressed as "draw" *(kuvuta)*, "speech" *(mdomo,* literally "mouth"), and sometimes "binding" *(kufunga)*. In contrast, businessmen are often suspected of using much more direct methods such as "stealing" *(kuiba)*, "killing" *(kuua)* or "buying a spirit" *(kununua jini)*. People make a mental distinction between men's and women's suspect paths to success; men's crooked ways are considered to derive from and demonstrate their lack of education, while trading women's enrichment is thought to draw from their market-derived education and knowledge *(maarifa)*.

In addition to the different forms of "concealment" integral to Chagga women's trading techniques, there is also more need for women to conceal the riches they accrue than there is for men. A woman's public display of wealth is readily taken as a sign of arrogance and is considered demeaning to her husband. In contrast, a public display of wealth is essential to men for attaining acknowledged status. The gendered differences in the acquisition and display of wealth reflect the fact that women, who are economically and socially in an inferior position to men from the start, have to be circumspect and delicate in both the making and using of money.

More than simply designating behavioral and personal distinctions, in using the concepts described above people also address and discuss changing economic and gender relations. *Ujanja* reflects the current need for women to "run around"—physically, socially, and intellectually—to make a living from outside the home *kihamba*. One of the few concepts employed for both genders is *ujinga* (stupidity), the opposite of *ujanja*, which signifies inactivity and unproductive immobility. The difference is that for men this state is considered unnatural and is usually caused externally by manipulation through witchcraft or womanly devices, whereas in the case of women it connotes a reliance on men to provide in economically difficult times. A wife who mostly stays at home fulfills the expectations of female settledness, but finds often that she has serious problems in fulfilling her wifely and motherly responsibilities of feeding her children and family. The trading women especially contrast the stay-at-home women's "naiveté" and "stupidity" with their own "experience" *(uzoefu)* and "cunning" as accrued through their economic activities outside the home.

Similar distinctions are found in other parts of Africa with different results. Among the Asante in Ghana, for instance, women who stay at home
and do not involve themselves in market trading are also considered "stupid." However, a woman's attachment to home, husband and marriage is
also disparaged as being self-indulgent and oriented towards sexual pleasure, whereas trading is considered a natural female occupation and a way
for a woman to provide for her children (Clark 1999). How the Asante associate marriage and pleasure, on the one hand, and trading, motherhood
and work, on the other, differs from the contemporary concerned Chagga
view that associates market trading with women's seeking of "enjoyment."
These differences are logical in the sense that among the matrilineal Asante
a husband and wife belong to two different lineages and a wife raises her
children for the lineage she shares with her brother, whereas among the patrilineal Chagga a wife and her children are affiliated with the wife's husband's lineage. In either case, it is a woman's suspected neglect of her responsibilities and loyalties to the lineage to which she and her children are
affiliated that creates concern and complaints about her "selfishness." The
Asante moral distinction is not, however, too far distant from the one emphasized currently by the Chagga market women. Indeed, in Kilimanjaro
the contemporary market women's constant talk about feeding and motherhood emphasizes and articulates the increasing importance of alternatives to patrilineal ties, that is, the practical kinship traced through women.

As among the Chagga, so too among the Asante is capital accumulation
a gendered category that is considered a more natural aspiration for men
than for women. However, Asante gender categories and qualities appear to
be more flexible than those among the Chagga because both genders can acquire the positive qualities of the other. Fathers who devote their income to
their children, and mothers who manage to accumulate money, are called
"nursing mothers" or "motherly men" and "manly women" respectively,
without disparagement (Clark 1999, 721–23). Transference of gender qualities like this among the Chagga is much more controversial: attributing any
female quality to a man is to mock him and a woman's adoption of male
qualities is a cause for moral concern. This is even truer today, because it is
seen as an increasing trend.

The term "stupidity" especially captures the ongoing restructuring of
gender relations in Kilimanjaro. Whether applied to men or women, stupidity is often a relational term; it reflects a husband's weaker economic
status in regard to his wife, or a wife's full reliance on what her husband
provides. Indeed, women's increased economic activity, importance, and
assertiveness are reflected on through the stories of "binding," a morally
questionable form of female agency that in essence means that men are
"stupefied" by women. "Binding" is thus an image used to reflect on the

contemporary situation, in which the economic and social strength of women is perceived as emasculating to some rural men especially. The restructuring of relations between men and the challenge that urban businessmen pose to the sociocultural order is most vividly expressed in the belief that they associate with *majini,* highly potent and capricious outside forces that ultimately bring destruction to rural home lineages and communities and result in "vanishing" *(kupotea/kuisha)* rather than in the consolidation of well-being and wealth *(kukaa/kuishi).*

In stories and conversations the contemporary situation—the increasing outward orientation from the home *kihamba* and its authority structure—is depicted as not simply threatening the social order, but also the entire continuity of life. This threat is portrayed as a failure to control the processes that are needed for the orderly and safe reproduction of life such as the phases of mobility and immobility in women's and men's life trajectories. *Ujanja,* denoting mobility in itself, and *kuzurura/kuzunguka* (to roam/wander about), used for women unattached to husbands, are terms employed to reflect upon the contemporary women's perceived lack of settledness. Urban men's alleged impatience to become rich and successful translates into images of their turning into ever-circulating, homeless, alienated creatures, vanishing with their descendants from their home communities and lineages. In their instability they resemble the restless character and fleeting value of the *majini* they are believed to acquire for rapid enrichment. The "heat" that women's mobility is thought to produce and the restless flickering and "vanishing" that men's impatient actions cause are the very antithesis of the "cool" peacefulness required for ordered reproduction and growth. The opposite of excessive mobility, that is, rural men's untimely immobilization as shown in their lack of activity and failure to fulfill their responsibilities, is considered to be equally "unnatural" and unproductive.

Money and its qualities contribute to current moral concerns in Kilimanjaro. Money is experienced as more individual, concealable, and convertible than the formerly important assets land, livestock, coffee, and food. It is also seen as a more vanishing, "hot," less gender-specific and generationally controlled resource. Because it is particularly unrestrained and open-ended in social terms, money enables social mobility. Recent research has often seen money and encroaching modernity and capitalism as the central causes for the moral alarm and increasing frequency of witchcraft accusations in contemporary Africa (e.g., Auslander 1993; Austen 1993; Comaroff and Comaroff 1993). Yet modernity, money, markets, and capitalism as universal principles are not adequate explanations for what causes moral concern in Kilimanjaro (cf. S. F. Moore 1996). The impact of these developments is intertwined with regional and national developments and concerns. The disquiet created by increasing economic freedoms in the post-socialist period is indeed expressed through their being popularly associated with "foreignness," not with some faraway global forces, however, but rather with the perceived Islamic influence—the more familiar "other" for the Chagga. The threatening "outside world" is imagined as infiltrating the mountain in the guise of mostly Islamic *majini* that ambitious Chagga men and some Chagga women are believed to ally themselves with. Rather than revealing anxiety about an increasing influence of the Islamic world as such, this association expresses a concern of "insiders", the rapidly enriched Chagga men especially, turning into strangers to their own home communities and values.

Yet it would be misleading to claim that the rural Chagga feel helpless or that theirs is a moral economy threatened by irresistible outside forces. Money and market liberalization are seen at the same time potentially alienating and emancipating, but not something akin to an uncontrollable "invisible hand." The circulating moral stories and gossip about failed businessmen and "selfish" trading women are attempts to make sense of the contemporary world and efforts to persuade and control ambitious individuals in their decisions about means of enrichment and the use of money. In their actions and their talk, trading women and businessmen, for their part, give meaning to money and reveal its flows. This is done, for instance, in the practice of turning money and commodities into more socially valued assets through gift-giving and feasting. Even if it is money that is given as a gift, the giver often names the purpose for which it is meant to be used. Aside from these kinds of "semantic conversions" (Werbner 1989, 66–69), there are the continuous rhetorical attempts to define and convert meaning, such as in the market women's conceptualization of their profit as "food" *(chakula)* and other family "necessities" *(riziki)*, as well as the way they call their trading capital a "hoe" *(jembe)*. Similarly, anyone selling a cow will justify withdrawing it from the more social meat-sharing use within the lineage by explaining how the money is badly needed for a family "necessity."

To define something as a family "necessity" is a vital way of justifying an economic undertaking and avoiding others' demands for a share in its proceeds. What is included in the "necessities" is negotiable and changing. These days, many market women include in "necessities" that they need to acquire many items customarily provided by men, as well as some support to friends. In the case of a man taking a cow to the butcher's, the scope of the family "necessities" has been enlarged to include such things as children's school fees and the need to replenish trading capital.

By defining and converting the meaning of money, people try to control its potentially alienating qualities. Through conceptualizations and

practices that draw on the ideas of moral economy in the domestic and kinship sphere, people try to avoid or they respond to criticism about their individualistic aspirations. By making their intentions and resources visible,
public, and transparent in their acts of giving and in their explanations for
their acts, traders and businessmen try to counter the gossip that attends
them. Such explanations and practices form the other side of the ongoing
dialogue about the moral value of trading, traders, and businessmen. Indeed, much of the contemporary moral dialogue is about attempts to reveal the economic situations and money flows of successful people and to
deal with the issue of what belongs to sharable wealth and what to individual riches. It involves negotiation over the scope, limit, and content of personal and sharable wealth, and about how new or ambiguous wealth (such
as cars, conspicuous houses, enclosed gardens, and women's wealth in general) should be culturally and morally categorized.

Much of this negotiation takes place indirectly and through the medium
of gossip. In the literature "indirection" is frequently seen as a way for
speakers to avoid full responsibility for their words by leaving both the
meanings and the sources of their "news" somewhat ambiguous. Gossip
and the opinions expressed by means of it are usually anonymous, with no
identifiable source. Gluckman (1963) saw anonymity and indirection in gossip as a means to avoid open conflict in a face-to-face society and thus to
maintain an image of outer harmony, and ultimately to maintain the group
itself. Indirection in talk as a fundamental means for maintaining equality
has also been described for egalitarian Pacific and Caribbean societies
(Brenneis 1984; Myers and Brenneis 1984, 2, 14). In these societies, indirection is used to protect individual autonomy, the very basis of egalitarianism,
by deliberately obscuring the identity of the gossipers and sometimes also
the subjects of the gossip. Because of the concern for individual autonomy,
gossiping is usually restricted to a small circle of intimates; it is meant to remain backstage and not to reach the ears of its subjects. Indeed, as a strictly
private event, gossiping on Nukulaelae in the Central Pacific is said to define
a private arena in distinction to a public arena (Besnier 1990, 295, 318).

In many societies, then, gossip has primary functions other than manipulating the reputations of absent others. Rather, gossiping forms a sphere
where the gossipers' own reputations are made by demonstrating knowledge of community matters, and especially through the display of artistic
skill and wit in the use of words when gossiping. This aspect of gossip, allowing personal distinctions to be made among men, is described, for instance, for peasants on the isle of St. Vincent in the Caribbean (Abrahams
1983, 85 –87) and for Indians living in Fiji (Brenneis 1984, 492). It is a wider-
spread phenomenon, however; the centrality of verbal art and performance
in creating men's reputations among their peers is found more generally

among Afro-Caribbeans and African Americans (e.g., Abrahams 1974, 1983; French and Kernan 1981).

In Abraham's (1983) and Brenneis's (1984) description, this kind of talk takes place in informal settings and creates a value system that counters the dominant value system. Reputation as an unofficial value system was first described by Wilson (1973) for the Caribbean. He distinguished a formal structure of respectability that is defined by the stratified system of classes imposed on the region by colonial rule, and an indigenous value system of reputation that levels the scarcity of respectability and depends on individual skills as measured by one's peers. Wilson used the phrase "crab antics" to describe the value system of reputation, referring to the constant efforts of individual men to climb crablike over others in their status and reputation, while others just as constantly pull the climbers down to a level equal with theirs. Comparably, in both Abraham's and Brenneis's descriptions, gossiping creates a communitas of men (cf. Turner 1969) in defiance of the morally high formal values of their societies; there is an atmosphere of licentious fun and intimacy between the men who together create narratives and compete in the skillful use of words. There is, then, a carnivalesque ambience to gossiping, and like the carnivals in Bakhtin's (1984) description and the gossip in Scott's (1985) study here, too, gossip and the reputations it helps to build remain on the unofficial and private side of social life, on the back stage, without presenting any real challenge to the official value system or social hierarchy.

The place and power of gossip is quite different in some Melanesian communities whose leaders are called big men. For instance, among the Kwanga of Papua New Guinea gossip has a publicly acknowledged role in creating and destroying the position of the leaders (Brison 1992). The Kwanga spend several hours a week in communal meetings where circulating gossip and rumors are openly addressed and their sources and truthfulness discussed. At these public meetings, both leaders and other members of the society try to clear their names by putting a stop to disparaging gossip about themselves (ibid., 7–8, 32). In contrast to the semipublic sphere that I have described for Kilimanjaro, gossip among the Kwanga therefore seems integral to the creation of a public sphere in which events and their interpretation, as well as people and the moral value of their actions, are openly discussed. This might first sound like Habermas's (1998) model of public sphere, that is, a discursive arena, in which people come to democratic decisions through open citizen debate, but in fact it is not that, because in Melanesia talk is often not considered a truthful reflection of speaker's intentions and thoughts.

The "truthfulness" distinction between talk and action has been discussed by several researchers who have studied Melanesia. Thoughts, feelings, intentions, and desires are believed to be hidden in a person's mind, for instance, in the Trobriand Islands (Weiner 1984), among the Melpa of Mount Hagen (Strathern 1979), or in a person's heart among the Urapmin in Papua New Guinea (Robbins 2001). Speech is usually not considered a reliable way to communicate such private thoughts and feelings, nor is the revelation desirable. Just as Brenneis (1987, 504) describes that for the Fijian Indians speaking "clearly" is considered brave and "hard," but foolish, Weiner reports that, among Trobrianders, speaking what one truly thinks about something is called "hard words," and that telling the truth in public is considered dangerous. The reason for this is the same as for why indirect talk is favored. "Hard" words penetrate the personal space of others and reveal one's own thinking, and in so doing strip away the ambiguity that shields the individual autonomy of both parties, the very basis of egalitarianism (Weiner 1984, 167). For this reason, actions such as an exchange of objects are considered a much more reliable way to express one's mind than are words. Exchanging objects is also a suitably subtle way to influence others since objects persuade but do not penetrate or control another person's mind (ibid., 173).

As I have discussed in this book, talk in Kilimanjaro is essential to the interpretation and discussion of the meaning and motive of exchange and other acts. Indeed, much of the force of persuasion accorded to objects in Melanesian societies seems to take place through talk in Kilimanjaro. However, indirection is a central characteristic in talk among the Chagga, too, although it seems to differ in its reasons, modes, and impact from what is described above for Melanesian and Caribbean societies. Indirection in Kilimanjaro involves some ambiguity in the meaning and source of information, but less often in the subject of talk. Indirection regarding the intended audience is an especially important feature and is crucial for forming what I have called a semipublic sphere in Kilimanjaro. This means that talk is often directed at someone else or to a larger audience than it would appear to. This aspect of indirection is also reported from Afro-Caribbean and African American talk. What is in Barbados called "dropping remarks" (Fisher 1976), among the Belizean Creole "throwing a phrase" (French and Kernan 1981, 249–53) and among some African Americans "signifying" (Mitchell-Kernan 1971, 89–90), means that a speaker makes a comment supposedly for one listener, with the intention that the one that overhears the comment understands it to have been directed at him personally.

In Kilimanjaro, the intended audience (or the desired "overhearers" of talk) is often wider than those present at the time of the talking. Gossip and responses to gossip seldom remain on the back stage, or are shared only between the primary speakers. The subject of gossip usually hears what has been said about him or her through the grapevine, as it were. The intended audience of a trader's casual market or bar conversation—which may more properly be a response to gossip—is often larger than those present. The subject of gossip tries to use the very medium that has spread the criticism about her to get her own position across, that is, the network of gossip. What is at stake is often an attempt to convince others about the speaker's own trustworthiness rather than the truthfulness of her words as such. The apparent spontaneity of bar or marketplace conversation is in itself a claim to disinterestedness and truthfulness. Similarly, when people recount other people's life histories by starting with "people say that . . ." this serves other purposes than merely avoiding responsibility and open conflict by making the source of the speaker's news ambiguous and anonymous. This opening line is frequently used to imply that the reported news—even if purportedly "secret"—is more widely shared and thus a more weighty piece of knowledge than just one individual's opinion.

The opinions and views conveyed by gossip and the responses to gossip are thus often aimed at convincing the greater public beyond the particular face-to-face situation, with the intent that they become solidified into more general and circulating "truths" and stories. In this sense, it is appropriate to say that the speakers themselves seek not only an immediate understanding of the participants to the specific conversation, but also a responsive understanding of "a third party" or "super-addressee" that is at some distance, and yet "invisibly present" and in that sense constitutive of the conversation (Bakhtin 1994 [1986], 126–27).

Gossiping also involves issues of equality and social differentiation in Kilimanjaro, where the upwardly mobile are often the subjects of gossip. The main motivation in gossiping and indirect talk is not, however, simply the hindrance of social differentiation, the "pulling-down" of aspiring social climbers to the same level as the gossipers and making them comply with the shared values. Rather than being a sanctioning force, gossip in Kilimanjaro is a means of persuasion. The more political objectives of gossip are quite often attempts to level differences in wealth, but the aim is more to share in the wealth of ambitious people than to hinder them from accumulating it. Most importantly, however, gossip and the semipublic sphere it creates enable a dialogue about moral reputations and value. Because of this sphere the wealthy and the ambitious remain aware of their subjection to community expectations, communal evaluation and persuasion. Material capital is therefore less directly and self-evidently translated into symbolic capital than Bourdieu (1977, 177–80) implies. Because it is socially produced, a moral reputation cannot simply be accumulated through individual calculation. At the same time, however, the semipublic sphere enables wealthy persons to respond to the circulating criticism regarding them, and thus to participate in building their own reputations either by an action or an explanation for their action. The dialogue taking place in the semipublic sphere can thus be characterized as a process of mutual persuasion, enabling people to indirectly discuss and argue with each other about their material needs and moral dispositions.

What might thus sound like the quintessential verification of some classic moral economic principles of sharing and suffering together like the constant appeals to motherhood and "feeding" by market women on the one hand, or of neoclassical economic principles like the popular criticism of traders' selfishness and profit-seeking mentality on the other, should be examined as a mutually constituting dialogue where moral reputations and value are debated and constructed. In this dialogue, moral value is conceptualized as a person's orientation to contribute to the social generation, whereas a morally deficient person is one who is seen as self-directed and appropriative.

Comparable images can be found in other post-socialist contexts, for instance, in Russia, where the moral value of business is often debated in terms of its "productivity" versus "nonproductivity" (Humphrey 2002, 74; Watts 2002, 69). Newly rich people, called the "New Russians," and public criticism about them, emerged in the post-socialist Russia of the 1990s. The "New Russians" became an epithet for men involved in diverse spheres of business, finance, services, and crime. Even though those who made their fortunes by outright crime and racketeering formed only one group of the newly rich, the entailed negative characteristics were readily related to anyone who was engaged in business or enjoying financial success. "New Russian" referred to someone who had money but lacked many other things, such as education, taste, morals, and patience (Balzer 2003, 16).

In various ways, the critical discussion focused on the perceived nonproductivity of their labor and efforts. However, just like in Kilimanjaro, the distinction between productive and nonproductive labor was not simply factual or descriptive, but was also highly moral; besides referring to the lack of physical labor and production, the distinction included an understanding of these men's motivations for their activities and use of their riches as being individualistic rather than social. As "productive labor" was categorized efforts that were seen to benefit the larger society, such as, for instance, peasant, artisan and manufacturing activities, as well as intellectual professions and the work of older local magnates who operated mills, factories or railroads (see Heyat 2002, 25; Humphrey 2002, 44, 59; Watts 2002, 65 –67). New Russians instead were characterized by what was seen as a new and aspirational mentality; they were considered rapacious, materialist and alienated from the Soviet values of honesty and social conscience. One aspect of their nonsociality was in their perceived orientation to the foreign instead of the local world, as shown in their sources of enrichment (such as import and export business) and in their consumption patterns, that is, in their inclination for Western goods, designer clothes, Mercedes and BMWs, and modern villas with prominent walls and gates (Balzer 2003, 16; Humphrey 2002, 58, 62, 182, 188).

The new economic elite in the 1990s was mainly male, and the New Russians were typically depicted as men with glamorous female dependents; feminine wives, mistresses, and high-class prostitutes (Humphrey, 178). Interestingly, the new female entrepreneurs in Russia used the same moral category of "production" to distinguish themselves from their male counterparts (see Bruno 1997). Against the New Russians' Western orientation the women entrepreneurs emphasized their use of local, Russian materials for their products and their aspirations to display "Russian soul" through their goods. Women also described their business as motivated by the social purposes of supporting their families, charitable functions and the needy people in general (ibid., 63–69).

The image of the New Russians and their perceived aspirations were thus used by other business people and the general public for making moral distinctions about acceptable labor and enterprise. That distinction was based on the perceived individualistic versus social orientation of the person; although the used terms are different from those in Kilimanjaro, they are comparable in their content, and in both cases are part of the negotiation that arises from the social mobility and change taking place in a postsocialist situation. Indeed, Humphrey (2002, 71) suggests that due to the relatively long historical absence of "normal" trade in Russia, the business activities of the New Russians do not have a vocabulary of their own legitimacy and are thus defined out of negation, from the outside, by the public. According to Humphrey (ibid., 72), this is shown where, in contrast to the passionate and vocal public criticism of traders, the traders themselves use such modest domestic expressions for their profit as *navar* (or the more colloquial *navarka*) meaning the grease that forms on the top of soup. Yet, might the use of such an expression refer to the new business people's tendency to rely on and modify familiar domestic concepts rather than their need to create a new vocabulary for their self-legitimization, and their failure to do so?

In Kilimanjaro, the moral value of trading and traders is largely debated through rather conventional concepts and practices, which does not indicate mere resistance to change or helplessness and a sense of alienation in the face of a new situation. In discussing new phenomena by using old concepts, people are at the same time rethinking the meaning of those concepts and practices. This discussion involves both political maneuvering and moral reflection. Therefore, it is important to combine aspects of political economy and moral economy in the study of a changing economic situation. As much as political economic changes engender moral discussion, moral arguments include attempts to steer politics. I have argued in this book that what ensues from this dialogue is a moral economy, not as some kind of static and defensive value system, but as something that is emerging in negotiations and interactions at the markets, bars, and neighborhoods.

Cultural ideas and moral values do not exist as abstract rules or conceptual codes. Gossip is a prime means for continuously opening the meaning of cultural categories for discussion and debate. A characteristic feature of gossip in Kilimanjaro is an unending curiosity and desire to question, deliberate, and meditate on the "real" nature of things and to create alternative perspectives on the apparent "reality." The words that the Chagga use for this attitude are *kuwaza* (to ponder/imagine) and *mawazo* (thoughts/ideas/notions), best summarized as "moral imagination." Such discussions, in which moral values and cultural meanings are contemplated, are the bases for cultural and socioeconomic transformation. Even though this talk begins on the back stage and remains informal, gossip does not form an unofficial sphere, one that comments on but has no effect on social hierarchies and cultural order. On the contrary, in expanding to form a semipublic sphere, gossip and the responses to it dialogically constitute and reconstitute cultural ideas and moral values.

# Notes

## Introduction

1. For a thorough account of the external and internal pressures that led to the reforms as well as of the political coalitions behind them, see Tripp 1997.

2. On the vigorous appropriation of and competition over the newly opened public arenas on the local level in Kilimanjaro, see S. F. Moore 1996.

3. The classical distinction made by Evans-Pritchard (1937) between witchcraft and sorcery is not usually made in Kilimanjaro. There is a notion of inherited witchcraft but often even that is described as "things" *(vitu)* given to a person and not as an embodied power. The Kiswahili word *uchawi* and the Kichagga word *usawi* are used both for inherited and acquired forms of occult forces. Therefore, I will use the word witchcraft in this book often also for those cases that fall into the category of sorcery in the classical terminology.

4. *Shamba* fields are located in the lower areas of the mountain and used for cultivating annual crops. Customarily *shamba* plots were allocated for use only by the chief, but during the twentieth century much of the *shamba* land became

permanently held and transferable through inheritance to the heirs like *kihamba* land.

5. By late 1993 there were more than two hundred privately owned newspapers in Tanzania (Sipola 1994, 37). In Mayanka the change was slower but visible; in 1994 one could choose between two government owned newspapers, in the beginning of 1997 there were variably one or two private newspapers and no government newspaper available. The variety was much bigger in larger centers such as Himo or Moshi town.

## 1. Domesticating the Market, Marketing the Domestic

1. The description of the market place in this chapter is mostly based on the situation in 1994. By 1997 the biggest change in the market was that the illegal cross-border beer trade had more or less ceased.

2. *Kanga* is a piece of colorful cloth that women wrap around their waist or chest, and sometimes another around their shoulders or head. It is considered a more traditional way for women to dress than in sewn dresses. Each *kanga* bears a slogan or a proverb in Kiswahili on it, and women often select a particular piece of *kanga* as much for the saying it carries as for its colors and designs. Nowadays *kangas* are mostly imported from India.

*Kitenge* is a multicolored wax print worn either by wrapping it around the body or by tailoring it into a dress. The cloth differs from *kanga* by being larger in size and thicker in quality, by the printing method of its designs, and in not having any printed slogans on it.

3. It is possible that men started to market cloth even earlier. According to Koponen (1994, 152–53) there were several Indian shops in Moshi and Marangu as early as 1898 where Africans could buy cloth and other imported goods. Indian traders also recruited itinerant African traders whom they supplied with cloth and other goods to be traded in the surrounding countryside.

4. Interview with author, 21 January 1995.

5. The boys have replaced the name of a bride and groom with the names of their sales items, and instead of "We are giving / have come with grace and mercy," they sing they are "selling with grace and mercy."

6. The idea of "marrying by force," which will be discussed in chapter 4, also creates and recreates the dominant ideas of (dominant) maleness. The same term *kwa nguvu*, "by force," used for this form of Chagga marriage was used by the woman above to describe men's behavior as they entered the rice trade.

7. Dictionaries give only negative meanings for the word *ujanja*, all referring to deceitfulness. Johnson's 1939 dictionary gives the following definitions: craftiness, cunning, roguery, deceit, fraud. The Swahili–Swahili dictionary *Kamusi ya Kiswahili Sanifu* (1981) gives several synonyms for the word, all referring to deceit, cunning, and slyness.

8. *Biashara ya sokoni ni udanganyifu.*

9. Interview with author, 1 September 1994.

10. This is very different from a Ghanaian marketplace, where, according to Clark (1994, 129), this kind of competition over the customers is disapproved of as

"stealing" another trader's customer. In Kilimanjaro the hostility and competition inherent in such a situation is again muted and dispelled by the jesting tone and theatrical style of the soliciting trader.

11. The Kenyan women who come to the market to buy large quantities of foodstuffs are often openly very demanding and arrogant. Chagga traders do not usually get provoked in these situations, but continue to behave as they do towards other customers. Afterwards, the Chagga sellers acknowledge the difference between themselves and the Kenyan women and consider the Kenyans "stern" *(mkali)* and "clever" *(mjanja)* in their habit of loudly and repeatedly demanding fairer measuring.

12. The root word *ku bemba* means "to wheedle / to fawn over / to cajole / to seduce."

13. In the literature, "bargaining" often refers to haggling over price, and the most perceptive analysts have seen it as a way to ameliorate price information between traders and customers in markets where such information is discontinuous and difficult to acquire (Alexander 1987, Geertz 1979, Uchendu 1967). The older assertion that foodstuffs are not generally subject to bargaining in peasant markets probably refers to an absence of price negotiation (e.g., Nadel 1965 [1942], 317).

14. For instance, the different sizes of Kenyan butter cans, all putatively but not actually holding one kilo, are used in the rice trade. It is common that the retailer uses a Cowboy brand can for buying the rice from the wholesaler and either a smaller Blue Band can or a cut Cowboy can for selling it. In this way the retailer is able to add 5 extra selling kilos to the purchased 100 kilos of rice.

15. See, for example, Appadurai 1986; Bourdieu 1977; Hart 1982, 45; Strathern 1992.

## 2. Feeding, Drinking, and Eating

1. For example, Barnes 1990, Clark 1994, Eames 1988, Ekechi 1995, Falola 1995, House-Midamba 1995, Mintz 1971, Musisi 1995, Robertson 1995, Tripp 1997.

2. The daily Radio Tanzania news is called *Habari na taarifa.*

3. The word *mjinga* has several interrelated but slightly differing meanings, such as "stupid, fool, foolish, naïve, ignorant, simple-minded." For consistency's sake I most often translate it as "stupid" in this book.

4. Compare this to the female vendors in the Kampala night markets and how they use slang expressions and language that are not understood by the general population (Musisi 1995, 132). And in Morocco the expression "words of the suq [market place]" refers to "dirty words" or "street talk" (Kapchan 1996, 36).

5. The old Chagga female traders whom I talked with were far more fluent in Kiswahili than those old women who had not done trading and who hardly spoke any Kiswahili, only Kichagga. Obviously this difference has to do with both the verbal liveliness and the "mixing" of different people(s) in the market places.

6. Raikes (1994, 37–39) has described how bars in Kisii, western Kenya, are important arenas for market transactions, to the extent that the value of trade agreed on in such places probably exceeds many times that of the market place.

7. *Mawazo* is derived from the verb *kuwaza*, which means, "to imagine, reflect, ponder, meditate."

8. Lecture given in Helsinki 2 December 1995.

9. The Chagga have appreciated education since its introduction by missionaries at the end of the nineteenth century, and during the colonial period benefited from a clear advantage over the other regions in access to schools. The average number of years of education of both men and women in Kilimanjaro region is higher than in any other region in Tanzania (Tanzania Demographic and Health Survey 1991/1992, 11–12).The puns common in sales talk ("this rice has gone through studies") and the jokes comparing markets and bars with schools derive from and make use of the value given to education.

10. Interestingly, *kuruka* means also "to pass over or beyond," "overstep," "trespass," referring to the crossing of borders or limits.

11. Interview with author, 2 September 1994.

12. See, for instance, Beidelman 1993, Clark 1994, Feldman-Savelsberg 1996, Masquelier 1995, Weiss 1996.

13. This probably derives from the Chagga idea that a man feeds a woman's vaginal mouth with his semen during intercourse (S. F. Moore 1976).

14. Interview with author, 14 December 1994.

15. Interviews with author, 16 August and 26 August 1994.

16. Gutmann (1926, 382–87) also refers to this kind of danger. He reported that a market was desecrated if even the scratch from a toenail spilled blood in it. All the wares automatically became taboo and had to be ritually cleansed before they could be carried off and used as food. The husband of the culprit had to bring a goat to the market, where it was killed as a sacrifice to the ancestors of the lineage controlling the market, and all the market women were sprinkled with a mixture of *jande* water and blood before they could go home. Gutmann's description is somewhat different from that of the old market women and some other elderly people I talked with in Mayanka. They said the danger fell only on the husbands and the male children of the two women involved. Most of the old women in Mayanka remained, however, unclear as to whom exactly the petition was made.

17. In the previous chapter I mentioned that, according to Gutmann (1926, 383–85), food that had not been pretasted in the market was potentially harmful for the children. Today, one hears many market women say as they moralize about others that they would not be able to feed their children with food earned by selling sexual services in the market.

18. Here by poison and harmful essences I mean food treated by sorcery; in Mayanka people acknowledged and told about some cases where purchased food, especially meat, was poisonous because it came from a diseased animal, and so was harmful to anyone who ate it.

19. According to Gutmann, a Chagga woman could accumulate cattle by inheriting part of her mother's herd. In marriage, the creation of a herd of her own required that she be "extremely industrious" and her husband good-natured. Through her skills in cultivation, raising the cattle and bartering, it was possible. According to Gutmann, however, "as a rule" the belongings of a woman consisted only of a few pieces of clothing, her cooking utensils, her hoe, sickle and perhaps some fruits harvested in the fields. (Gutmann 1926, 55–56.)

20. For explanation of the term "self-reliance," see note 24.

21. Feldman-Savelsberg (1996) examines a case in West Africa where women emphasize matrilineal connections in a putatively patrilineal society.

22. According to the literature (S. F. Moore 1977, 365; Hasu 1999), the Chagga understanding of conception is that the child forms from the mother's blood and the father's semen. Some of the elder Chagga people in Mayanka hold this view, yet sometimes maintain that the bones come from the father. Many people in Mayanka, even some of those who were as old as sixty years, were not, however, familiar with this notion. Often people said that to their understanding the child gets "seeds" *(mbegu)* from both the mother and the father. Jørgensen (1983, 9), who writes about conception ideologies in Papua New Guinea, says that rather than being shared and one, the ideologies form a lively arena in the realm of gender politics; "there's always another story." In Mayanka, cases of sterility especially brought to open discussion and disputation the issues of what conception requires and the reasons for its failure.

23. The contemporary economic necessity for both men and women to "run around" is also reflected in the idea of "bound" men and stay-at-home women as "stupid" *(mjinga, pl. wajinga)*.

24. "Self-reliance" *(kujitegemea)* was what Nyerere promoted as the most important and highly moral aim for the newly independent nation in the Arusha Declaration in 1967. The word *mapinduzi* comes from the name of the governing and, until 1992, the only party CCM, Chama Cha Mapinduzi ("Revolutionary Party"). The party was established in 1977, when the original mainland party, the Tanganyika African National Union (TANU), which had governed since independence in 1961, merged with Zanzibar's Afro Shirazi Party. The word *mageuzi* ("reform") became the catchword for multiparty politics and the more liberal political era in the 1990s.

25. Nadel (1965 [1942], 1952) studied the Nupe in northern Nigeria, McCall (1961) studied the Akan in Ashanti Kingdom, and Little (1948) the Mende in Sierra Leone Protectorate.

26. See e.g., LeVine 1970, Mintz 1971, Ottenberg 1959, and Sudarkasa 1973.

27. Boserup's (1970) book was a groundbreaking work for the research in this period because it emphasized the importance of African women's economic roles through their predominance in agricultural and farming activities, and yet their decreasing share in the benefits of global economic growth. Hay (1988) has described the changing tone and focus in the historical writing on African women during the 1970s as a shift from an emphasis on successful elite women (queens) to prostitutes, i.e., from a view of women as heroines to one of them as victims.

28. See Clark 1994; Hill 1969; Ogbomo 1995; Sudarkasa 1973, 26 –32

29. Clark 1994, 88 –89; Eames 1988, 82–83; Ekechi 1995, 43; Falola 1995, 35; Sudarkasa, 1973.

30. See Hay 1976; House-Midamba 1995, 86; Kongstad and Mönsted 1980, 119 –20; Koponen 1988, 103 –4; Robertson 1997.

31. E.g., House-Midamba 1995, Musisi 1995, Tripp 1997. King (1996) studied the *jua kali* sector in Kenya; although women were estimated to make up 46 percent of the microenterprise sector (ibid., 40), they appear very little in his study, however.

32. See e. g. Bryceson 1994, 21; Hansen 1989, 151, 154; House-Midamba 1995, 88; Kongstad and Mönsted 1980, 131; Robertson 1995; Schuster 1982.

33. Robertson conducted fieldwork in Ghana in the 1970s, and in Kenya in the late 1980s.

34. See Barnes 1990, 262; Clark 1994, 368; Mintz 1971, 252–53; Sudarkasa 1973; and White 1987, 90–97.

35. See e.g. Barnes 1990; Bledsoe 1980; Bujra 1975; Kongstad and Mönsted 1980, 122–23; LaFontaine 1974, 107; Mintz 1971, 255; Obbo 1975; Pittin 1983; Tripp 1997; Van Donge 1992, 197; White 1987, 90.

36. In the early African settlement in Nairobi, called Pangani, women owned 42 percent of the houses in 1932. Pangani was demolished and Pumwani emerged where by 1943 women owned 41 percent of the houses. In the beginning of the 1970s half of the houses of Pumwani were owned by women. (Bujra 1975, 213–14.)

37. There was a more general tendency to label single female migrants to the colonial towns as prostitutes (Obbo 1980, 26; Ogden 1996; White 1990). According to Jeater (1993), this moral labeling was a combination of the strict patriarchal or patrilineal social organization of the rural areas, and the Victorian, middle-class, Christian morality.

38. As indications of the traders' marginal status Schuster (1982, 123) lists "their passivity and appearance at work, their limited hope for improvement, their ambiguous role as both wife and provider."

## 3. Constructing Moral Reputation

1. See e.g., Apter 1993; Austen 1993; Comaroff and Comaroff 1993; Drucker-Brown 1993; Fisiy and Geschiere 1991, 1996; Weiss 1996; White 2000.

2. E.g., Drucker-Brown 1993, Englund 1996, Green 1997, Rowlands and Warnier 1988.

3. E.g., Auslander 1993, Austen 1993, Comaroff and Comaroff 1993, Geschiere 2000, Weiss 1996, White 2000.

4. Chagga spouses do not usually call each other by their first names, but by their lineage names or by attaching the name of the first child to the title of *Mama* (mother) or *Baba* (father).

5. Interview with author, 3 January 1995.

6. Ibid.

7. "Carrying" refers to a marriage by capture; see chapter 4.

8. *Pombe* is Kiswahili and is used as a general term for beer, both traditional and bottled.

9. Interview with author, 3 January 1995.

10. Ibid.

11. Ibid.

12. Ibid.

13. Ibid.

14. Interview with author, 15 January 1995.

15. Interview with author, 3 January 1995.

16. Interview with author, 15 January 1995.

17. Ibid.

18. Ibid.

19. Interview with author, 3 January 1995.

20. She uses the concept "binding" to refer to keeping cattle in the shed. See more about this concept and its use in chapter 4.

21. Ibid.

22. Ibid.

23. Basically *pori* is an environmental term meaning plains land in distinction to mountain, forest, and grassland areas. As a moral category it is, however, usually contrasted with *migombani* (banana land), representing Kilimanjaro. It can be used for almost any location outside Kilimanjaro in reference to a cultural "other," and it often includes a reference to moral inadequacy and lack of civilization, which among other things includes the tendency to use witchcraft.

24. Interview with author, 3 January 1995.

25. Ibid.

26. A Chagga woman should not say "I built the house," or "I bought a car," or "I bought a *shamba*," because it is understood as a deliberate humiliation of her husband. As shown by Mary's account, she is constantly talking in that way, however.

27. The basic verb *Kukaa* has both the meaning of "to stay" and "to sit." In Kiswahili the basic form of the verbs start with "ku-."

28. Interview with author, 15 January 1995.

29. Ibid.

30. *Konyagi* is a distilled ginlike liquor produced in Tanzania.

31. In 1997 the general economic situation was tighter than it was in 1994. One visible indication of this was the relative emptiness of many bars that in 1994 used to be lively with people in the evenings. Mary's bar was no exception.

32. "Drying up" refers to a situation where a person suffers from inadequate food and care, the typical signs of which are physical weakness and weight loss. Additionally, when used in reference to a woman it can refer to her being sexually deprived and needy (see also Emanatian 1996).

33. Also the fact that the Mpare's young son was living with Mary complicated the Mpare's position; would her son later acknowledge the Mpare as his "mother" if he was raised by Mary?

34. Interview with author, 15 January 1995.

35. Ibid.

36. Ibid.

37. Interview with author, 23 December 1994.

38. Cf. Abrahams (1970, 299–300) on gossip as a genre.

39. Buying such "medicines" or "spirits" is considered a new method of enrichment and sorcery, and they are much more usually related to men than women. See more in chapter 6.

40. *Machalare* is a customary meal prepared by cooking meat with *mchare* bananas.

41. See more on the credit system in the market in chapter 1.

## 4. From Captured Wives to Bound Men

1. A substantial increase in elopements, informal unions, and single-motherhood has been noted in many studies concerning Eastern and Southern Africa; see for example Gulbrandsen 1986, Håkansson 1994, Taylor 1992. Also see

H. Moore and Vaughan (1994, 164–72) on the difficulty of quantifying such changes.

2. Interview with author, 28 October 1994.

3. Interview with author, 22 October 1994.

4. Interview with author, 30 October 1994.

5. Interview with author, 21 January 1995.

6. Interview with author, 28 October 1994. *Li* in *limama* is a diminutive.

7. Interview with author, 27 November 1994.

8. Interview with author, 12 October 1994.

9. A girl *(msichana)* becomes a woman *(mwanamke)* by marriage.

10. Interview with author, 27 November 1994.

11. Interview with author, 28 October 1994.

12. Interview with author, 27 November 1994.

13. Interview with author, 12 October 1994.

14. Interview with author, 22 October 1994.

15. Interview with author, 21 January 1995.

16. On the importance of unblemished and shining skin in the judgment of a person's character and personhood, especially those of young girls, see Fortes (1987, 261) for the Tallensi people, and Weiss (1997) for the Haya.

17. Virginity can also be a social construct in a very literal sense as shown by the practices of infibulation and reinfibulation that is done, for instance, after each delivery in Sudan and that also a divorced or widowed woman can undergo (Boddy 1989, 54). Hymen repair is practiced in some other areas, too (Lindisfarne 1994). At least for these places, it is succinct to say, "virgins are made, not born" (Hayes 1975; quoted in Boddy 1989, 54).

18. To give birth is in Kiswahili *kujifungua,* that is, "to open oneself," and in Kichagga *naenengo mana.*

19. This transference is not complete and does not take place overnight. A woman retains her links to the natal home and kin and her membership in the husband's lineage strengthens only gradually.

20. For an analysis of the symbolic construction of patrilineal kinship system through the marital exchange and transformation of matrilineal and patrilineal substances among the Chagga in the early German period, see Hasu 1999.

21. To affiliate a pre- or extramarital child, its father's patrilineage has to pay a compensation of a cow and a goat to the mother's side, cover the expenses of feeding the mother during the postparturition seclusion, and the feeding and medicine expenses as well as the school fees the child amassed by the time it is taken to the father's home. Sometimes long lineage discussions and/or court cases are required before the father acknowledges the child. The acknowledgement is in the interest of the girl and her natal family, since she cannot take the children of another man with her should she get married but usually leaves them at her natal home. With the acknowledgement comes the claims for the father's provision for the child; if the child is male, the father is to provide him a plot of land just like for his male children born in wedlock. There is much effort among the Chagga for the acknowledgement of the child by its father; often enough also the close relatives urge the reluctant father to do so. This seemingly "biological" idea is based on the cultural

understanding of the father's "feeding" starting already in intercourse (see S. F. Moore 1977, 365).

22. A very old (circa ninety years of age) woman's reflections on the changed times summarizes well common opinions on the subject: "In the olden days, after giving birth to a child, a woman does not leave from her husband. After giving birth, it is not easy for the husband to throw the woman away [amtupe]. The man asks, 'where would I take these children?' 'Do you understand: A child is a tie to bind a woman not to leave her husband. There are men who bear a lot of trouble because of a child. Likewise, there are women who bear a lot of trouble because of a child. But in the olden days women used to be beaten a lot! Women used to be beaten and did she go to her [natal] home, she will certainly be returned and the case will be returned to be talked with her husband. But if her father returned her to her husband today, she will tell him: 'Are you playing with me, father? Not with me!' Thus, today women are not treated like they used to be. Today they say,' Now I have decided to like him [the husband/a man]; now I have decided to leave him'" (Interview with author, 24 August 1994).

23. Hutchinson (1990, 400–401) mentions briefly that among the Western Leek Nuer in Sudan a term for a divorced woman (ciek mi keegh) encompasses unmarried mothers as well. Hutchinson does not discuss the moral implications of this term, but the semantic combination of the two conditions is interesting.

24. Interview with author, 26 August 1994.

25. Interview with author, 17 August 1994.

26. A curse concerning the girl's future inability to bear children was also involved in the case brought to the local court in 1994 referenced above.

27. In the field I heard one such reference during a wedding ceremony involving a very well-off family in Dar es Salaam where the bridegroom's categorical paternal aunt sang and praised the bride by calling her "a modern cow" (ng'ombe wa kisasa).

28. The Kiswahili word for marrying is different for men and women. The active form kuoa ("to marry") is used for men and the passive form kuolewa na ("to become married by") is used for women.

29. Compare to what Luise White (1990) says about prostitutes in colonial Nairobi. These women sold not only sex, but also domestic services to male wage-earners and prostitution was thus a form of illegal marriage.

30. Masquelier (1995, 894–95) finds comparable images among the Hausaphone Mawri in Niger. One of the spirits possessing Mawri women is called Maria. According to Masquelier, "the spirit symbolizes female sexuality in its most dangerous state, detached from reproduction . . . no longer contained by the rules of marriage and maternity. . . . It objectifies deceitful and destructive attractiveness; Maria devotees concentrate on appearance rather than substance, on sugar rather than food, and on prostitution rather than motherhood."

31. In one case where the wife was believed to have built a "career" of binding and finally killing her husband, the long period preceding his death, when he lay paralyzed in his bed and was unable to articulate words, was believed by many to have been caused by the wife's medicines.

32. Interview with author, 4 December 1994.

33. Interview with author, 15 December 1994.

34. See, for example, Auslander 1993; Comaroff and Comaroff 1993; Englund 1996, 1999; Piot 1999. See Fisiy and Geschiere (1996) and Geschiere (2000 [1997]), who relate witchcraft discourses to economy and politics.

## 5. Urban Men in Their Home Lineages

1. See Fernandes et al. 1984, 85; Schneider-Barthold et al. 1983, 27–28, 48–51, 83; Swantz 1985, 92.

2. With the shrinking of land plots, households have had to diversify their income sources. In a study made in the beginning of the 1960s, a third of the farms were found to have incomes outside agriculture (Ruthenberg 1964, 215–16). In the beginning of the 1980s practically all the households had at least one source of income outside agriculture (GDI 1983, 41, 45, 65; Kerner 1988, 177; S. F. Moore 1986, 237, 307.)

3. In his interview among rural farmers in Kilimanjaro in the 1970s, Maro found that only 23 percent of the men had had temporary work experience outside Moshi District and another 12 percent had served in the British Army. Some 65 percent of the men had not ventured outside the district, and half of those who had been away had stayed away for less than a year (Maro 1974, 190; cited in S. F. Moore 1986, 140). Annual migration from rural areas reached 25 percent among young men in the 1970s (Maro 1975).

4. Cultural inclinations influence what is seen as the most important and preferable occupation. In the census that I took in Mayanka at the end of 1994, men tended to give "cultivation" as a secondary occupation if they had any other occupation, even a prior one, to mention. Only in cases where men did not have any other work to mention or were very old was "cultivation" given as the primary occupation. The difference when compared to the results of the national census of 1967 reveals both the change in the economic bases and the aspirations of the Chagga. In 1967, in Kilimanjaro about 50 percent of the household heads stated as their primary occupation "coffee farming," 33 percent indicated "other agriculture," while only 17 percent gave "non-farming" as their occupation (Tanzania. 1967 population census, vol. 4, table 321, p. 413; cited in Samoff 1979, 67).

5. One of the implications of the close relations between paternal grandfather and first-born male grandchild is that sometimes the grandfather decides to give his house to the grandson instead of his own son. This practice was noted by Gutmann (1926, 48) and still exists today.

6. On the basis of these inheritance patterns, Gutmann (1926, 22) concluded that the last-born son was the representative of the maternal lineage, whereas the first-born son was the primary representative of the father's lineage. In Mayanka, however, both men and women rejected that interpretation, and said that the last son firmly belongs to the father's patrilineage. The last-born son is often, even today, called *Lja mkeku,* which is translated in Gutmann (ibid.) as "the one from the breast of the old woman." Rather than being associated with his mother's lineage, the association might be with the "old woman" whose social belonging to and position in her husband's lineage are firm and strong, unlike that of a young wife. Also, as the caretaker of the core patrilineal land and the ancestral graves, the youngest

son is strongly associated with his father's lineage. The youngest son might thus be rather thought of as "bi-gendered." Matrilineal connections are acknowledged in different ways, however, for instance, in name-giving. The children are given names alternately from the paternal and maternal side, every other child thus inheriting its name from the mother's side. This establishes a special connection between those two persons and it remains all through their lives.

7. I witnessed one inheritance meeting in Mayanka where a daughter was given land in accordance with her father's final will. The land plot was acquired by purchase and was thus not yet effective lineage land, and the father was a wealthy man able to leave land plots to all of his many sons as well.

8. The planting of the trees was apparently a strategic act since, although he was now his mother's only remaining son, Petro had several stepbrothers who needed land.

9. The political power of Chagga men living outside in lineage affairs is acknowledged by S. F. Moore (1986, 216, 250). Yet she (ibid., 254, 306) maintains that the middle sons, because of their position in the inheritance system, belong to the social category of persons "structurally selected for failure." Kerner (1988, 183) has challenged this contention and defines the middle sons rather as the "internal strangers" who, precisely because of being forced to leave, have ensured the resources, knowledge, and connections that maintain the local community. It seems to me that with the increased discrepancy between urban and rural economic possibilities and the changed inheritance practices, the position of the middle sons has been enhanced within the extended family and lineage.

10. S. F. Moore (1986, 283–84) mentions that in the lineage that she studied there were several examples of guardians cheating their wards. For this reason, she includes fatherless young men in the category of people who are in a "structurally weak position" (ibid., 305–6).

11. The same unfinished building was used only for the biggest church events such as the Christmas and confirmation services usually held in December. One sign of the lavishness of Henry's father's funeral was that the local church had not been able to acquire plastic sheets to replace the missing roof or loudspeakers for its major occasions, as Henry did.

12. Wearing uniform colors distinguished Henry, his mother, sisters, wife, and daughter as a group; Henry's brother and his family were not dressed in black.

13. Henry's original name is Lyatonga (both are pseudonyms here), which was the name of an old lineage elder that is to continue from generation to generation by the practice of naming each first-born son of a first-born son after him. Whereas some of the men named Lyatonga preferred using it to their individual names, Henry had at some point changed his name from Lyatonga to Henry, which he considered more international. This was another way to distinguish himself from the lineage men, and the "Lyatonga men."

14. When a bull was slaughtered for his father after the burial, Henry constantly consulted the elders for the right procedures. One of his lineage mates nevertheless complained afterwards that the portions of the bull's meat sent to people's homes were usually folded inside banana leaves and not in plastic bags as was done this time. The man added that Henry did not know or care for the customs. It was common to

hear people, both relatives and others, call Henry an upstart who could not behave respectfully.

15. At that time the minimum monthly wage was 10,000 TZS and the common monthly wage range in government jobs was 15,000–40,000 TZS.

16. See Comaroff (1985, 54) on round shapes and arcs as signifying enclosure and domestication in Tswana houses and H. Moore (1986, 132–37) on square and round houses among the Endo people.

17. Guyer reviews the "wealth in people" model in Equatorial Africa and emphasizes the valuation of different qualities of people or the "multiple dimensions of the value accorded to persons," and not only the accumulative logic of increasing the number of dependents (Guyer 1993, 259).

18. Barnes (1962) originally raised the question of whether the concepts of the African lineage and descent models were applicable in New Guinea societies. This initiated a debate that finally also developed into a critique and rethinking of the African materials themselves. For the discussion and analyses see e.g., Sahlins 1965, A. Strathern 1973, Karp 1978, Verdon 1980.

## 6. Making Sense of Failure

1. One case that involved suspicion of a person having bought a spirit in Tanga is related by S. F. Moore (1986, 295). It transpired in 1979 and the bought spirit was believed to have been acquired for bewitching another person, not for enrichment.

2. Interview with author, 20 January 1995.

3. Ibid.

4. *Kumbe lilimwingizia mali, lakini sasa linaharibu vitu vyake, watoto wake sio watu wazuri, linazunguka zunguka tu, na kulirudisha hawezi tena . . . linaranda-randa huko barabarani.*

5. Interview with author, 20 January 1995.

6. *Amepotea kabisa, hana nyumba, hana pesa, hana hata nguo, na mke wake . . . hali yao mbaya, watakufa.* Interview with author, 4 January 1995.

7. Interview with author, 9 July 1994.

8. Taylor (1992) has shown the importance of the dialectic of flow and blockage in Rwandan healing practice. He studies the historical transformation of imagery with commodification and capitalization. He does not consider how the valuation of flow/blockage and rest/mobility changes according to the life phase, however, but says that flows are positively valued and blockage negatively (Taylor 1992, 11).

9. Kichagga: *Lukombe kiaru*; Kiswahili: *Tulambe kiatu chako*.

10. See Weiss (1996) for an interesting account of how the physical conditions and symptoms are interpreted as expressions of more general states of being among the Haya.

11. This is comparable with Bloch's writing on the meaning of the ancestral tombs in Madagascar (1992, 11): "Among the Merina the monumental tombs represent the immortality of the descent group, its unchanging permanence through time, but also its immobile localization in a piece of territory with which it has been and will always be placed forever."

12. In the rituals described by Gutmann (1926) there are many benedictions on the person becoming firm like Mount Kibo.

13. The connection between slowness, coolness, peaceful continuity, and growth is echoed in older ritual speech (see e.g., Gutmann 1926, 235–70, 571).

14. *Kuisha* means "to finish," "to end," and "to complete."

15. *Rusha* means "doing someone out of his right." The root verb *ruka* means "to fly up," "fly away," "pass somebody over," "pass over or beyond," "overstep the limit," thus expressing personal and social boundaries in a spatial image. Note the meaningfulness of the personal boundaries also above in Upendo's account of her meeting with the wandering spirit by her repeating usage of such terms as "back," "ahead," "at the side," "to turn," "to pass."

16. An old woman related both restlessness and a meager harvest to the illegitimacy of land. She explained that after cultivating even a small area, her mother used to harvest a lot, "because earlier there was a lot of food, not like today: they cultivate but it does not show." In her mind, this change was not due to the shrinking size of land plots; productivity was better since "a lot of land was legitimate, and the soil too was moist." She explained: "Now the land has lost much of its strength. . . . Today you sell and the one to whom you sell does not stay long before he sells it to another person. Such land is not legitimate, and that is the reason why it gets sold again and again. And if you cultivate there you will not get a thing." Interview with author, 16 August 1994.

17. A parallel interpretation of cursed land and household turmoil caused by a bought spirit is related in one case by S. F. Moore (1986, 295; see above, n.1). In that case, suspicions of a bought spirit arose as one house was found "beaten" and in disarray, and the alternative explanation for the situation was that the land was cursed.

18. See more on the moral distinctions between different areas and peoples in the chapter on Mental Geography in Pietilä 1999.

19. Swantz (1985) found affirmation in her research in Kilimanjaro during the 1970s on the assertion of Dundas (1968 [1924]) that a curse is the weapon of weak members of society. According to Swantz (1985, 88–89), her data indicated that the use of curses was limited entirely to women and usually used against other women. She interprets this as an expression of the inferior social position of women and cursing as their only weapon for expressing oppression and wielding power. In Mayanka, a curse can be uttered by both women and men, but it is often held that the curses of women tend to be more severe and steadfast. For this reason, women's curses—especially those of old women—are feared, not the least by their sons.

20. See, for instance, Comaroff and Comaroff 1993, xxvi; Fisiy and Geschiere 1996, 206; Weiss 1996; and Taussig 1980 for a case in South America.

21. White interprets the stories as popular debates about labor and inadequate remuneration and thus as discourses of new forms of violence and exploitation.

22. For its fluidity money was sometimes conceptualized as "hot" in Mayanka (cf. Weiss on Haya 1996, 231). For instance, I was once sitting in the office of a female civil servant when a man came in, handed her a brown envelope, and left. The woman lifted the envelope against the sunny window and as she saw that it enclosed

a note, she slipped it into her pocket, and tapping it she smiled at me and said, "I'm happy to get this soup money to warm my pocket." The "warmth" in the woman's usage had a double meaning, however, referring not only to the quality of the money but also, through the reference to soup and by its enclosure in the pocket, to its immediate "domestication."

23. See Weiss (1996) and Comaroff and Comaroff (1993, xx–xxiv) on modernity and commodities as experienced processes. Weiss (1996) examines them as new fields of signification that are conceived to alter the temporal and thermal dimensions of the basic processes of growth, production, and consumption.

24. Nowadays, these kinds of images of power are also related to affluent women traders; in an earlier chapter the frightening power of a self-sufficient woman enriched by her trading was expressed as her being able to "choose any man she happens to like."

25. According to Gibbon (1995, 16), in the mid-1990s there were widely held concerns about the upsurge of "wild capitalism" brought about by the process of economic liberalization in Tanzania. This meant the reappearance in free market guises, and on a larger and less controlled scale, of earlier forms of "rent-seeking behavior"; that is, rather than by real economic production and progress, profits were created by manipulating the economic environment, especially by utilizing government relations and/or state resources for business ventures.

26. See more in chapter on Mental Geography in Pietilä 1999.

27. The Arusha Declaration, which was largely based on the ideas of President Julius Nyerere, formulated African socialism *(ujamaa)* and self-reliance as the basis for the country's development path. This came to mean an extensive centralization of economic and political power on the state and organization of population into village cooperatives during the 1970s. In many areas a mass of the rural population was physically moved into new villages, but in densely populated areas, such as Kilimanjaro, "villagization" more often meant drawing administrative borders for the already existing settlements rather than relocation of people.

# Glossary

All the words below are in Kiswahili. Verbs are listed in their basic form, which starts with *ku-*.

| | |
|---|---|
| aibu | shame, dishonor |
| akili | intellect, intelligence |
| biashara | business, trade |
| dawa, pl. madawa | medicine |
| faida | profit, gain |
| hawara | mistress, concubine |
| heshima | respect, honor |
| jini, pl. majini | spirit (in this book refers to a bought spirit) |
| kanga | piece of cotton cloth with a printed saying and colorful designs, worn by women |
| kihamba, pl. vihamba | patrilineally inherited plot of land on which typically bananas and coffee are grown |
| kitenge, pl. vitenge | printed cotton wrap, of heavier fabric than *kanga* |

| | |
|---|---|
| klabu/kilabu, pl. vilabu | bar |
| Konyagi | distilled ginlike liquor made in Tanzania |
| kubembeleza | to coax, to persuade, to soothe |
| kudanganya | to deceive, to cheat |
| kufuga | to domesticate, to keep cattle |
| kufunga | to bind, to close |
| kuisha | to finish, to vanish, to cease |
| kuishi | to live, to remain |
| kujitegemea | to be self-reliant |
| kukaa | to stay, to sit |
| kukauka | to dry up, also used for a person who suffers from inadequate food and care, and for a sexually deprived woman |
| kulima | to cultivate |
| kupotea | to vanish, to get lost |
| kurusha | to deprive someone of his/ her right |
| kutembea | to wander, to walk, to lead an irregular life |
| kuvuta | to draw, to attract |
| kuwaza | to meditate, to ponder, to imagine, to reflect, to think |
| kuzunguka | to wander around (aimlessly) |
| kuzurura | to roam, to wander around |
| maarifa | knowledge, erudition, experience |
| machalare | customary meal made of meat and *mchare* bananas |
| maelewano | mutual understanding |
| mageuzi | reform, change |
| mama | mother |
| mangi | chief |
| mapinduzi | revolution |
| matanga | ceremony in which the property and the social relations and obligations of a deceased and his/ her home are discussed and arranged |
| mbege | finger millet (eleusine), also local beer (made of bananas and finger millet) |
| mbishi | an obstinate person |
| mdomo | mouth, speech |
| mganga, pl. waganga | healer |
| mhuni, pl. wahuni | a shameless person, vagabond |
| mjanja, pl. wajanja | a cunning person |
| mjinga, pl. wajinga | a person who is stupid/ fool/ foolish/ ignorant/ naïve/ simple-minded |
| mkali | a stern or tough person |
| mzima | a person who is well/ healthy/ sound/ unhurt |
| mzungukaji | a person who wanders around (aimlessly) |
| mzururaji | a person who roams/ wanders around |
| nyongeza | supplement, an increase |
| panga | large bush knife, machete |
| pombe | beer (both traditional and bottled) |

| | |
|---|---|
| pori | forest, wilderness; also used to refer to a cultural "other" |
| riziki | basic necessities or needs |
| sale, pl. masale | dracaena plant used to mark a *kihamba* boundary and a grave |
| shamba | land on the lower belt used for cultivating annual crops, such as maize, eleusine, and beans; used to be temporarily held land but nowadays often passed on as inheritance from father to offspring like *kihamba* land |
| shilingi, pl. shilingi | Tanzanian monetary unit: Tanzanian Shilling, TZS |
| siri, pl. siri | secret |
| soko, pl. masoko | market, marketplace |
| tamaa | greed, desire, avarice |
| uchawi | sorcery, witchcraft |
| ujamaa | familyhood (African) socialism |
| ujanja | cunning, craftiness, cleverness |
| ujinga | stupidity, ignorance, naivety, foolishness, simple-mindedness |
| ukoo, pl. koo | lineage |
| ulezi | finger millet: eleusine coracana |
| uzima | wholeness, soundness, completeness |
| uzoefu | experience |
| wazo, pl. mawazo | idea, opinion, reflection, view, thought |

# Bibliography

Abrahams, Roger D. 1970. "A Performance-Centered Approach to Gossip." *Man* 5, no. 2: 290–301.

———. 1974. "Black Talking on the Streets." In *Explorations in the Ethnography of Speaking*, eds. Richard Bauman and J. Sherzer, pp. 240–63. Cambridge: Cambridge University Press.

———. 1983. *The Man-of-Words in the West Indies: Performance and the Emergence of Creole Culture*. Baltimore: Johns Hopkins University Press.

Alexander, Jennifer. 1987. *Trade, Traders and Trading in Rural Java*. Singapore: Oxford University Press.

Appadurai, Arjun. 1986. "Introduction: Commodities and the Politics of Value." In *The Social Life of Things: Commodities in Cultural Perspective*, ed. Arjun Appadurai, pp. 3–63. Cambridge: Cambridge University Press.

Appleby, Gordon. 1985. "Marketplace Development in the Gambia River Basin." In *Markets and Marketing: Monographs in Economic Anthropology* No. 4, ed. Stuart Plattner, pp. 79–97. Lanham, Md.: University Press of America and Society for Economic Anthropology.

Apter, Andrew. 1993. "Atinga Revisited: Yoruba Witchcraft and the Cocoa Economy, 1950–1951." In *Modernity and Its Malcontents: Ritual and Power in Postcolonial Africa,* eds. Jean Comaroff and John Comaroff, pp. 113 –23. Chicago: University of Chicago Press.

Ardener, Edwin. 1975. "Belief and the Problem of Women and the 'Problem' Revisited." In *Perceiving Women,* ed. Shirley Arderner, pp. 1–28. London: J. M. Dent.

Auslander, Mark. 1993. "'Open the Wombs!': The Symbolic Politics of Modern Ngoni Witchfinding." In *Modernity and Its Malcontents: Ritual and Power in Postcolonial Africa,* eds. Jean Comaroff and John Comaroff, pp. 167–92. Chicago: University of Chicago Press.

Austen, Ralph. 1993. "The Moral Economy of Witchcraft: An Essay in Comparative History." In *Modernity and Its Malcontents: Ritual and Power in Postcolonial Africa,* eds. Jean Comaroff and John Comaroff, pp. 89 –110. Chicago: University of Chicago Press.

Babb, Florence. 1989. *Between Field and Cooking Pot: The Political Economy of Marketwomen in Peru.* Austin: University of Texas Press.

Bakhtin, Mikhail M. 1981. *The Dialogic Imagination: Four Essays.* Edited by Michael Holquist. Translated by Michael Holquist and Caryl Emerson. Austin: University of Texas Press.

———. 1984. *Rabelais and His World.* Translated by Hélène Iswolsky. Bloomington: Indiana University Press.

———. 1994 [1986]. *Speech Genres and Other Late Essays.* Edited by Michael Holquist and Caryl Emerson. Translated by Vern McGee. Austin: University of Texas Press.

Balzer, Harley. 2003. "Routinization of the New Russians?" *The Russian Review* 62: 15 –36.

Barnes, J. A. 1962. "African Models in the New Guinea Highlands." *Man* 52: 5 –9.

Barnes, Sandra. 1990. "Women, Property, and Power." In *Beyond the Second Sex,* eds. P. R. Sanday and R. G. Goodenough, pp. 253 –80. Philadelphia: University of Pennsylvania Press.

Bastian, Misty L. 1992. "The World as Marketplace: Historical, Cosmological, and Popular Constructions of the Onitsha Market System." Ph.D. diss., University of Chicago.

Beidelman, T. O. 1993 [1986]. *Moral Imagination in Kaguru Modes of Thought.* Washington, D.C.: Smithsonian Institution Press.

Bergmann, Jörg R. 1993. *Discreet Indiscretions: The Social Organization of Gossip.* New York: Aldine de Gruyter.

Berry, Sara. 1995. "Stable Prices, Unstable Values: Some Thoughts on Monetization and the Meaning of Transaction in West African Economies." In *Money Matters: Instability, Values and Social Payments in the Modern History of West African Communities,* ed. Jane Guyer, pp. 299 –313. London: James Currey.

Besnier, Niko. 1990. "Conflict Management, Gossip, and Affective Meaning in Nukulaelae." In *Disentangling Conflict Discourse in Pacific Societies,* eds. Karen Ann Watson-Gegeo and Geoffrey M. White, pp. 290–334. Stanford, Calif.: Stanford University Press.

Bledsoe, C. 1980. *Women and Marriage in Kpelle Society.* Stanford, Calif.: Stanford University Press.

Bloch, Maurice. 1992. "Internal and External Memory: Different Ways of Being in History." *Suomen Antropologi* 1: 3 –15.

Bohannan, Paul. 1955. "Some Principles of Exchange and Investment among the Tiv." *American Anthropologist* 57, no. 5: 60–70.

———. 1959. "The Impact of Money on an African Subsistence Economy." *The Journal of Economic History* 19, no. 4: 491–503.

———. 1963. " 'Land,' 'Tenure' and Land-Tenure." In *African Agrarian Systems,* ed. D. Biebuyck, pp. 110–15. Oxford: Oxford University Press.

Bohannan, Paul, and George Dalton, eds. 1968 [1962]. *Markets in Africa.* Evanston, Ill.: Northwestern University Press.

Boddy, Janice. 1989. *Wombs and Alien Spirits: Women, Men, and the Zar Cult in Northern Sudan.* Madison: University of Wisconsin Press.

Boserup, Esther. 1970. *Women's Role in Economic Development.* New York: St. Martin's.

Bourdieu, Pierre. 1977. *Outline of a Theory of Practice.* Cambridge: Cambridge University Press.

BP Tanzania Limited. 1990. *BP Map of Tanzania.* Dar es Salaam: BP Tanzania Limited.

Brenneis, Donald. 1984. "Grog and Gossip in Bhatgaon: Style and Substance in Fiji Indian Conversation." *American Ethnologist* 11, no. 3: 487–506.

———. 1987. "Talk and Transformation." *Man* 22, no. 3: 499 –510.

Brison, Karen J. 1992. *Just Talk: Gossip, Meetings, and Power in a Papua New Guinea Village.* Berkeley: University of California Press.

Bruno, Marta. 1997. "Women and the Culture of Entrepreneurship." In *Post-Soviet Women: From the Baltic to Central Asia,* ed. Mary Buckley, pp. 56 –73. Cambridge: Cambridge University Press.

Bryceson, Deborah. 1994. "Trade Roots in Tanzania: Evolution of Urban Grain Markets Under Structural Adjustment." *Sociologia Ruralis* 34, no. 1: 13 –25.

Bujra, Janet. 1975. "Women 'Entrepreneurs' of Early Nairobi." *Canadian Journal of African Studies* 9, no. 2: 213 –34.

Bureau of Statistics, Planning Commission, Dar es Salaam, Tanzania. 1993. *Tanzania Demographic and Health Survey 1991/1992.* Edited by Ngallaba, S., Kapiga S., Ruyobya, I. and Boerma J. Columbia, Md.: Macro International Inc.

Caplan, Pat. 1997. *African Voices, African Lives: Personal Narratives From a Swahili Village.* London: Routledge.

Carsten, Janet. 1995. "The Substance of Kinship and the Heat of the Hearth: Feeding, Personhood, and Relatedness among Malays in Pulau Langkawi." *American Ethnologist* 22, no. 2: 223 –41.

Clark, Gracia. 1994. *Onions Are My Husband: Survival and Accumulation by West African Market Women.* Chicago: University of Chicago Press.

———. 1999. "Mothering, Work, and Gender in Urban Asante Ideology and Practice." *American Anthropologist* 101, no. 4: 717 –29.

———. 2001. "Gender and Profiteering: Ghana's Market Women as Devoted Mothers and "Human Vampire Bats." In *"Wicked" Women and the Reconfiguration of*

*Gender in Africa*, eds. Hodgson Dorothy and Sheryl McCurdy, pp. 293–311. Portsmouth, N.H.: Heinemann.

Colson, E. 1971. "The Impact of the Colonial Period on the Definition of Land Rights." In *Colonialism in Africa*. Vol. 3, *Profiles of Change*, ed. Victor Turner, pp. 193–215. Cambridge: Cambridge University Press.

Comaroff, Jean. 1985. *Body of Power, Spirit of Resistance: The Culture and History of a South African People*. Chicago: University of Chicago Press.

Comaroff, Jean, and John Comaroff. 1992. "Goodly Beasts, Beastly Goods." In *Ethnography and the Historical Imagination*, Jean Comaroff and John Comaroff, pp. 127–54. Boulder, Colo.: Westview Press.

———. 1993. Introduction to *Modernity and Its Malcontents: Ritual and Power in Postcolonial Africa*, eds. Jean Comaroff and John Comaroff, pp. xi–xxxvii. Chicago: University of Chicago Press.

Comaroff, John, and S. A. Roberts. 1981. *Rules and Processes: The Cultural Logic of Dispute in an African Context*. Chicago: University of Chicago Press.

Coplan, David. 2001. "You Have Left Me Wandering About: Basotho Women and the Culture of Mobility." In *"Wicked" Women and the Reconfiguration of Gender in Africa*, eds. Hodgson Dorothy and Sheryl McCurdy, pp. 188–211. Portsmouth, N.H.: Heinemann.

Cornwall, Andrea. 2001. "Wayward Women and Useless Men: Contest and Change in Gender Relations in Ado-Odo, S. W. Nigeria." In *"Wicked" Women and the Reconfiguration of Gender in Africa*, eds. Hodgson Dorothy and Sheryl McCurdy, pp. 67–84. Portsmouth, N.H.: Heinemann.

Cowen, Michael. 1981. "The Agrarian Problem." *Review of African Political Economy* 20: 57–73.

Drucker-Brown, Susan. 1993. "Mamprusi Witchcraft: Subversion and Changing Gender Relations." *Africa* 63, no. 4: 531–49.

Dundas, Charles. 1968 [1924]. *Kilimanjaro and its people*. London: Frank Cass and Co. Ltd.

Dwyer, K. 1982. *Moroccan Dialogue: Anthropology in Question*. Baltimore: Johns Hopkins University Press.

Eames, Elizabeth. 1988. "Why the Women Went to War: Women and Wealth in Ondo Town, Southwestern Nigeria." In *Traders versus the State: Anthropological Approaches to Unofficial Economies*, ed. Gracia Clark, pp. 81–97. Boulder, Colo.: Westview Press.

Ekechi, Felix. 1995. "Gender and Economic Power: The Case of Igbo Market Women of Eastern Nigeria." In *African Market Women and Economic Power: The Role of Women in African Economic Development*, eds. Bessie House-Midamba and Felix K. Ekechi, pp. 41–58. Westport, Conn.: Greenwood Press.

Emanatian, Michele. 1996. "Everyday Metaphors of Lust and Sex in Chagga." *Ethos* 24, no. 2: 195–236.

Englund, Harri. 1996. "Witchcraft, Modernity and the Person. The Morality of Accumulation in Central Malawi." *Critique of Anthropology* 16, no. 3: 257–79.

———. 1999. "The Self in Self-Interest: Land, Labour and Temporalities in Malawi's Agrarian Change." *Africa* 69, no. 1: 139–59.

Epstein, A. L. 1969. "Gossip, Norms and Social Network." In *Social Networks in Urban Situations: Analysis of personal relationships in Central African Towns,* ed. Clyde Mitchell, pp. 117–27. Manchester: Manchester University Press.

Evans-Pritchard, E. E. 1937. *Witchcraft, Oracles and Magic among the Azande.* Oxford: Clarendon Press.

FAO (Food and Agriculture Organization of the United Nations) GeoNetwork. 2001a. *Major Cities of Africa.* Rome: FAO. http://www.fao.org/geonetwork/srv/en/main.search (accessed 2 June 2006).

———. 2001b. *Rivers of Tanzania.* Rome: FAO. http://www.fao.org/geonetwork/srv/en/main.search (accessed 2 June 2006).

———. 2001c. *Sub-National Boundaries of Africa.* Rome: FAO. http://www.fao.org/geonetwork/srv/en/main.search (accessed 2 June 2006).

Fabian, Johannes. 1995. "Language and Popular in Africa." Paper presented in the postgraduate seminar days of anthropological and ethnological sciences at the University of Helsinki, Finland, 12 February.

———. 1996. *Remembering the Present: Painting and Popular History in Zaire.* Berkeley: University of California Press.

Falola, Toyin. 1995. "Gender, Business, and Space Control: Yoruba Market Women and Power." In *African Market Women and Economic Power: The Role of Women in African Economic Development,* eds. Bessie House-Midamba and Felix K. Ekechi, pp. 23–40. Westport, Conn.: Greenwood Press.

Feldman-Savelsberg, Pamela. 1996. "Cooking Inside: Kinship and Gender in Bangangté Idioms of Marriage and Procreation." In *Gender, Kinship, Power: A Comparative and Interdisciplinary History,* eds. Maynes, Waltner, Soland and Strasser, pp. 117–97. New York: Routledge.

Ferguson, James. 1985. "The Bovine Mystique: Power, Property and Livestock in Rural Lesotho." *Man* 20: 647–74.

Ferguson, James. 1992. "The Cultural Topography of Wealth: Commodity Paths and the Structure of Property in Rural Lesotho. *American Anthropologist* 94: 55–73.

Fernandes, Oktingati, and Maghembe. 1984. "The Chagga Homegardens: a Multistoreyd Agroforestry Cropping System on Mt. Kilimanjaro." *Agroforestry Systems* 2: 73–86.

Fernandez, James. 1982. *Bwiti: An Ethnography of the Religious Imagination in Africa.* Princeton, N.J.: Princeton University Press.

Fisher, Lawrence E. 1976. "Dropping Remarks and the Barbadian Audience." *American Ethnologist* 3, no. 2: 227–42.

Fisiy, Cyprian, and Peter Geschiere. 1991. "Sorcery, Witchcraft and Accumulation—Regional Variations in South and West Cameroon." *Critique of Anthropology* 11, no. 3: 251–78.

———. 1996. "Witchcraft, Violence and Identity: Different Trajectories in Postcolonial Cameroon." In *Postcolonial Identities in Africa,* eds. Richard Werbner and Terence Ranger, pp. 193–210. London: Zed Books Ltd.

Fortes, Meyer. 1987. "The Concept of the Person." In *Religion, Morality and the Person: Essays on Tallensi Religion,* ed. Jack Goody, pp. 247–86. Cambridge: Cambridge University Press.

French, Robert, and Keith T. Kernan. 1981. "Art and Artifice in Belizean Creole." *American Ethnologist* 8, no. 2: 238–58.

Geertz, Clifford. 1979. "Suq: the bazaar economy in Sefrou." In *Meaning and Order in Moroccan Society: Three Essays in Cultural Analysis,* eds. Clifford Geertz, Hildred Geertz, and Lawrence Rosen, pp. 123–264. Cambridge: Cambridge University Press.

Geschiere, Peter. 2000 [1997]. *The Modernity of Witchcraft: Politics and Occult in Postcolonial Africa.* Charlottesville: University Press of Virginia.

Gibbon, Peter. 1995. "Mechanization of Production and Privatization of Development in Post-Ujamaa Tanzania: An Introduction." In *Liberalised Development in Tanzania,* ed. Peter Gibbon, pp. 9–36. Uppsala: The Scandinavian Institute of African Studies.

Glassman, Jonathon. 1995. *Feasts and Riot: Revelry, Rebellion, and Popular Consciousness on the Swahili Coast, 1856–1888.* Portsmouth, N.H.: Heinemann.

Gluckman, Max. 1963. "Gossip and Scandal." *Current Anthropology* 4, no. 3: 307–16.

———. 1972 [1965]. *The Ideas in Barotse Jurisprudence.* Manchester: Manchester University Press.

Godelier, Maurice. 1986. *The Making of Great Men: Male Domination and Power Among the New Guinea Baruya.* Translated by Rupert Swyer. Cambridge: Cambridge University Press.

Green, Maia. 1997. "Witchcraft Suppression Practices and Movements: Public Politics and the Logic of Purification." *Comparative Studies in Society and History* 39, no. 2: 319–45.

Gregory, C. A. 1982. *Gifts and Commodities.* London: Academic Press.

Gulbrandsen, Ornulf. 1986. "To Marry—or Not to Marry: Marital Strategies and Sexual Relations in a Tswana Society." *Ethnos* 1–2: 7–28.

Gutmann, Bruno. 1907. "Die Frau bei den Wadschagga." *Globus* 92: 49–51.

———. 1926. *Das Recht der Dschagga.* München: C. H. Beck. English translation by A. M. Nagler, Human Relations Area Files (HRAF), New Haven, Conn.: Yale University Press.

Guyer, Jane. 1993. "Wealth in People and Self-realisation in Equatorial Africa." *Man* 28, no. 2: 243–65.

———. 1995. Introduction to *Money Matters: Instability, Values and Social Payments in the Modern History of West African Communities,* ed. Jane Guyer, pp. 1–37. London: James Currey.

Guyer, Jane, and Samuel Belinga. 1995. "Wealth in People as Wealth in Knowledge: Accumulation and Composition in Equatorial Africa." *Journal of African History* 36, no. 1: 91–120.

Habermas, Jürgen. 1998. *On the Pragmatics of Communication.* Cambridge, MA: MIT Press.

Hansen, Karen Tranberg. 1989. "The Black Market and Women Traders in Lusaka, Zambia." In *Women and the State in Africa,* eds. Jane Parpart and Kathleen Staudt, pp. 143–60. Boulder: Lynne Rienner Publishers.

Hart, Keith. 1982. "On Commoditization." In *From Craft to Industry: The Ethnography of Proto-industrial Cloth Production,* ed. Esther N. Goody, pp. 38–49. Cambridge: Cambridge University Press.

Hasu, Päivi. 1999. *Desire and Death: History through Ritual Practice in Kilimanjaro.* Helsinki: Transactions of the Finnish Anthropological Society.

Haviland, John. 1977. *Gossip, Reputation, and Knowledge in Zinacantan.* Chicago: University of Chicago Press.

Hay, Jean. 1976. "Luo Women and Economic Change during the Colonial Period." In *Women in Africa: Studies in Social and Economic Change,* eds. Nancy Hafkin and Edna Bay, pp. 87–109. Stanford, Calif.: Stanford University Press.

———. 1988. "Queens, Prostitutes, and Peasants: Historical Perspectives on African Women, 1971–1986." *Canadian Journal of African Studies* 22, no. 3: 431–47.

Hayes, Rose. 1975. "Female Genital Mutilation, Fertility Control, Women's Roles, and the Patrilineage in Modern Sudan: A Functional Analysis." *American Ethnologist* 2: 617–33.

Heyat, Farideh. 2002. "Women and the Culture of Entrepreneurship in Soviet and Post-Soviet Azerbaijan." In *Markets and Moralities: Ethnographies of Postsocialism,* eds. Ruth Mandel and Caroline Humphrey, pp. 19–32. Oxford: Berg.

Hill, Polly. 1963. "Markets in Africa." *The Journal of Modern African Studies* 1, no. 4: 441–53.

———. 1969. "Hidden Trade in Hausaland." *Man* 4: 392–409.

Hodgson, Dorothy, and Sheryl McCurdy. 2001. Introduction to *Wicked" Women and the Reconfiguration of Gender in Africa,* eds. Hodgson Dorothy and Sheryl McCurdy, pp. 1–24. Portsmouth, N.H.: Heinemann.

House-Midamba, Bessie. 1995. "Kikuyu Market Women Traders and the Struggle for Economic Empowerment in Kenya." In *African Market Women and Economic Power: The Role of Women in African Economic Development,* eds. Bessie House-Midamba and Felix K. Ekechi, pp. 81–98. Westport, Conn.: Greenwood Press.

House-Midamba, Bessie, and Felix K. Ekechi. 1995. Introduction to *African Market Women and Economic Power: The Role of Women in African Economic Development,* eds. Bessie House-Midamba and Felix K. Ekechi, pp. xi–xix. Westport, Conn.: Greenwood Press.

Howard, Mary, and Ann Millard. 1997. *Hunger and Shame: Child Malnutrition and Poverty on Mount Kilimanjaro.* New York: Routledge.

Humphrey, Caroline. 2002. *The Unmaking of Soviet Life: Everyday Economies after Socialism.* Ithaca, N.Y.: Cornell University Press.

Hutchinson, Sharon. 1990. "Rising Divorce among the Nuer, 1936–1983." *Man* 25, no. 3: 393–411.

Håkansson, Thomas. 1994. "The Detachability of Women: Gender and Kinship in Processes of Socioeconomic Change among the Gusii of Kenya." *American Ethnologist* 21, no. 3: 516–38.

International Monetary Fund. 1995. *Statement by the IMF Staff Representative.* Paris: Tanzania Consultative Group.

Jackson, Michael. 1989. *Paths Toward a Clearing: Radical Empiricism and Ethnographic Inquiry.* Bloomington: Indiana University Press.

Jackson, Michael, and Ivan Karp, eds. 1990. *Personhood and Agency: The Experience of Self and Other in African Cultures.* Uppsala: Acta Universitatis Upsaliensis.

Jacobson-Widding, Anita., 1990. "The Shadow as an Expression of Individuality in Congolese Conceptions of Personhood." In *Personhood and Agency: The*

*Experience of Self and Other in African Cultures,* eds. Michael Jackson and Ivan Karp, pp. 31–58. Uppsala: Acta Universitatis Upsaliensis.

Jeater, D., 1993. *Marriage, Perversion and Power: The Construction of Moral Discourse in Southern Rhodesia, 1894–1930.* Oxford: Clarendon Press.

Jørgensen, Dan. 1983. "The Facts of Life, Papua New Guinea Style." *Mankind* 14, no. 1: 1–12.

*Kamusi ya Kiswahili Sanifu.* 1981. Dar es Salaam: Oxford University Press.

Kapchan, Deborah. 1996. *Gender on the Market: Moroccan Women and the Revoicing of Tradition.* Philadelphia: University of Pennsylvania Press.

Karp, Ivan. 1978. "New Guinea Models in the African Savannah." *Africa* 48, no. 1: 1–16.

Kerner, Donna. 1988. "The Social Uses of Knowledge in Contemporary Tanzania." Ph.D. diss., City University of New York.

King, Kenneth. 1996. *Jua Kali Kenya: Change and Development in an Informal Economy 1970–95.* London: James Currey Ltd.

Kongstad, P., and M. Mönsted. 1980. *Family, Labor and Trade in Western Kenya.* Centre for Development Research, Publication No. 3. Uppsala: Scandinavian Institute for African Studies.

Koponen, Juhani. 1988. *People and Production in Late Precolonial Tanzania: History and Structures.* Helsinki: Finnish Society for Development Studies, Finnish Anthropological Society in cooperation with Scandinavian Institute of African Studies.

———. 1994. *Development for Exploitation: German colonial policies in Mainland Tanzania, 1884–1914.* Helsinki and Hamburg: Finnish Historical Society and Lit Verlag.

Krapf, J. L. 1860. *Travels, Researches and Missionary Labours during an Eighteen Years' Residence in Eastern Africa.* London.

Kuper, Adam. 1982. "Lineage Theory: A Critical Retrospect." *Annual Review of Anthropology* 11: 71–95.

La Fontaine, Jean. 1974. "The Free Women of Kinshasa: Prostitution in a City in Zaire." In *Choice and Change: Essays in Honour of Lucy Mair,* ed. J. Davis, pp. 89–113. Monographs on Social Anthropology, No 50. London: Athlone Press.

LeVine, Robert. 1970. "Sex Roles and Economic Change in Africa." In *Black Africa: Its Peoples and Cultures Today,* ed. John Middleton, pp. 174–80. London: Macmillan and Co.

Lewis, Oscar. 1959. *Five Families: Mexican Case Studies in the Culture of Poverty.* London: Souvenir Press.

———. 1961. *The Children of Sanhez: Autobiography of a Mexican Family.* Harmondsworth: Penguin Books.

Lindisfarne, Nancy. 1994. "Variant Masculinities, Variant Virginities: Rethinking 'Honour and Shame.'" In *Dislocating Masculinity: Comparative Ethnographies,* eds. A. Cornwall and N. Lindisfarne, pp. 82–96. London: Routledge.

Little, K. L. 1948. "The Changing Position of Women in the Sierra Leone Protectorate." *Africa* 18, no. 1: 1–17.

Lovett, Margot. 2001. "'She Thinks She's Like a Man': Marriage and (De)constructing Gender Identity in Colonial Buha, Tanzania, 1943–1960." In *"Wicked" Women and the Reconfiguration of Gender in Africa,* eds. Hodgson Dorothy and Sheryl McCurdy, pp. 47–66. Portsmouth, N.H.: Heinemann.

MacGaffey, Janet. 1987. *Entrepreneurs and Parasites: The struggle for indigenous capitalism in Zaire.* Camridge: Cambridge University Press.

Malinowski, Bronislav. 1961 [1922]. *Argonauts of the Western Pacific.* New York: Dutton and Co.

Maro, Paul. 1975. *Population Growth and Agricultural Change in Kilimanjaro 1920–1970.* Research Paper no. 40. Dar es Salaam: Bureau of Resource Assessment and Land Use Planning.

Marwick, Max. 1965. *Sorcery in its Social Setting: A Study of Northern Rhodesian Cewa.* Manchester: Manchester University Press.

Masquelier, Adeline. 1995. "Consumption, Prostitution, and Reproduction: the Poetics of Sweetness in Bori." *American Ethnologist* 22, no. 4: 883–906.

Mauss, Marcel. 1985 [1938]. "A Category of the Human Mind: the Notion of Person; the Notion of Self." Translated by W. D. Halls. In *The Category of the Person: Anthropology, Philosophy, History,* eds. Michael Carrithers, Steven Collins and Steven Lukes, pp. 1–25. Cambridge: Cambridge University Press.

———. 1990 [1925]. *The Gift: The Form and Reason for Exchange in Archaic Societies.* London: Routledge.

Mbembe, Achille. 1992. "Provisional Notes on the Postcolony." *Africa* 62, no. 1: 3–37.

McCall, D. 1961. "Trade and the Role of Wife in a Modern West African Town." In *Social Change in Modern Africa,* ed. Aidan Southall, pp. 286–99. London: Oxford University Press.

McCurdy, Sheryl A. 2001. "Urban Threats: Manyema Women, Low Fertility, and Venereal Diseases in Tanganyika, 1926–1936." In *"Wicked" Women and the Reconfiguration of Gender in Africa,* eds. Hodgson Dorothy and Sheryl McCurdy, pp. 212–33. Portsmouth, N.H.: Heinemann.

Meyer, Hans. 1891. *Across East African Glaciers.* Translated from German by E. H. S. Calder. London: George Philip and Son.

Microsoft MapPoint Web Service. 2005. *World Atlas.* Washington, D.C. http://encarta.msn.com/encnet/features/MapCenter/Map.aspx (accessed 2 June 2006).

Middleton, John, and E. H. Winter, eds. 1963. *Witchcraft and Sorcery in East Africa.* London: Routledge and Kegan Paul.

Ministry of Finance, Economic Affairs and Planning, Bureau of Statistics. 1989. *Tanzania Population Census 1989.* Dar es Salaam: Ministry of Finance, Economic Affairs and Planning, Bureau of Statistics.

Mintz, Sidney. 1971. "Men, Women, and Trade." *Comparative Studies in Society and History* 13: 247–69.

Mitchell-Kernan, Claudia. 1971. *Language Behavior in a Black Urban Community.* Monographs of the Language-Behavior Research Laboratory, no. 2. Berkeley: University of California.

Moore, Henrietta. 1986. *Space, Text and Gender: An Anthropological Study of the Marakwet of Kenya.* New York: Guilford Press.

Moore, Henrietta, and Vaughan, Megan. 1994. *Cutting Down Trees: Gender, Nutrition, and Agricultural Change in the Northern Province of Zambia, 1890–1990.* London: James Currey Ltd.

Moore, Sally Falk. 1976. "The Secret of the Men: A Fiction of Chagga Initiation and Its Relation to the Logic of Chagga Symbolism." *Africa* 46, no. 4: 357–70.

———. 1986. *Social Facts and Fabrications: "Customary" Law on Kilimanjaro, 1880–1980.* Cambridge: Cambridge University Press.

———. 1996. "Post-Socialist Micro-Politics: Kilimanjaro, 1993." *Africa* 66, no. 4: 587–605.

Munro William A. 1998. *The Moral Economy of the State Conservation, Community Development, and State Making in Zimbabwe.* Athens: Ohio University Press, Center for International Studies.

Musisi, Nakanyike B. 1995. "Baganda Women's Night Market Activities." In *African Market Women and Economic Power: The Role of Women in African Economic Development,* eds. Bessie House-Midamba and Felix K. Ekechi, pp. 121–39. Westport, Conn.: Greenwood Press.

Myers, Fred R., and Donald Brenneis. 1984. Introduction to *Dangerous Words: Language and Politics in the Pacific,* eds. Donald Brenneis and Fred R. Myers, pp. 1–29. Prospect Heights, Ill.: Waveland Press.

Nadel, S. F. 1965 [1942]. *A Black Byzantium: The Kingdom of Nupe in Nigeria.* London: Oxford University Press.

———. 1952. "Witchcraft in Four African Societies: An Essay in Comparison." *American Anthropologist* 54, no. 1: 18–29.

Ngolé, Jean-Pierre. 1986. "Social Relations and Group Identity among Women Fishsellers in the Congo." *Women's Studies International Forum* 9, no. 3: 287–93.

Obbo, Christine. 1975. "Women's Careers in Low Income Areas as Indicators of Country and Town Dynamics." In *Town and Country in Central and Eastern Africa,* ed. David Parkin, pp. 288–93. Oxford: Oxford University Press for International African Institute.

———. 1980. *African Women: Their Struggle for Economic Independence.* London: Zed Press.

Ogden, Jessica. 1996. "'Producing' Respect: the 'proper woman' in Postcolonial Kampala." In *Postcolonial Identities in Africa,* eds. Richard Werbner and Terence Ranger, pp. 165–92. London: Zed Books Ltd.

Ogbomo, Onaiwu. 1995. "Esan Women Traders and Precolonial Economic Power." In *African Market Women and Economic Power: The Role of Women in African Economic Development,* eds. Bessie House-Midamba and Felix K. Ekechi, pp. 1–22. Westport. Conn.: Greenwood Press.

Okely, Judith, and Helen Callaway. 1997. *Anthropology and Autobiography.* London: Routledge.

Oliver, R. A., and J. D. Fage. 1962. *A Short History of Africa.* Harmondsworth: Penguin African Library.

Ottenberg, Phoebe V. 1959 "The Changing Economic Position of Women Among the Afikpo Ibo." In *Continuity and Change in African Cultures,* eds. William R. Bascom and Melville J. Herskovits, pp. 205–23. Chicago: University of Chicago Press.

Paine, Robert. 1967. "What Is Gossip About? An Alternative Hypothesis." *Man* 2, no. 2: 278–85.

Parpart, Jane. 2001. "'Wicked Women' and 'Respectable Ladies': Reconfiguring Gender on the Zambian Copperbelt, 1936 –1964." In *"Wicked" Women and the Reconfiguration of Gender in Africa,* eds. Hodgson Dorothy and Sheryl McCurdy, pp. 274 –92. Portsmouth, N.H.: Heinemann.

Parry, Jonathan, and Maurice Bloch. 1989. Introduction to *Money and the Morality of Exchange,* eds. Jonathan Parry and Maurice Bloch, pp. 1–32. Cambridge: Cambridge University Press.

Parsalaw, Willy. 1996. "Liberalisation of Maize Marketing in the Arusha Region in Tanzania." In *Constraints on the Success of Structural Adjustment Programmes in Africa,* ed. Charles Harvey. London: MacMillan Press Ltd.

Pietilä, Tuulikki. 1999. *Gossip, Markets and Gender: The Dialogical Construction of Morality in Kilimanjaro.* Research Report No. 233, Department of Sociology, University of Helsinki.

Pietilä, Tuulikki, Sanna Ojalammi-Wamai, and Liisa Laakso. 2002. "Elections at the Borderland. Voter Opinion in Arusha and Kilimanjaro, Tanzania." In *Multi-party Elections in Africa,* eds. Michael Cowen and Liisa Laakso, pp. 278 –98. Oxford: James Currey.

Piot, Charles. 1999. *Remotely Global: Village Modernity in West Africa.* Chicago: University of Chicago Press.

Pittin, Renée. 1983. "Houses of Women: A Focus on Alternative Life-Styles in Katsina City." In *Female and Male in West Africa,* ed. Christine Oppong, pp. 291– 302. London: George Allen and Unwin Ltd.

Polanyi, Karl. 1957. "The Economy as an Instituted Process." In *Trade and Market in the Early Empires: Economies in History and Theory,* eds. Karl Polanyi, C. M. Arensberg and H. C. V. Pearson, pp. 243 –70. Glencoe, Ill.: Free Press.

President's office, Planning Commission, Bureau of Statistics. 1994. *Kilimanjaro Regional Statistical Abstract 1993.* . Dar es Salaam.

Radcliffe-Brown, A. R. 1952. "On Social Structure." In *Structure and Function in Primitive Society,* pp. 188 –204. London: Cohen and West.

Raikes, Philip. 1994. "Business as Usual: Some 'Real' Food Markets in Kenya." *Sociologia Ruralis* 34, no. 1: 26 –44.

Rekdal, Ole B. 1996. "Money, Milk and Sorghum Beer: Change and Continuity among the Iraqw of Tanzania." *Africa* 66, no. 3: 367 –85.

Robbins, Joel. 2001. "God Is Nothing but Talk: Modernity, Language, and Prayer in a Papua New Guinea Society." *American Anthropologist* 103, no. 4: 901–12.

Robertson, Claire. 1974. "Economic Woman in Africa: Profit-Making Techniques of Accra Market Women." *The Journal of Modern African Studies* 12, no. 4: 657 –64.

———. 1984. *Sharing the Same Bowl: a Socioeconomic History of Women and Class in Accra, Ghana.* Bloomington: Indiana University Press.

———. 1995. "Comparative Advantage: Women in Trade in Accra, Ghana, and Nairobi, Kenya." In *African Market Women and Economic Power: The Role of Women in African Economic Development,* eds. Bessie House-Midamba and Felix K. Ekechi, pp. 99 –119 . Westport, Conn.: Greenwood Press.

———. 1997. *Trouble Showed the Way: Women, Men, and Trade in the Nairobi Area, 1890–1990.* Bloomington: Indiana University Press.

Rowlands, M., and J. P. Warnier. 1988. "Sorcery, Power and the Modern State in Cameroon." *Man* 23: 118–32.

Rubert, Steven C. 1998. *A Most Promising Weed: A History of Tobacco Farming and Labor in Colonial Zimbabwe, 1890–1945.* Athens: Ohio University Center for International Studies.

Rudé, George. 1972 [1959]. *The Crowd in the French Revolution.* London, Oxford, New York: Oxford University Press.

Ruthenberg, Hans. 1964. *Agricultural Development in Tanganyika.* Berlin: Springer-Verlag.

Sahlins, Marshall. 1965. "On the Ideology and Composition of Descent Groups." *Man* 65: 104–7.

———. 1972. *Stone Age Economics.* Chicago: Aldine-Atherton Inc.

Samoff, Joel. 1974. *Tanzania: Local Politics and the Structure of Power.* Madison: University of Wisconsin Press.

———. 1979. "Education in Tanzania: Local Politics and the Structure of Power." *The Journal of Modern African Studies* 17, no. 1: 47–70.

Sawayael, Blandina. 1993. "The Pastoral Analysis of the Situation of Women in Kiboriloni Parish of the Northern Diocece of the Evangelical Lutheran Church in Tanzania." Master's thesis, Lutheran Theological College, Makumira, Tanzania, June.

Schmoll, Pamela. 1991. "Searching for Health in a World of Disease." Ph.D. diss., University of Chicago.

Schneider-Barthold, Wolfgang, Nina Boschmann, Stefan Gruchmann, Wolfgang Hehn, Wolfgang Leidig, and Michael Plesch. 1983. *Farmers' Reactions to the Present Economic Situation in Tanzania with Respect to Production and Marketing: A Case Study of Five Villages in the Kilimanjaro Region.* Berlin: German Development Institute.

Schuster, Ilsa. 1979. *New Women of Lusaka.* Palo Alto, Calif.: Mayfield Publishing Company.

———. 1982. "Marginal Lives: Conflict and Contradiction in the Position of Female Traders in Lusaka, Zambia." In *Women and Work in Africa,* ed. Edna Bay, pp. 105–26. Boulder, Colo.: Westview Press.

Scott, James. 1976. *The Moral Economy of the Peasant: Rebellion and Subsistence in Southeast Asia.* New Haven, Conn.: Yale University Press.

———. 1985. *Weapons of the Weak: Everyday Forms of Peasant Resistance.* New Haven, Conn.: Yale University Press.

———. 1990. *Domination and the Arts of Resistance: Hidden Transcripts.* New Haven, Conn.: Yale University Press.

Setel, Philip. 1996. "AIDS as a Paradox of Manhood and Development in Kilimanjaro, Tanzania." *Social Science and Medicine* 43, no. 8: 1169–78.

Shand, Mike. 2004. *Tanzania Digital National Atlas. Political Sheet: Administrative Divisions.* University of Glasgow. http://mshand.geog.gla.ac.uk/ATLAS%20 F%20TANZANIA/atlas.htm (accessed 2 June 2006).

Sipola, Simo. 1994. "Lehdistö Taistelee Vapaudestaan Tansaniassa." *Kehitys* (Finnida) 4: 36–37.

Skinner, G. 1964. "Marketing and Social Structure in Rural China, Part I." *Journal of Asian Studies* 24: 3 –43.

Smith, Carol. 1985. "How to Count Onions: Methods for a Regional Analysis of Marketing." In *Markets and Marketing*, ed. Stuart Plattner, pp. 49 –78. Monographs in Economic Anthropology, No 4. Lanham, Md.: University Press of America and Society for Economic Anthropology.

Spear, Thomas. 1997. *Mountain Farmers: Moral Economies of Land and Agricultural Development in Arusha and Meru.* Oxford: James Currey.

Stahl, Kathleen. 1964. *History of the Chagga People of Kilimanjaro.* London: Mouton and Co.

——. 1974. "Outline of Chagga History." *Tanzania Notes and Records* 64: 35 –49.

*A Standard Swahili-English Dictionary.* 1993 [1939]. Nairobi: Oxford University Press.

Stoller, Paul. 1995. *Embodying Colonial Memories: Spirit Possession, Power and the Hauka in West Africa.* New York: Routledge.

Strathern, Andrew. 1973. "Kinship, Descent and Locality: Some New Guinea Examples." In *The Character of Kinship*, ed. Jack Goody, pp. 21–33. Cambridge: Cambridge University Press.

Strathern, Marilyn. 1979. "The Self in Self–Decorating." *Oceania* 49: 241–57.

——. 1988. *The Gender of the Gift: Problems with Women and Problems with Society in Melanesia.* Berkeley: University of California Press.

——. 1991. Introduction to *Big Men and Great Men: Personifications of Power in Melanesia*, eds. Maurice Godelier and Marilyn Strathern, pp. 1–4. Cambridge: Cambridge University Press.

——. 1992. "Qualified Value: the Perspective of Gift Exchange." In *Barter, Exchange and Value: An Anthropological Approach*, eds. Caroline Humphrey and Stephen Hugh-Jones, pp. 169 –91. Cambridge: Cambridge University Press.

Sudarkasa, Niara. 1973. *Where Women Work: A Study of Yoruba Women in the Marketplace and in the Home.* Ann Arbor: University of Michigan Press.

Swantz, Marja-Liisa. 1985. *Women in Development: A Creative Role Denied?* London: C. Hurst and Company.

*Tanzania Population Census 1967.* 1969 –1971. Ministry of Economic Affairs and Development Planning, Bureau of Statistics. Dar es Salaam: Government Printer.

Taussig, Michael. 1980. *The Devil and Commodity Fetishism in South America.* Chapel Hill: University of North Carolina Press.

Taylor, Christopher. 1992. *Milk, Honey and Money: Changing Concepts in Rwandan Healing.* Washington, D.C.: Smithsonian Institution Press.

Thompson, E. P. 1971. "The Moral Economy of the Crowd in the Eighteenth Century." *Past and Present* 50: 76 –136.

Tripp, Aili Mari. 1997. *Changing the Rules: The Politics of Liberalization and the Urban Informal Economy in Tanzania.* Berkeley: University of California Press.

Turner, Victor. 1969. *The Ritual Process: Structure and Anti-Structure.* Chicago: Aldine.

Uchendu, Victor. 1967. "Some Principles of Haggling in Peasant Markets." *Economic Development and Cultural Change* 16, no. 1: 37 –50.

Van Donge, Jan Kees. 1992. "Waluguru Traders in Dar es Salaam: An Analysis of the Social Constitution of Economic Life." *African Affairs* 91: 181–205.

Verdon, M. 1980. "Descent: An Operational View." *Man* 15: 129–50.

Wagner, Roy. 1991. "The Fractal Person." In *Big Men and Great Men: Personifications of Power in Melanesia,* eds. Maurice Godelier and Marilyn Strathern, pp. 159–73. Cambridge: Cambridge University Press.

Watts, Julian. 2002. "Heritage and Enterprise Culture in Archangel, Northern Russia." In *Markets and Moralities: Ethnographies of Postsocialism,* eds. Ruth Mandel and Caroline Humphrey, pp. 53–74. Oxford: Berg.

Weiner, Annette. 1984. "From Words to Objects to Magic: 'Hard Words' and the Boundaries of Social Interaction." In *Dangerous Words: Language and Politics in the Pacific,* eds. Donald Brenneis and Fred R. Myers, pp. 161–91. Prospect Heights, Ill.: Waveland Press.

Weiss, Brad. 1996. *The Making and Unmaking of the Haya Lived World: Consumption, Commoditization, and Everyday Practice.* Durham, N.C.: Duke University Press.

———. 1997. "Northwestern Tanzania on a Single Shilling: Sociality, Embodiment, Valuation." *Cultural Anthropology* 12, no. 3: 335–61.

Werbner, Richard. 1989. *Ritual Passage, Sacred Journey.* Washington, D.C.: Smithsonian Books.

———. 1996 [1991]. *Tears of the Dead: The Social Biography of an African Family.* Washington, D.C.: Smithsonian Institution Press.

White, Frances. 1987. *Sierra Leone's Settler Women Traders: Women on the Afro-European Frontier.* Ann Arbor: University of Michigan Press.

White, Luise. 1990. *The Comforts of Home: Prostitution in Colonial Nairobi.* Chicago: University of Chicago Press.

———. 2000. *Speaking With Vampires: Rumor and History in Colonial Africa.* Berkeley: University of California Press.

Wilson, Peter. 1973. *Crab Antics: The Social Anthropology of English-Speaking Negro Societies of the Caribbean.* New Haven, Conn.: Yale University Press.

Yang, Mayfair Mei-hui. 2000. "Putting Global Capitalism in Its Place. Economic Hybridity, Bataille, and Ritual Expenditure." *Current Anthropology* 41, no. 4: 477–509.

# Index

Accumulation: conceptualization of, 86; as a gendered category, 74, 116, 167, 184, 193; and individualism, 73, 85–86, 90, 182, 189, 191; of market qualities and relations, 65, 66, 68, 188; morality of, in theories, 12, 90, 182; and reputation, 115, 163, 199; as the suspected motive of market women, 70, 71, 73–75, 191–92; by women, 73, 74, 85, 87, 97, 113, 206 n.19. *See also* Money, conceptualization of; Witchcraft

*Akili,* 38, 40, 65, 69, 188

Bakhtin, Mikhail, 8, 9, 60, 91, 197, 199

Bars *(klabu/vilabu):* bar food, 113; as culturally specific spheres, 38, 65, 66, 68, 70; and "feeding," 74; gendered attendance at, 74, 75, 76, 81, 106, 109, 111, 156; gendered ownership of, 35; and gender-reversal, 70, 71, 74, 109, 111; locations and lively hours of, 21, 22, 33, 69; Mary's bar, 100, 104, 105, 106, 112, 113; reflective conversations in, 5, 9, 13, 24, 66, 100, 101, 106, 199, 202; and sex, 70, 71, 72, 74, 76, 79, 80, 106, 109. *See also Mawazo*

Beer: bottled, 22, 113, 158; as a gendered item, 74, 75, 76, 103; as a gift, 23, 47, 57, 151, 156, 162, 163; Kenyan, 33, 36, 204 n.1; *pombe,* meaning of, 208 n.8. *See also* Bars, and gender-reversal; Bars, and sex; *Mbege*

Belinga, Samuel, 43, 68, 189

Berry, Sara, 59

Big men, 156, 163

Binding *(kufunga):* "binding women," 119,
135, 136, 138, 190, 192, 193, 211 n.31; of a
bought spirit, 172; of cattle, 209 n.20;
and markets, 65; of men by women,
68, 71, 74, 75, 100, 132, 133, 134, 176,
177; of people, 111; in women's life
cycle, 126, 132. *See also* Domestication;
Enclosing

Bloch, Maurice, 42, 43, 182

Blockage: accumulation as, 189; curse as,
177; inside body, 177; in male life cycle,
175, 177, 214 n.8

Bohannan, Paul, 32, 41, 42, 43, 82, 145

Bought spirits *(majini):* domestic and kinship value and, 174, 180, 184, 189, 190;
for enrichment, 110, 117, 171, 172–73,
178, 192, 194; as foreign forces, 181,
186, 194, 195; as an idiom in moral
discussion, 166, 189, 190; and individual assets, 172–74, 178, 189, 214 n.1, 215
n.17; liberalization era and, 186; nonnegotiable character of, 175, 180; and
restlessness, 178, 194; as socially unconstrained force, 174, 181–82, 189

Bourdieu, Pierre, 11, 32, 41, 59, 60, 78, 163,
199, 205 n.15

Businessmen, 5, 26, 165; education or intelligence and, 166, 188, 192, 200; as an
idiom in moral discussion 166, 187–
90; moral discussion about, 5, 9, 25,
165–66, 185, 191–92, 195; and occult
or foreign forces, 186, 192, 194

Clark, Gracia, 50, 55, 59, 64, 86, 193, 204 n.10,
205 n.1, 206 n.12, 207 nn.28 29, 208 n.34

Coffee: as a cash generator, 4, 104, 144, 212
n.4; as a gendered and generational resource, 7, 104, 144, 149–50, 194; history of cultivation of, 4, 143–44, 149;
*kihamba* and, 18, 161, 178; as marking
ownership of land, 150

Comaroff, Jean, 12, 43, 130, 176, 182, 194,
208 nn.1 3, 212 n.34, 214 n.16, 215 n.20,
216 n.23

Comaroff, John, 12, 43, 176, 182, 194, 208 nn.1
3, 212 n.34, 215 n.20, 216 n.23

Coolness, value of, 69, 130, 177, 194, 215 n.13

Cattle: business, 170, 173, 176; children's
lineage affiliation and, 210 n.21; as

equated with women, 132, 211 n.27; as
a form of wealth, 176, 183; as a household asset, 97, 104, 112, 206 n.19; selling
and meat-sharing of, 183, 195. *See also*
Meat

Concealing: of economic resources, 6, 48,
73, 77, 184, 192; in market trade, 48, 50,
58–61, 69. *See also* Talk, and concealing; *Ujanja,* and concealing in measuring techniques; *Ujanja,* and market
trading;

Cultivation, as a moral category, 32, 99,
187–90, 212 n.4

Cunning (or craftiness): in market trading, 32, 38–39, 60, 69, 192; as related
to market women, 39, 40, 66, 71, 188,
192. See also *Ujanja*

Curse: as an afflicting force, 169, 170, 171,
177, 178, 180–81, 190, 215 n.19; versus
bought spirits, 180–81; and fighting
in markets, 72; versus witchcraft, 180;
in wife capture, 131, 211 n.26;

Dialogue: about African trading women's
motives, 82, 87; in Bakhtin's sense, 9,
91, 199; ethnographic method as, 91–
92; indirect dialogue, 8, 9, 12, 25, 64,
65, 76, 87, 90, 92, 109, 117, 196, 199,
200; about moral value and reputations, 3, 5, 9, 12, 31, 82, 87, 90, 109, 191,
196, 200, 202. *See also* Gossip

Domestication: of a bought spirit *(kufuga),*
174; of cattle *(kufuga),* 132, 209 n.20;
of economic flows, 189, 216 n.22; of a
man by a woman *(kufuga),* 132; of
marketplace, 32, 44, 46, 59, 61; of a
woman by a man *(kufuga),* 132. *See
also* Binding

Education: businessmen and, 166, 188, 192,
200; of children as the aim of African
women, 85–86; of children as the responsibility of Chagga men, 77, 105–
6, 112, 134, 155, 156, 210 n.21; of children as the responsibility of Chagga
market women, 76, 77, 101, 103, 105,
114; early exposure of the Chagga to,
4, 206 n.9; as a failed plan, 121, 123,
156; as a family necessity, 183, 195; importance of, for the Chagga, 4, 144,

206 n.9; markets as, 38, 65–66, 68, 188, 192; as a moral category, 166, 185, 187–90; restrictions on the Chagga for, 4. *See also Akili;* Knowledge

Enclosing: a girl or woman by a man, 126, 127, 132, 134; round architectural forms as, 160, 162, 214 n.16

Englund, Harri, 11, 12, 182, 189, 208 n.2, 212 n.34

Epstein, A. I., 7, 90

Exchange: in Chagga history, 4, 30–31; in personhood theories, 11, 138, 198; persuasion through, 198; spheres in theories, 11, 32, 41–43, 82; of thoughts and ideas, 13, 66, 138, 202. *See also Mawazo;* Bars, reflective conversations in

Fabian, Johannes, 13, 66

Feeding: creation of lineage and kinship identities through, 77–78, 82, 88, 126–27, 137–38, 192, 193, 210–11 n.21; in market women's talk and practices, 32, 48, 76–79, 82, 85, 88, 137, 190, 192, 193, 200; as taking care of or providing for, 11, 12, 74, 77, 82. *See also* Kinship; Personhood

Ferguson, James, 43, 182

Fisiy, Cyprian, 208 n.1, 212 n.34, 215 n.20

Geschiere, Peter, 12, 182, 189, 208 nn.1 3, 212 n.34, 215 n.20

Gift: customary way of asking for, 175; given by a boy to woo a girl, 93, 121, 126; given by a man to *hawara,* 134; given to mark engagement, 126; in theories, 11–12, 32, 42, 60–61, 183, 189; practices and rhetoric in the markets, 23, 32, 47–48, 59–62. *See also* Money, as a gift; Patronage

Glassman, Jonathon, 44, 61

Gluckman, Max, 7, 90, 145, 196

Gossip: construction of moral reputations through, 10, 25–26, 90, 109, 110, 113, 116–17, 156, 159, 196; construction of moral value through, 6, 9; front and back stage, 7, 8, 9, 197–98, 202; indirect dialogue through, 8, 9, 92, 102, 115, 196, 198–99, 202; as moral imagination, 13–14, 88, 117; as persuasion, 116, 119, 164, 189, 195, 199; as revealing,

8, 10, 13, 91, 116, 166, 196; secrets and, 6, 76, 116, 166; as semipublic sphere, 9, 197, 199, 202; theories, 7, 8, 90–91, 196–97, 209 n.38. *See also* Dialogue; Moral value, dialogical construction of; Talk, and indirection

Gutmann, Bruno, 30, 52, 57, 58, 71, 72, 82, 119, 127, 132, 147, 152, 177, 206 nn.16 17 19, 212 nn.5 6, 215 nn.12 13

Guyer, Jane, 43, 59, 68, 162, 164, 189, 214 n.17

Heat/Hotness *(moto):* of "loose" girls or women, 130, 134, 194; of market women, 69, 127; of money, 194, 215 n.22

Houses: African women and ownership of, 85–87, 135, 137; built for *hawara,* 133, 134; empty houses, 171, 174; and inheritance, 146–47; in *kihamba,* 18–20; as male resource and wealth, 77, 130, 145–46, 149, 155, 159–60, 162–64, 168; marking ownership of land, 150; modern houses, 20, 22, 112, 115, 159–62, 186, 196; revealing owner's immoral deeds, 172, 173, 174, 178, 189, 192; women and building of, 71, 74, 76, 96–97, 107

Kerner, Donna, 6, 187, 212 n.2, 213 n.9

*Kihamba (vihamba):* as a collective asset, 7, 162–64, 178, 183, 194; crops and trees grown on, 18, 104, 143–44, 149, 161, 178; as a customary male resource, 74, 75, 77, 80, 90, 99, 103, 133, 137, 144, 149, 150; decreasing sizes of, 5, 18, 144, 149, 162, 164, 185, 192, 194, 212 n.2; as a domestic sphere, 38, 69, 70, 80, 192, 194; and family livelihood, 64, 80, 103, 104, 112, 185, 192, 194, 212 n.2; graves in, 145, 147, 157, 166, 175, 212n.6; illegitimately acquired, 178, 179, 180, 188, 215 nn.16 17; inheritance of, 18, 103, 107, 137, 144, 146–47, 149–50, 151, 153–54, 210 n.21, 212n.6, 213 nn.7 8; lineage identity and, 145, 162, 163; middle brothers and, 147, 149, 151, 152; restlessness and, 171, 178–79, 185, 215 n.16; selling of, 150, 215 n.16; spreading in Kilimanjaro, 143; as symbolizing stability and continuity, 166, 175, 177–78, 187, 194; trading women and, 74, 75, 77, 85; urban men and,

*Kihamba (continued)*
   145–46, 152, 162, 164; widows and, 150–
   54; women's access through marriage,
   69, 80, 99, 127; and women's work, 89,
   107, 144
Kilimanjaro: administrative units in, 14;
   and civilization/development, 180,
   209 n.23; economic differences in, 8,
   22, 162, 164, 185; and economic history,
   4–5, 30, 143–44, 170, 185, 212 n.3 4; history of marketplaces in, 4, 30; importance of trading in, 4–5, 30, 136; levels
   of education in, 206 n.9; and modernity, 4, 12; state politics and, 4, 216 n.27.
   *See also* Education
Kinship: official (patrilineal) kinship, 78,
   127, 210 n.20; practical kinship, 78, 79,
   81, 193; terms and values as used in
   markets, 32, 44, 45, 47, 48, 59, 61, 79,
   196. *See also* Feeding; Lineage
Knowledge: as a quality accumulated in
   market, 64, 66, 68, 74, 86, 188, 192;
   about markets, 49, 66; and personhood, 66, 68, 74, 86, 134, 177, 188, 196,
   213 n.9. *See also* Education
Koponen, Juhani, 4, 204 n.3, 207 n.30
*Kubembeleza* (coaxing), 45–46, 49, 57, 58,
   70, 79, 133, 205 n.12. *See also* Talk, as
   persuasion

Land: scarcity of, 107, 143–44, 148–49, 185;
   and spatial control, 74, 75, 162–64. See
   *Kihamba; Shamba*
Liberalization policies, 3–5, 13, 29, 37, 44,
   144, 162, 185, 186, 189, 195, 203 n.1, 207
   n.24, 216 n.25
Lineage: matrilineal, 193, 207 n.21, 210 n.20,
   212–13 n.6; meetings, 6, 25, 146, 149,
   150, 154, 158, 213 n.7; patrilineages/
   patrilineal, 26, 69, 73–75, 77–81, 110,
   124, 127, 145–47, 149–52, 154–55, 157–
   59, 162–63, 166, 169, 171, 177–78, 180,
   183, 187, 189, 193–95, 206 n.16, 207
   n.21, 208 nn.37 4, 210 nn.19 20 21, 212
   n.6, 213 nn.7 9 10 13 14; theories, 145–
   46, 164, 214 n.18; women's natal lineage
   connections, 75, 78, 79, 80, 81, 92, 124,
   126, 127, 129, 130, 131, 137, 208 n.4, 210
   nn.19 21, 211 n.22. *See also Kihamba;*
   Kinship; Motherhood

"Loose": as used about a bought spirit, 172;
   as used about women, 81, 82–83, 87,
   118, 119, 130, 135, 136, 190, 194. *See also*
   "Settledness"
Lost/to become lost *(kupotea):* about children, 81, 102; about men or property,
   169, 178, 179, 194, 214 n.6; "to lose oneself," 136. *See also* Staying; Vanish

Marketplaces: bargaining in, 49, 50, 205
   n.13; as centers of social life, 21, 30,
   80; as culturally specific sites, 34, 38,
   41, 62, 65, 66, 69, 72, 80, 199, 205 n.4,
   206 nn.9 16; domestication of, 32, 44,
   46, 59, 61; importance in food marketing of, 29–30; importance of negotiation in, 32, 41, 46, 47, 49, 50, 55, 58, 61,
   64, 70, 80, 88; market ring, 4, 21, 30;
   men in, 30, 31, 35, 36, 37, 39, 49, 56, 57,
   65, 70, 72, 76, 204 nn.3 6; "mixing" of
   people in, 30, 38, 41, 65, 72, 80; and
   morality of exchange, 31, 32, 41 4, 58–
   62, 65, 73–74, 191–92, 200, 202, 204–5
   n.10; one-day credit system in, 55, 114;
   taxes in, 33, 56–58, 202; trade supple-
   ments/add-ons *(nyongeza)*, 49, 52, 62,
   78; as women's sphere, 30–31, 35, 37.
   *See also* Kilimanjaro, history of marketplaces in
Market women: and gendered behavior, 31,
   32, 62, 63, 64–66, 68, 69, 70, 71–72, 75–
   76, 80, 82, 88, 131, 184, 191–93, 205 nn.11
   5, 206 n.17; research on African trading
   women, 64, 84–87. *See also* Bars; Feeding; Knowledge; Motherhood; *Ujanja*
Mauss, Marcel, 10, 11, 32, 42
*Mawazo/Kuwaza:* and market and bar conversations, 13, 66, 138; as reflective discussion or imaginative thinking, 13,
   66, 202, 205 n.7. *See also* Bars; Gossip,
   as moral imagination
*Mbege:* 22, 66, 69, 103, 113; in customary
   exchanges, 74, 94, 150, 154, 178; as a
   gift, 47, 151, 162; the importance of
   sharing of, 74, 113, 154, 158; and mobility, 178; and poison, 73. *See also* Beer;
   Patronage
Meat: domestic and bar meat, 113, 206 n.18,
   209 n.40; eating by market women, 70,
   74, 89, 111; as a household necessity, 112,

183, 195; as a male item of provision
and relating, 74, 77, 151, 154, 162, 183,
195, 213 n.14; as prepared by women,
106, 133–34

Medicines, as household necessities for
treating illness, 76, 77, 210 n.21. *See
also* Witchcraft, medicines

Middle brothers/Middle sons, 5, 147, 149,
150–52, 162, 213 n.9

*Mjinga* (stupid)/*Ujinga* (stupidity): as inactivity, 192, 193, 207 n.23; about markets,
41; meaning of the word, 205 n.3; men
and colonial drugs in East Africa, 135;
men stupefied by women, 71, 111, 135,
176, 193, 207 n.23; stay-at-home women
as, 65, 68, 75, 76, 96, 192, 193, 207 n.23;
women's dependence on men as, 76,
193. See also *Ujanja*

Mobility: African women's, 83, 86; and heat,
127, 130, 194; increased need for, to
earn subsistence, 5, 13, 189, 207 n.23;
intellectual, 69–70, 176, 194; and market women, 69, 70, 71, 74, 133, 192, 194;
and men, 143, 144, 175, 177, 178, 179, 192,
194, 214 nn.8 11; restrictions in men's,
132, 133, 175, 176, 177, 194; social, 194,
199, 201. *See also* Binding; Staying

Money: acquired by illegitimate means,
67–70, 173, 174; conceptualization of/
conceptual conversion of, 64, 86, 97,
114, 115, 163, 182–84, 195–96; early acceptance of money economy by the
Chagga, 4, 182; as an empowering resource, 5, 20, 75, 181, 184, 194; as the
exchange medium in markets, 59, 72,
73; experienced qualities of, 7, 73, 176,
181, 184, 194, 215–16 n.22; as a gendered
resource, 96, 99, 134, 183, 184, 192–93;
and gender-reversal, 71, 74, 132, 134,
193; as a gift, 93, 163, 183, 195; and greed,
70, 75, 170, 176, 182; and household
economy, 76, 97, 99, 100, 102, 103, 104,
111, 112, 117, 144, 151, 183; increased need
of, 5, 12–13, 64, 80, 144, 184; investment
of, by African women, 85, 87; and liberalization era, 5, 186, 195; and loans,
114; market women and, 46, 48, 56, 64,
66, 70–71, 73–76, 78, 97–98; middle
brothers and, 5, 151–52; and moral
persuasion in stories, 184, 195–96; and

restlessness, 174, 178, 179; and savings
society, 113, 114; and status, 64, 86, 183,
188, 190, 200; in theories, 7, 42, 182–83,
194; and urban men, 5, 151–52, 160, 186.
*See also* Accumulation

Moore, Sally Falk, 4, 6, 30, 146, 150, 152, 154,
166, 180–81, 183, 194, 203 n.2, 206 n.13,
207 n.22, 211 n.21, 212 nn.2 3, 213 nn.9
10, 214 n.1, 215 n.17

Moral economy: and household economy,
112, 117; as ideas and practices, 44, 59,
60–62, 195–96, 202; in Kilimanjaro
markets, 44, 46, 59–62, 202; and liberalization era, 189, 195, 201; in theories,
11–12, 42–44, 59, 60, 61, 182. *See also*
Marketplaces, domestication of

Moral imagination. *See* Gossip, as moral
imagination; *Mawazo/Kuwaza*

Moral value: in a changing economy, 5, 6,
14, 117, 119, 139, 196, 201–2; claims for,
12, 48, 88, 102, 109, 115, 128–29, 137–
39; dialogical construction of, 8–9, 90,
119, 139, 196, 197, 202; gendered, 25, 117,
129, 146, 164–65; idioms for discussing,
of person, 82, 87–88, 92, 108–9, 116,
128, 135–38, 163–64, 190, 193–95, 200–
1; of *ujanja*, 38–41, 69–70, 192, 194; of
women's relations with men, 136. *See
also* Dialogue; Gossip; Personhood;
Reputation; Respect

Motherhood/Mother *(mama):* economic/
social importance of, 78, 79, 137, 193;
in market women's talk, 32, 45, 46, 48,
57, 137, 139, 193, 200; single/unmarried
mothers 81, 129, 130, 138, 139, 209 n.1,
210 n.21, 211 n.23; as a sociomoral sign,
108, 109, 116, 122, 130, 138, 200, 208 n.4,
210 n.6, 211 n.30. *See also* Feeding; Kinship, practical; Necessity

Necessity/Necessities: in literature about
African trading women, 84–88; in
market women's talk and practices,
46, 73, 76, 77, 88, 195; and men, 130,
195. *See also* Feeding

Parry, Jonathan, 42, 43, 182

Patrilineages. *See* Lineage; Kinship; Feeding

Patronage: and men, 12, 162, 163; and
women, 46–48, 59

Personhood/Person: and feeding, 11, 48, 77,
    86, 88; gendered, 25 –26, 65 –66, 68,
    74, 81, 86, 116 –17, 126 –28, 130, 135, 159,
    162–64, 165, 171, 175 –78, 180, 187–88,
    209 n.32, 210 n.16, 215 n.12; and moral
    value, 9, 10–11, 12, 25, 39, 41, 48, 81, 88,
    102, 109, 115 –16, 126, 129, 135, 138, 156,
    163 –65, 167, 170–71, 180, 187–88, 190,
    200–1, 210 n.16; in theories, 10 11, 148,
    162, 198, 214 n.17. *See also* Accumula-
    tion; Dialogue; Feeding; Moral value;
    Motherhood; Reputation; Witchcraft
Persuasion: through exchange objects, 198;
    through talk: *see* Gossip, as persuasion;
    *Kubembeleza*; Talk, as persuasion
Piot, Charles, 11, 32, 41, 189, 212 n.34
Polanyi, Karl, 11, 32, 41
*Pori*, 98, 209 n.23
Profit: and liberalization, 5, 73, 186, 191, 216
    n.25; in markets, 46, 52, 54, 56, 66, 73,
    90, 114; in market women's talk, 24, 32,
    40, 46, 48, 184, 195; and moral value of
    person, 48, 188, 192, 200; and negotia-
    tion, 32, 49; in research about African
    trading women, 84 –85; in theories, 12,
    32, 41. *See also* Accumulation

Reputation: and cultural ideas and values,
    13, 197, 202; dialogical construction of,
    5, 9, 10, 12, 26, 90, 92, 116, 163, 193, 197,
    199 –200; of families and lineages, 163;
    of a girl or a woman, 90, 109, 131, 139;
    of a man, 190, 196, 197. *See also* Gossip;
    Personhood; Moral value
Respect *(heshima):* as described for the
    Caribbean, 197; and girls or women,
    46, 68, 81, 82, 87, 99, 115 –16, 118 –20,
    124, 126, 127, 129, 134, 137 –39; and
    men, 164, 166, 175, 177, 185, 187, 213 –
    14 n.14; as shown towards a customer
    in market, 45. *See also* Moral value,
    gendered; Moral value, idioms for
    discussing; "Settledness;" Shame
Robertson, Claire, 64, 83, 84, 85, 87, 205 n.1,
    207 nn.30 32, 208 n.33

Sahlins, Marshall, 11, 41, 43, 60, 61, 214 n.18
Schuster, Ilsa, 87, 139, 207 n.32, 208 n.38
Scott, James, 7 –9, 11, 42, 43, 59, 61, 90, 197

Self-reliance *(kujitegemea),* 76, 81, 207 n.24,
    216 n.27
Setel, Philip, 144, 167, 185
"Settledness": of girls or women, 69, 119,
    120, 124, 127, 192, 194; of men, 74, 136.
    *See also* Binding; Stay; Staying
*Shamba*, 18, 89, 103 –4, 178, 203 –4 n.4, 209
    n.26
Shame *(aibu):* and girls or women, 94, 122–
    24, 129 –31; lack of, in girls or women,
    119, 128 –29; and men, 177; secrets and,
    76, 77. *See also* Respect
Socialist period, 3, 4, 6, 187, 216 n.27
Spear, Thomas, 43
Stahl, Kathleen, 4, 15, 30
Stay/Sit *(kukaa):* at home, about women,
    65, 68, 75, 76, 99, 101, 131, 159, 192, 193,
    207 n.23; meaning of the word, 209
    n.27; about men, 71, 136, 177, 207 n.23;
    about seclusion period, 95, 96, 97, 126,
    127; "sit on husband," 133
Staying/Remaining *(kukaa/kuishi),* as the
    value of stability, 137, 166, 171, 175, 177,
    178, 194, 215 n.16.
Straddling (strategies), 156, 175
Strathern, Marilyn, 11, 61, 162, 163, 198, 205
    n.15
Stupid/Stupidity. See *Mjinga/Ujinga*
Swantz, Marja-Liisa, 181, 182, 212 n.1, 215
    n.19

Talk: and concealing, 41, 48, 58, 60, 61, 77;
    and indirection, 24, 38, 39, 77, 100, 103,
    109, 115, 116, 136, 138, 196, 198, 199, 200;
    as persuasion, 12, 23, 46, 59, 60, 62, 70,
    93, 116, 119, 121, 122, 133, 189, 192, 195,
    198, 199, 200; and revealing, 12, 58, 80,
    116, 189, 195, 196, 198. *See also* Dialogue;
    Gossip; *Kubembeleza*
*Tamaa,* 167, 170, 190
Taylor, Christopher, 11, 183, 188, 209 n.1, 214
    n.8
Tripp, Aili Mari, 43 –44, 84, 86, 203 n.1, 205
    n.1, 207 n.31, 208 n.35

*Ujanja* (cunning): and *akili,* 38, 40, 65,
    69; and concealing in measuring tech-
    niques, 41, 48, 50, 58, 61, 69; as defined
    in dictionaries, 204 n.7; as a gendered

quality, 39, 65; and knowledge, 65, 68; and *kuwaza*, 66; and market trading, 38, 60, 192; and *mdomo* (mouth), 40–41, 72; as mobility, 69, 192, 194; moral quality of, 38–41, 62, 69, 192; as negotiation skills, 58, 70

Urban men, 5, 26, 80, 136, 146, 152, 156, 162, 185, 194, 213 n.9

Vanish *(kupotea/kuisha)*: as an idiom used about property/people, 166, 169, 170, 175, 178–79, 184, 194; as used to exorcise a spirit, 172–73. *See also* Lost/to become lost

Weiss, Brad, 124, 126, 130, 206 n.12, 208 nn.1 3, 210 n.16, 214 n.10, 215 nn.20 22, 216 n.23

Werbner, Richard, 92, 183, 195

White, Luise, 7, 10, 87, 135, 139, 182, 208 nn.37 1 3, 211 n.29, 215 n.21

Wholeness *(uzima)*, 124, 126, 127, 128, 177

Widows: inheritance of, 154; social power of, as old mothers/grandmothers, 78, 150–51, 154, 155, 190; as trustees of property, 152–54

Witchcraft: and accumulation, 7, 11–12, 90–91, 110, 117, 182, 189, 209 n.39, 212 n.34; versus Christianity, 172, 173, 180; versus curse, 177, 180–81, 190; medicines, and women, 70, 71, 101, 108–11, 117, 132–36, 211 n.31; medicines, historical changes in forms of, 181, 209 n.39; and moral value of person, 12, 108–9, 138; and poisoned food, 58, 73, 177, 181, 206 n.18; as a reference to cultural "other," 172, 180, 194, 209 nn.23 39; and reflections on reality, 13, 24, 91, 117, 189, 190; theories, 12, 90–91, 138, 182, 194, 212 n.34; about the used concepts, 203 n.3; and women, 90–91, 100, 102, 110, 117, 132, 192. *See also* Bought spirits; Moral value, idioms for discussing; Personhood, and moral value

WOMEN IN AFRICA AND

THE DIASPORA

*Engaging Modernity: Muslim Women and the Politics of Agency in Postcolonial Niger*
Ousseina D. Alidou

*Tired of Weeping: Mother Love, Child Death, and Poverty in Guinea-Bissau*
Jónína Einarsdóttir

*Women's Organizations and Democracy in South Africa: Contesting Authority*
Shireen Hassim

*Gossip, Markets, and Gender: The Dialogical Construction of Moral Value in Post-Socialist Kilimanjaro*
Tuulikki Pietilä

*Surviving the Slaughter: The Ordeal of a Rwandan Refugee in Zaire*
Marie Béatrice Umutesi; translated by Julia Emerson